RADICAL PHILOSOPHY

2.01
Series 2 / 2018

Editorial	2
Crimes of solidarity	
Martina Tazzioli	4
Postmodernity, not yet	
Nathan Brown	11
Hegel and the advent of modernity	
Jamila M. H. Mascat	29
Dossier: On the 1917 commemorations	47
Revolutionary commemoration	
Hannah Proctor	47
Order in disorder	
Ilya Budraitskis	58
All power to the soviets	
Lars T. Lih	64
Marx in Algiers	
Sandro Mezzadra	79
The realism of our time	
Kim Stanley Robinson and Helena Feder	87
Reviews	99
Bernard Stiegler, *Automatic Society*	
Douglas Spencer	99
Angela Nagle, *Kill All Normies*	
Jen Isakson and Ross Speer	102
William MacAskill, *Doing Good Better*, Peter Singer, *The Most Good You Can Do*	
Rupert Read	106
Judith Roof, *What Gender Is, What Gender Does*	
Sam McBean	109
Bojana Cvejić, *Choreographing Problems*	
Austin Gross	112
Rosie Warren, ed., *The Debate on* Postcolonial Theory and the Specter of Capital	
Marie Louise Krogh	115
Finn Brunton and Helen Nissenbaum, *Obfuscation*	
Matthew Fluck	118
Simone Browne, *Dark Matters*	
Gloria González Fuster	120
Christopher Watkin, *French Philosophy Today*	
Peter Hallward	122
Kate Eichhorn, *Adjusted Margin*	
Victoria Horne	124
Sarah Kember, *iMedia*	
Neda Genova	126

Editorial collective
Claudia Aradau
Brenna Bhandar
Victoria Browne
David Cunningham
Peter Hallward
Stewart Martin
Lucie Mercier
Daniel Nemenyi
Hannah Proctor
Rahul Rao
Martina Tazzioli
Chris Wilbert

Engineering collective
Austin Gross
Daniel Nemenyi
Lara Mancinelli
Alex Sassmanshausen
Joseph Villwock

Creative Commons BY-NC-ND
Radical Philosophy, 2018.

ISSN 0300-211X
ISBN 978-1-9999793-0-0

Editorial

Critical projects that seek to sustain themselves over a long stretch of time have to change if they are to avoid becoming part of an establishment. And if they are prepared to change, they have to change more than once. *Radical Philosophy* emerged out of the long 1960s, framed politically by the student movement and the New Left, and intellectually by a rebellion against what the first issue of the journal termed 'the poverty of so much that now passes for philosophy'. In the 1980s and 1990s, this was refashioned by a more profound engagement with feminism, ecology and the new social movements, as well as by an attempt to get to grips with both the changing forms of what was then called 'continental philosophy' and the consequences of the Thatcherite and Reaganite counter-revolutions. From the early 2000s, when the first version of the radicalphilosophy.com website went live, the journal sought consistently to expand its geopolitical horizons, with contributions from Latin America, Africa and East Asia - albeit never enough - while publishing important articles that brought philosophical perspectives to a range of new disciplinary and cross-disciplinary areas from media theory, geography and film studies to architecture, literary and art theory. Throughout this history, we have tried to remain true to our founding ambition to 'free ourselves from the restricting institutions and orthodoxies of the academic world, and thereby to encourage important philosophical work to develop'.

One of many self-published left-wing journals that were founded in Britain in the early 1970s, *Radical Philosophy* is today, however, more or less alone in its continuing independence from corporate publishing and in its political commitment to a collective editorial project. The reasons for this are not hard to see. The material, intellectual and political contexts within which a publication such as ours operates have clearly changed beyond all recognition. We began as a magazine produced on typewriters and photocopiers, with images literally cut and pasted into the text, mailed out by the collective to our readers. The changing shapes and fortunes of independent spaces of the left, and the general penetration of the computer and the internet into everyday practices of writing and reading, have since then dramatically transformed what it means to autonomously produce and distribute a publication like *RP*. In particular, it became apparent that, for a radical journal committed to the construction of as wide a community of readers and contributors as possible – including those outside the West European and North American academy – it was getting harder and harder to justify the access restrictions under which the magazine had come to operate. Given the new possibilities made available via the internet and 'print-on-demand', making a commitment to an equally radical form of openness – in a context where, too often, 'open access' has simply meant the revivification of the zombie forms of commercial academic publishing – became an increasingly pressing priority. By the end of 2016, as we approached both our forty-fifth birthday and our 200th issue, it thus became evident that we required a renewed confrontation with the altered demands of the philosophical and political present. As such, when five members of the previous editorial group stepped down in early 2017, we took the opportunity not only to open up and diversify membership of the collective, but also to commit ourselves to rethinking our own means and relations of production – editorial as well as technical – in order to bring new life to the project.

The means of producing *Radical Philosophy* evolved from its original DIY ethic to proprietary publishing software that required not simply costly licences and machines for its operation but also an outsourcing of labour and a paywall system to finance itself. To shake this and the greater problem of centralising the collective's power around those with the relevant skills and licences, we reconceived our means of production around Free and Open Source Software that inherently accommodates a distribution of labour, and created a new in-house engineering collective to work alongside our editors to develop the journal's tools and distribution channels. Taking our cue mostly from science publications, we have now turned to the markup language LaTeX to produce our print edition and to interface with our newly designed website. Where we formerly relied on software developed according to a logic of capital accumulation, we now operate more autonomously thanks to that developed by our own engineering collective.

In this new form, *Radical Philosophy* remains, as it has always been, a collectively edited, independently published and self-produced journal – but one with what is, we hope, a renewed editorial energy and collaborative ethos (if with no less philosophical rigour or critical bite). The longer and newly designed print journal, which will generally appear three times a year, is accompanied by a new website through which we will now be publishing *all* of our content in freely available form. At the same time, the archive of the last forty-five years of *Radical Philosophy*, all the way from issue 1 to 200, is being made fully open with downloadable pdfs of everything that we have published since 1972.

In the Founding Statement of the Collective published in our first issue, the journal's aim was articulated as one of challenging a situation in which philosophy had been made 'into a narrow and specialised academic subject of little relevance or interest to anyone outside the small circle of Professional Philosophers'. Yet such a challenge was never about just a simple widening of the discipline. Instead, *Radical Philosophy* has always been about a breaking down of those fundamental institutional divisions that have so impoverished philosophy itself by separating it off both from other knowledges and from a wider political and intellectual culture of the left. The need to elaborate what Adorno once called a philosophising beyond philosophy, whether or not it originates in actual departments of academic philosophy, remains as relevant a task today as it did in 1972.

There are many reasons for this. In an editorial published on the occasion of our 100th issue, it was remarked that for all the changes it has seen, institutionally, 'philosophy remains the most traditional and least reformed discipline in the humanities; not least with regard to race and gender'. Sadly, little has changed in this respect over the subsequent years. Amidst the current groundswell of demand for the decolonisation of knowledge, philosophy remains a central battleground, stubbornly resistant to the change that those storming its bastions wish to see. The analysis of how philosophical texts are entangled in the sordidness of the world and the evaluation of what, if anything, might be salvaged from their disentanglement, can be destabilising for a whiteness and a patriarchy that regard such texts as foundational to their very self-conception. We hope that, among other things, the pages of *Radical Philosophy* will become a venue for reflection upon the question of what it might mean to decolonise philosophy today. Alongside the translation and introduction of new authors, such an enterprise entails a profound questioning of the very notion of canonicity and the essence of the method of reason that calls itself philosophical. It is in keeping forever open the question of what it might mean *to do* philosophy that the project of a radical philosophy can remain truly radical.

Crimes of solidarity
Migration and containment through rescue
Martina Tazzioli

'Solidarity is not a crime.' This is a slogan that has circulated widely across Europe in response to legal prosecutions and municipal decrees, which, especially in Italy and France, have been intended to act against citizens who provide logistical and humanitarian support to transiting migrants. Such criminalisation of individual acts of solidarity and coordinated platforms of refugee support is undertaken both in the name of national and European laws, in opposition to the facilitation of irregular entries, and through arbitrary police measures. In Calais on the French coast, for example, locals have been prohibited from allowing migrants to take showers in their homes or to recharge their mobile phones, while in the Roya Valley at the Italian-French border, many locals have been placed on trial, including the now famous ploughman Cedric Herrou. Responding to accusations that he has been one of the main facilitators along the French-Italian underground migrant route, Herrou has replied that 'it is the State that is acting illegally, not me', referring to the French State's own human rights violations.[1]

'Crimes of solidarity', to use the expression employed by activists and human rights organisations, are defined and prosecuted according to the 2002 EU Directive which prevents and penalises 'the facilitation of unauthorised entry, transit and residence' of migrants. In both Italy and France there are national laws that criminalise the facilitation and the support of 'irregular' migration; what in France activists call '*délit de solidarité*'. Notably, citizens who help migrants to cross national borders are prosecuted in Italy under the same law that punishes smugglers who take money from migrants. In France, the 'humanitarian clause', which exempts from sanctions citizens who support migrants whose life, dignity and physical integrity is at risk, is often disregarded. Nonetheless, the expression 'crimes of solidarity' should not lead us to overstate the legal dimension of what is at stake in this. Indeed, the 'crime' that is posited here goes well beyond the legal boundaries of European law, as well as national ones, and acquires an ethical and political dimension. In particular, the criminalisation of individuals and groups who are facilitating the crossing of migrants, without making a profit from doing so, opens up the critical question of exactly 'who is a smuggler?' today. Significantly, the very definition of 'smuggling' in European and international documents is a fairly slippery one, as the boundaries between supporting migrants for one's own financial benefit or for 'humanitarian' reasons are consistently blurred.[2]

In a 1979 interview, Michel Foucault stressed the potential strategic role that might be played by 'rights' to 'mark out for a government its limit'.[3] In this way, Foucault gestured towards an extralegal conceptualisation and use of rights as actual limits to be set against governments. In the case of crimes of solidarity, we are confronted less, however, with the mobilisation of rights as limits to states' action than with what Foucault calls 'infra-legal illegalisms';[4] namely, with practices of an active refusal of states' arbitrary measures that are taken in the name of migration containment, regardless of whether or not the latter are legally grounded or in violation of the law.

NGOs and independent organisations that undertake search and rescue activities to save migrants in the Mediterranean have also been under attack, accused of collaborating with smuggling networks, of constituting a pull-factor for migrants, and of ferrying them to Europe. Three years after the end of the military-humanitarian operation Mare Nostrum, which was deployed by the Italian Navy to save migrant lives at sea, the Mediterranean has become the site of a sort of naval battle in which the obligation to rescue migrants in distress is no longer the priority. The fight against smugglers and traffickers has taken central stage, and the figure of the shipwrecked refugee has consequently vanished little by little. Today, the war on smugglers is presented as *the* primary goal and, at the same time, as a strategy to protect migrants from 'traffickers'. The criminalisation of NGOs, like Doctors without Borders, Save the Children and SOS Mediterranee, and of independent actors, including Sea-Eye, Sea-Watch, Jugend-Rettet and Arms Pro-Activa, who conduct search and rescue operations, started with the simultaneous implementation of the Libyan mobile sea-barrier, which charges the Libyan Coast Guard with responsibility for intercepting migrant vessels and bringing them back to Libya. As a consequence of this agreement, being rescued means *being captured and contained*.

Following the signing of a new bilateral agreement between Libya and Italy in March 2017, in July, the Italian government put pressure on one of the three Libyan governments (the one led by Fayez al-Serraj) demanding better cooperation in intercepting and returning migrants who head to Europe by sea. In order to accelerate this process, Italy sent two Navy ships into Libyan national waters, with the purpose of 'strengthening Libyan sovereignty by helping the country to keep control of its national waters'.[5]

Far from being a smooth negotiation, however, the Libyan government led by General Khalifa Haftar threatened to shoot in the direction of the Italian ships if they were to violate Libya's sovereignty by entering their national territory.[6]

Overall, the 'migration deal' has been made by the EU and Italy in the context of different asymmetric relationships: on the one hand, with a 'rogue state' such as Libya, characterised by a fragmented sovereignty, and on the other, with non-state actors, and more precisely with the same smugglers that Europe has supposedly declared war on. Indeed, as various journalistic investigations have proved, Italy has paid Libyan militias and smuggling networks to block migrants' departures temporarily in exchange for fewer controls on other smuggling channels, specifically those involving drugs and weapons. In this way, smugglers have been incorporated into a politics of migration containment. Governing migration through and with smugglers has become fully part of the EU's political agenda. As such, a critical appraisal of the criminalisation of migrant smuggling requires undoing the existing narrative of a war on smugglers, as well as challenging those analyses that simply posit smugglers as the straightforward enemies of society.

The naval battle in the Mediterranean has not been an exclusive affair of Italy and Libya. On the contrary, it is within this type of geopolitical context that the escalating criminalisation of sea rescue is more broadly taking place.[7] On July 31, at the request of the European Commission, the Italian Home Office released a 'Code of Conduct' that NGOs have been asked to sign if they want to continue search and rescue activities. Given that the code of conduct imposes on NGOs the obligation to have armed judicial police on board,[8] some organisations, including Doctors without Borders, Sea Watch and Jugend Rettet, have refused to sign, arguing that through the enforcement of the Code of Conduct, and under pressure from the European Commission, Italy has turned towards a militarisation of humanitarianism and of independent actors. As a consequence of the refusal to sign, their ships have been prevented from docking in Italian ports and the rescuers of the Jugend Rettet are currently on trial, accused of collaborating with Libyan smugglers. On August 11, Libya traced new virtual restrictive sea borders for NGOs, declaring that search and rescue ships will not be allowed to get closer than one hundred miles from the Libyan coast. The humanitarian scene of rescue has been shrunk.

In such a political context, two interrelated aspects emerging from the multiplication of attacks against refugee support activities and against search and rescue operations are worth considering. The first concerns a need to unpack what is now meant by the very expression 'crime of solidarity' within the framework of this shift towards the priority of fighting smugglers over saving migrants. This requires an engagement with the biopolitical predicaments that sustain a debate centered on the question of to what extent, and up to which point, rescuing migrants at sea is deemed legitimate. The second, related point concerns the modes of containment through rescue that are currently at work in the Mediterranean. One consequence of this is that the reframing of the debate around migrant deaths at sea has lowered the level of critique of a contemporary politics of migration more generally: the fight against smugglers has become *the* unquestioned and unyielding point of agreement, supported across more or less the entire European political arena.

The criminalisation of NGOs, accused of ferrying migrants to Europe, should be read in partial continuity with the attack against other forms of support given to migrants in many European countries. The use of the term 'solidarity' is helpful in this context insofar as it helps to highlight both actions undertaken by citizens in support of refugees and, more importantly, the transversal alliances between migrants and non-migrants. In fact, acting in solidarity entails supporting migrant struggles – for example, as struggles for movement or struggles to stay in a certain place – more than it does acting in order to save or bring help to them.[9] As Chandra Mohanty argues, practices of solidarity are predicated upon the recognition of 'common differences',[10] and in this sense they entail a certain shared political space and the awareness of being governed by the same mechanisms of precaritisation and exploitation.[11] In other words, solidarity does not at all imply a simple politics of identity, but requires building transversal alliances and networks in support of certain struggles. The reduction of migrants to bodies to be fished out of the water, simultaneous with the vanishing of the figure of the refugee, preemptively denies the possibility of establishing a common ground in struggling for freedom of movement and equal access to mobility.

Despite the many continuities and similarities between the criminalisation of refugee support activities on the mainland and at sea, if we shift the attention to the Mediterranean Sea, what is specifically at stake here is a biopolitics of rescuing or 'letting drown'. Under attack in the Mediterranean scene of rescue and drowning are what could be termed crimes of humanitarianism; or, that is, crimes of rescue. Humanitarianism as such, precisely in its acts of taking migrants out of the sea through independent search and rescue operations that exercise an active refusal of the geographical restrictions imposed by nation states, has become an uncomfortable and unbearable mode of intervention in the Mediterranean.

Geographies of ungrievability

The criminalisation of alliances and initiatives in support of migrants' transit should not lead us to imagine a stark opposition between 'good humanitarians', on the one side, and bad military actors or national authorities, on the other. On the contrary, it is important to keep in mind the many entanglements between military and humanitarian measures, as well as the role played by military actors, such as the Navy, in performing tasks like rescuing migrants at sea that could fall under the category of what Cuttitta terms 'military-humanitarianism'.[12] Moreover, the Code of Conduct enforced by the Italian government actually *strengthens* the divide between 'good' NGOs and 'treacherous' humanitarian actors. Thus, far from building a cohesive front, the obligation to sign the Code of Conduct produced a split among those NGOs involved in search and rescue operations.

In the meantime, the figure of the *refugee* at sea has arguably faded away: sea rescue operations are in fact currently deployed with the twofold task of not letting migrants drown and of fighting smugglers, which *de facto* entails undermining the only effective channels of sea passage for migrants across the Mediterranean. From a military-humanitarian approach that, under Mare Nostrum, considered refugees at sea as shipwrecked lives, the unconditionality of rescue is now subjected to the aim of dismantling the migrants' logistics of crossing. At the same time, the migrant drowning at sea is ultimately not seen any longer *as* a refugee, i.e. as a subject of rights who is seeking protection, but as a life to be rescued in the technical sense of being fished out of the sea. In other words, the migrant at sea is the subject who eventually needs to be rescued, but not thereby placed into safety by granting them protection and refuge in Europe. What happens 'after landing' is something not considered within the framework of a biopolitics of rescuing and of letting drown.[13] Indeed, the latter is not only about saving (or not saving) migrants at sea, but also, in a more proactive way, about aiming at human targets. In manhunting, Gregoire Chamayou explains, 'the combat zone tends to be reduced to the body of the enemy'.[14] Yet who is the human target of migrant hunts in the Mediterranean? It is not only the migrant in distress at sea, who in fact is rescued and captured at the same time; rather, migrants and smugglers are both considered the 'prey' of contemporary military-humanitarianism.

Public debate in Europe about the criminalisation of NGOs and sea rescue is characterised by a polarisation between those who posit the non-negotiable obligation to rescue migrants and those who want to limit rescue operations in the name of regaining control over migrant arrivals, stemming the flows and keeping them in Libya. What remains outside the order of this discourse is the shrinking and disappearing figure of the refugee, who is superseded by the figure of the migrant to be taken out of the sea.

Relatedly, the exclusive focus on the Mediterranean Sea itself contributes to strengthening *geographies of ungrievability*. By this I mean those produced hierarchies of migrant deaths that are essentially dependent on their more or less consistent geographic distance from Europe's spotlight and, at the same time, on the assumption of shipwrecked migrants as the most embodied refugee subjectivities. More precisely, the recent multiplication of bilateral agreements between EU member states and African countries has moved back deadly frontiers from the Mediterranean Sea to the Libyan and Niger desert. As a consequence, migrants who do not die at sea but who manage to arrive in Libya are kept in Libyan prisons.

Containment through rescue

On 12 August 2017, Doctors without Borders decided to stop search and rescue operations in the Mediterranean after Libya enforced its sea-barrier by forbidding NGOs to go closer than about one hundred miles from the Libyan coast, and threatening to shoot at those ships that sought to violate the ban. In the space of two days, even Save the Children and the independent German organisation Sea-Eye declared that they would also suspend search and rescue activities. The NGOs' Mediterranean exit has been presented by humanitarian actors as a refusal to be coopted into the EU-Libyan enforcement of a sea barrier against migrants. Yet, in truth, both the Italian government and the EU have been rather obviously pleased by the humanitarians' withdrawal from the Mediterranean scene of drown and rescue.

Should we therefore understand the ongoing criminalisation of NGOs as the attempt to fully block migrant flows? Does it indicate a return from the staging of a 'good scene of rescue' back to an overt militarisation of the Mediterranean? The problem is that such an analytical angle risks, first, corroborating the misleading opposition between military intervention and humanitarianism in the field of migration governmentality. Second, it re-instantiates the image of a Fortress Europe, while disregarding the huge 'migration industry' that is flourishing both in Libya, with the smuggling-and-detention market, and on the Northern shore of the Mediterranean.[15] With the empty space left by the NGOs at sea, the biopolitics of rescuing or letting drown has been reshaped by new modes of containment *through* rescue: migrants who manage to leave the Libyan coast are 'rescued' – that is, intercepted and blocked – by the Libyan Coast Guard and taken back to Libya. Yet containment should not be confused with detention nor with a total blockage of migrants' movements and departures. Rather, by 'containment' I refer to the substantial disruptions and decelerations of migrant movements, as well as to the effects of more or less temporary spatial confinement. Modes of containment through rescue were already in place, to some extent, when migrants used to be 'ferried' to Italy in a smoother way, by the Navy or by NGOs. Indeed, from the moment of rescue onward, migrants were transferred and channelled into the Hotspot System, where many were denied international protection and, thus, rendered 'illegal' and constructed as deportable subjects.[16] The distinction between intercepting vessels sailing to Europe and saving migrants in distress has become blurred: with the enforcement of the Libyan sea barrier, rescue and capture can hardly be separated any longer. In this sense, visibility can be a trap: if images taken by drones or radars are sent to Italian authorities before migrants enter international waters, the Italian Coast Guard has to inform Libyan authorities who are in charge of rescuing migrants and thus taking them back to Libya.

This entails a spatial rerouting of military-humanitarianism, in which migrants are paradoxically *rescued to Libya*. Rather than vanishing from the Mediterranean scene, the politics of rescue, conceived in terms of not letting people die, has been reshaped as a technique of capture. At the same time, the geographic orientation of humanitarianism has been inverted: migrants are 'saved' and dropped in Libya. Despite the fact that various journalistic investigations and UN reports have shown that after being intercepted, rescued and taken back to Libya, migrants are kept in detention in abysmal conditions and are blackmailed by smugglers,[17] the public discussion remains substantially polarised around the questions of deaths at sea. Should migrants be saved unconditionally? Or, should rescue be secondary to measures against smugglers and balanced against the risk of 'migrant invasion'? A hierarchy of the spaces of death and confinement is in part determined by the criterion of geographical proximity, which contributes to the sidelining of mechanisms of exploitation and of a politics of letting die that takes place beyond the geopolitical borders of Europe. The biopolitical hold over migrants becomes apparent at sea: practices of solidarity are transformed into a relationship between rescuers and drowned.[18]

The criminalisation of refugee support activities cannot be separated from the increasing criminalisation of refugees as such: not only those who are labelled and declared illegal as 'economic migrants', but also those people who are accorded the status of refugees. Both are targets of restrictive and racialised measures of control. The migrant at sea is presented as part of a continuum of 'tricky subjectivities'[19] – which include the smuggler, the potential terrorist and the refugee – and as both a 'risky subject' and a 'subject at risk' at the same time.[20] In this regard, it is noticeable that the criminalisation of refugees as such has been achieved precisely through the major role played by the figure of the smuggler. In the EU's declared fight against smuggling networks, migrants at sea are seen not only as shipwrecked lives to be rescued but also as potential fake refugees, as concealed terrorists or as traffickers. At the same time, the fight against smugglers has been used to enact a further shift in the criminalisation of refugees, which goes beyond the alleged dangerousness of migrants. Indeed, in the name of the war against the 'illegal' smuggling economy, as a shared priority of both left- and right-wing political parties in Europe, the strategy of letting migrants drown comes, in the end, to be justified. As Doctors without Borders have pointed out, 'by declaring Libya a *safe country,* European governments are ultimately pushing forward the humanitarianisation of what appears at the threshold of the inhuman.'[21]

The migrant at sea, who is the subject of humanitarianism par excellence, is no longer an individual to be saved at all costs, but rather the object of thorny calculations about the tolerated number of migrant arrivals and the migrant-money exchange with Libya. *Who is (in) danger(ous)?* The legal prosecutions and the political condemnation of 'crimes of rescue' and of 'crimes of solidarity' bring to the fore the undesirability of refugees *as* refugees. This does not depend so much on a logic of social dangerousness as such, but, rather, on the practices of spatial disobedience that they enact, against the restrictions imposed by the European Union. Thus, it is precisely the irreducibility of migrants to lives to be rescued that makes the refugee the main figure of a continuum of tricky subjectivities in a time of economic crisis. Yet, a critical engagement with the biopolitics of rescuing and drowning cannot stick to a North-South gaze on Mediterranean migrations. In order not to fall into a Eurocentric (or EU-centric) perspective on asylum, analyses of crimes of solidarity should also be articulated through an inquiry into the Libyan economy of migration and the modes of commodification of migrant bodies, considering what Brett Neilson calls 'migration as a currency';[22] that is, as an entity of exchange and as a source of value extraction.

Crimes of solidarity put in place critical infrastructures to support migrants' acts of spatial disobedience. These infra-legal crimes shed light on the inadequacy of human rights claims and of the legal framework in a time of hyper-visible and escalating border violence. Crimes of solidarity consist of individual and collective active refusals of states' interventions, which are specifically carried out at the very edges of the law. In this way, crimes of solidarity manage to undo the biopolitics of rescuing and letting drown by acting beyond the existing scripts of 'crisis' and 'security'. Rather than being 'rescued' from the sea or 'saved' from smugglers, migrants are supported in their unbearable practices of freedom, unsettling the contemporary hierarchies of lives and populations.

Martina Tazzioli is a member of the Radical Philosophy *editorial collective, and author of* Spaces of Governmentality: Autonomous Migration and the Arab Uprisings *(2014).*

Notes

1. See the interview with Herrou in *l'Humanité*, accessed 30 September 2017, https://www.humanite.fr/cedric-herrou-cest-letat-qui-est-dans-lillegalite-pas-moi-629732.
2. Economic profit is an essential dimension of 'smuggling', as it is defined by the United Nations Conventions against Transnational Organised Crime (2000). However, it is not in the 2002 EU Council Directive defining the facilitation of unauthorised entry, transit and residence.
3. Michel Foucault, 'There can't be societies without uprisings', trans. Farès Sassine, in *Foucault and the Making of Subjects*, ed. Laura Cremonesi, Orazio Irrera, Daniele Lorenzini and Martina Tazzioli (London: Rowman & Littlefield, 2016), 40.
4. See Michel Foucault, *The Punitive Society: Lectures at the Collège de France, 1972-1973*, trans. Graham Burchell (Houndmills and New York: Palgrave, 2015).
5. See 'Il governo vara la missione navale, prima nave italiana in Libia', *La Stampa*, 18 July 2017, http://www.ilsecoloxix.it/p/italia/2017/07/28/ASBvqlal-parlamento_missione_italiana.shtml.
6. See, for example, the report in *Al Arabiya*, 3 August 2017, http://english.alarabiya.net/en/News/middle-east/2017/08/03/Haftar-instructs-bombing-Italian-warships-requested-by-Fayez-al-Sarraj.html
7. See Liz Fekete, 'Europe: crimes of solidarity', *Race & Class* 50:4 (2009), 83 – 97; and Eric Fassin, 'Le procès politique de la solidarité (3/4): les ONG en Méditerranée' (2017), *Mediapart*, accessed 30 September 2017, https://blogs.mediapart.fr/eric-fassin/blog/170817/le-proces-politique-de-la-solidarite-34-les-ong-en-mediterranee
8. The Code of Conduct can be found at: http://www.interno.gov.it/sites/default/files/allegati/codice_condotta_ong.pdf; see also the transcript by *Euronews*, 3 August 2017, http://www.euronews.com/2017/08/03/text-of-italys-code-of-conduct-for-ngos-involved-in-migrant-rescue
9. Sandro Mezzadra and Mario Neumann, 'Al di la dell'opposizione tra interesse e identità. Per una politica di classe all'altezza dei tempi' (2017), *Euronomade*, accessed September 30 2017, http://www.euronomade.info/?p=9402
10. Chandra Mohanty, '"Under western eyes" revisited: feminist solidarity through anticapitalist struggles', in *Signs: Journal of Women in Culture and Society* 28:2 (2003), 499–535.
11. As Foucault puts it, 'In the end, we are all governed, and in this sense we all act in solidarity'. Michel Foucault, 'Face aux gouvernement, les droits de l'homme', in *Dits et Ecrits II* (Paris: Gallimard, 2000), 1526.
12. P. Cuttitta, 'From the Cap Anamur to Mare Nostrum: Humanitarianism and migration controls at the EU's Maritime borders', in *The Common European Asylum System and Human Rights: Enhancing Protection in Times of Emergency*, ed. Claudio Matera and Amanda Taylor (The Hague: Asser Institute, 2014), 21–38. See also Martina Tazzioli, 'The desultory politics of mobility and the humanitarian-military border in the Mediterranean: Mare Nostrum beyond the sea', *REMHU: Revista Interdisciplinar da Mobilidade Humana* 23:44 (2015), 61–82.
13. See Lucia Ciabarri and Barbara Pinelli, eds, *Dopo l'Approdo: Un racconto per immagini e parole sui richiedenti asilo in Italia* (Firenze: Editpress, 2016).
14. Gregoire Chamayou, 'The Manhunt Doctrine', *Radical Philosophy* 169 (2011), 3.
15. As a matter of fact, the vessels of the EU naval operation EU Navfor Med and the vessels of the Frontex operation 'Triton' were increased in number a few days after the pull-out of the NGOs.
16. Nicholas De Genova, 'Spectacles of migrant "illegality": the scene of exclusion, the obscene of inclusion', *Ethnic and Racial Studies* 36:7 (2013), 1180–1198.
17. See, for instance, the UN Report on Libya (2017), accessed 30 September 2017, http://reliefweb.int/sites/reliefweb.int/files/resources/N1711623.pdf.
18. Tugba Basaran, 'The saved and the drowned: Governing indifference in the name of security', *Security Dialogue* 46:3 (2015), 205 – 220.
19. Glenda Garelli and Martina Tazzioli, 'The Biopolitical Warfare on Migrants: EU Naval Force and NATO Operations of migration government in the Mediterranean', in *Critical Military Studies*, forthcoming 2017.
20. Claudia Aradau, 'The perverse politics of four-letter words: risk and pity in the securitisation of human trafficking', *Millennium* 33:2 (2004), 251–277.
21. Interview with Doctors without Borders, Rome, 21 August 2017.
22. Brett Neilson, 'The Currency of Migration', in *South Atlantic Quarterly*, forthcoming 2018.

Postmodernity, not yet
Toward a new periodisation
Nathan Brown

> To take an attitude of partisanship towards key struggles of the past does not mean either choosing sides, or seeking to harmonise irreconcilable differences. In such extinct yet still virulent intellectual conflicts, the fundamental contradiction is between history itself and the conceptual apparatus which, seeking to grasp its realities, only succeeds in reproducing their discord within itself in the form of an enigma for thought, an aporia. It is to this aporia that we must hold, which contains within its structure the crux of a history beyond which we have not yet passed.
>
> Fredric Jameson

The term 'postmodernism' may no longer seem to tell us much about the present. In his 1996 preface to the third edition of his classic survey, *Modern Architecture Since 1900*, William J.R. Curtis remarks that '"postmodernism" proved to be a temporary and localised phenomenon, while the string of "isms" since then have continued in the usual way to distort history for their own purposes.'[1] Likewise, Peter Osborne has more recently remarked that, in the context of art criticism, 'the category of postmodernism is now well and truly buried', and, in a 2014 article in this journal, argues that 'those, like [Fredric] Jameson, who took the road called postmodernism have long since had to retrace their steps or accustom themselves to life in a historical and intellectual cul-de-sac.'[2] From the morass of debates concerning the significance of 'postmodernism' during the 1970s and '80s, Jameson's account of the cultural logic of late capitalism emerged as a framework capable of integrating the descriptive and ideological aspects of the periodising label within a wide-ranging practice of Marxist criticism. The salutary gesture of Jameson's 1984 programme essay was to displace merely celebratory or derogatory references to the 'postmodern', both of which failed to understand the structural causes of its prevalence. His subsequent work has been a primary and productive point of reference for discussions of our major periodising categories, pushing us to situate these as mediating terms between cultural and economic production. This work having been accomplished, however, it is now unclear what will become of the categories of postmodernity and postmodernism themselves. Do they retain the conjunctural utility for critical reflection upon the present that Jameson lent them in the 1980s and early '90s? Or are they now to be located within their limits, not as the names of historical and cultural situations extending into an unknown future, but rather as designators of a bygone era – in the same manner as they putatively consigned modernity and modernism to the past? And if the latter is the case, how are we to periodise the present? An uninviting answer to this last question involves a simple terminological redoubling of our posteriority to modernity and to modernism. This is the manouevre of Jeffrey Nealon's 2012 book, *Post-Postmodernism, or, the Cultural Logic of Just-In-Time Capitalism*, in which he characterises twenty-first century culture and economics as an 'intensification and mutation within postmodernism' correlated to just-in-time production.[3] Nealon thus positions the cultural logic of contemporary capitalism both 'within' and beyond postmodernism, while the terminological posteriority of the latter with respect to modernism is simply redoubled. The implicit ambivalence attendant upon this redoubling (within yet beyond) is suggested as well by the title of a 2007 collection, *The Mourning After: Attending the Wake of Postmodernism*. Here we find N. Katherine Hayles and Todd Gannon opening their contribution to the volume by declaring that 'On or about August 1995, postmodernism died', citing as the cause of death a routinisation of informational complexity by Netscape, the first user-friendly internet browser.[4] And it was in 1996, just five years after the publication of Jameson's signal book, that landscape architect Tom Turner published *City as Landscape: A Post-Postmodern View of Design and Planning*, in which he suggests (from a very different perspective) that 'there are signs of post-postmodern life, in urban design, architecture, and elsewhere', by which he means an attitude that 'seeks to temper reason with faith'.[5] With this attitude in mind, Turner goes so far as to equate sensibilities he refers to indifferently as 'post-Postmodern, or pre-Modern'.[6]

'Giving names to periods is difficult', Turner acknowledges. Nevertheless, to periodise the present as post-postmodern is to surrender the project of historicising cultural production to the same impulses of ahistorical thought that Jameson's account was meant to displace. To periodise the present through the redoubled application of a prefix marking it as after what was after what came before is not to think history, rupture or negation, but rather to perpetuate a narrative of sequential succession that reduces the past to a terminological prop for the indeterminacy of the present. To recognise this is to recognise the same problem with the term 'postmodern' itself. Indeed, this problem was among the motives for Jameson's complex ground-clearing operation, his effort to account for the symptomatic sense of this term while retaining it through critical transformation. Nevertheless, in what follows I will offer a prescription for treating the contemporary impasse of periodisation by diagnosing the symptomatic ambivalence of Jameson's own pivotal theory of the postmodern; an ambivalence that I think both occludes and implicitly indicates the way toward a coherent understanding of the historical relation between capitalism, modernity and modernism. The remedy I will suggest is a minor terminological shift in our reference to the cultural situation of the late twentieth and early twenty-first century – but one that has major consequences for a historical materialist grasp of what is at stake in the wrenching passage of the present through the crux of the past's intersection with the future. Thus, the point of my suggestion is not to attempt a belated and opportunistic 'correction' of a major thinker and critic; rather, it is to take up the generative contradictions of Jameson's work in order to pass through the discrepancy between the conjuncture in which it was articulated and our own.

The Post and the Late

The symptomatic ambivalence of Jameson's account lies in the tension between the 'post' and the 'late' that it inscribes in the periodisation of 'postmodernism' and 'postmodernity' as the cultural and historical logic of 'late capitalism'. Interestingly, Jameson does not refer to 'postmodernity' at all in his 1984 essay, but he will tell us in *Archaeologies of the Future* that 'the presumption of the existence of something like postmodernity was always based on the evidence of those thoroughgoing modifications of all levels of the system we call late capitalism.'[7] Thus, while Jameson acknowledges that 'for Marx modernity is simply capitalism itself', he periodises *late* capitalism as *posterior* to modernity.[8] That is, diverging from Marx's identification of capitalism and modernity, Jameson wants to hold that capitalism continues in the late twentieth and early twenty-first century, but that it continues after – and enacts, through its 'thoroughgoing modifications' – the end of modernity. Indeed, Jameson will refer in his 1991 book to his 'systematic comparison between the modern and the postmodern moments of capital.'[9] This putative disjunction between the end of modernity and the continuation of capitalism was always central to Jameson's intervention in debates about the category of the postmodern. Jameson's deployment of the term 'late capitalism', drawn from Ernest Mandel, was meant to 'mark its continuity with what preceded it rather than the break, rupture, and mutation that concepts like "postindustrial society" wished to underscore.'[10] Against the ideological presumption that 'society' had somehow moved beyond the contradictions of capitalism, Jameson wanted to underscore the continuity of capitalism under transformed structural conditions – which transformation he thus emphasises by aligning the *lateness* of contemporary capitalism with a periodising break between the modern and the postmodern. Thus the terminological tension between the 'late' and the 'post' in Jameson's account, the condition of being *within* capitalism but *after* modernity, constitutes an effort to mark both continuity and rupture, against the notion that everything is different or that nothing has changed.

Yet Jameson will also recommend, in *A Singular Modernity*, 'the experimental procedure of substituting capitalism for modernity in all the contexts in which the latter appears.' This, he tells us, is 'a therapeutic rather than a dogmatic recommendation, designed to exclude old problems (and to produce new and more interesting ones).'[11]

It is in this therapeutic spirit that I want to subject Jameson's own periodising terminology to this substitution, thus aligning *postmodernity* with *postcapitalism* rather than with late capitalism – precisely the alignment he hoped to counter in the 1980s. My methodological model for this 'experiment', however, would not be the vulgar sociological obfuscation of the continuing contradictions of capitalist modernity, but rather Marx's own identification of modernity with capitalism. From this perspective, modernity would necessarily continue throughout the history of capitalism, precisely as the history of its contradictions – the history of what Marx called 'the moving contradiction' – while postmodernity could only mark a radically transformed cultural and historical situation after capitalism had well and truly ended. From this perspective, postmodernity is not a *fait accompli* but a state of affairs to be struggled toward; nor would the end of capitalism be something already achieved, as in the ideological model Jameson attempted to counter, but rather a historical horizon. 'The condition of postmodernity' would attend the end of capitalism, not its late phase. We can thus condense the political significance of the therapeutic terminological substitution that Jameson himself recommends in a slogan: No Postmodernity Without Postcapitalism! We could condense the periodising significance of this slogan still further: Postmodernity, Not Yet.

As an intervention into the periodising framework of Jameson's work, the advantage of this position is that it acknowledges the conjunctural constraints under which his account was developed while also shifting it in accordance with his own Marxist recognition that modernity is the history of capitalism. But if we carry out this intervention, we are immediately tasked with rethinking the problem that Jameson was attempting to solve, its terminological poles now reversed: how to think the transformation of capitalism in accordance with the continuity of modernity as the still-unfolding history of its contradictions? This involves theorising – grounding through a structurally adequate account – the relationship between what Jameson calls 'late capitalism' and what we would call 'late modernity', an economic and historical period whose cultural logic we could call 'late modernism'. We are then drawn back, as if by a gravitational field, into the question of the relation not only between capitalism and modernity, but also modernism and modernity. If we try to address the ambivalence of Jameson's theory (its tension between the late and the post) by applying to it the therapy he prescribes (aligning modernity with capitalism, thus postmodernity with a postcapitalism yet to come, and thus late capitalism with late modernity), how will we then work through the transformation of historical and cultural theory this involves? In what follows I want to suggest a historical materialist framework within which to pursue this problem, one that specifies the relation between modernism and modernity in such a way that we can think the transformation of both categories in the late twentieth century while also thinking the continuity of modernity with capitalism, through what we could indeed call their late phases.[12]

Mattick v. Mandel

One effect of the symptomatic tension between the *post* and the *late* in Jameson's account is the exaggerated emphasis he places upon the absolute elimination of nature and earlier social forms within late capitalism. 'Postmodernism', he famously writes, 'is what you have when the modernization process is complete and nature is gone for good.'[13] Jameson identifies modernity with a completed process of 'modernization' such that 'the postmodern must be characterized as a situation in which the survival, the residue, the holdover, the archaic has finally been swept away without a trace.'[14] As he acknowledges, understanding the postmodern as *entirely* modern draws us into paradox: 'this is the sense in which we can affirm, either that modernism is characterized by a situation of incomplete *modernization*, or that postmodernism is *more* modern than modernism itself.'[15] The postmodern is 'more modern' because, Jameson declares:

> everything is now organized and planned; nature has been triumphantly blotted out, along with peasants, petit-bourgeois commerce, handicraft, feudal aristocracies and imperial bureaucracies. Ours is a more homogeneously modernized condition. We no longer are encumbered with the embarrassment of non-simultaneities and non-synchronicities. Everything has reached the same hour on the great clock of development or rationalization (at least from the perspective of the 'West').[16]

Perhaps this last parenthetical qualification should give us pause. Can uneven development really have been resolved into absolute synchrony ('the same hour on the great clock of development') if one must append the qualification 'at least from the perspective of the "West"'? Such a claim would seem to implicitly recognise, by delimiting a homogenous occidental perspective, the continuing heterogeneity of 'development' that it cancels through the very perspectival delimitation it has to impose.

In characterising postmodernity as completed modernisation, Jameson has in mind Arno Mayer's account of the persistence of the old regime within modernity.[17] Jameson's strategy for dealing with the tension between the late and the post is to splice Mayer's cultural and historical account of modernity's pre-modern survivals with Ernest Mandel's account of the economic structure of late capitalism so as to identify a 'third stage' of development (Mandel) in which the persistence of the *ancien régime* ceases to persist, thus ending the asynchrony of modernity that Mayer elucidates and inaugurating postmodernity. Mandel himself argues that 'late capitalism, far from representing a "post-industrial society", thus appears as the period in which all branches of the economy are fully industrialised for the first time.'[18] Jameson maps Mandel's stagist theory of capitalist 'long waves' onto his own periodisation of cultural production into Realist, Modernist, and Postmodernist phases. He thus lauds Mandel's work as a condition of possibility for the articulation of his periodising schema:

> Ernest Mandel's book *Late Capitalism* ... for the first time theorized a third stage of capitalism from a usably Marxian perspective. This is what made my own thoughts on 'postmodernism' possible, which are therefore to be understood as an attempt to theorize the specific logic of the cultural production of that third state, and not as yet another disembodied cultural critique or diagnosis of the spirit of the age.[19]

For Jameson, *post*modernity can correspond with *late* capitalism because the latter is a 'third stage' during which the 'fully industrialised' economy corresponds with the end of uneven development – and thus with the end of modernity, understood as the uneven process of modernisation.

Let us dwell for a moment upon the status of Mandel's account as the *sine qua non* of Jameson's periodisation. Jameson values Mandel's 'great book' because it offers a 'usably Marxian perspective' on historical periodisation, yet he does not seem very concerned with challenges, on Marxist grounds, to Mandel's framework.[20] He dismissively refers to 'the scholastic, I am tempted to say theological, debates on whether the various notions of "late capitalism" are really consistent with Marxism itself.'[21] If we want to take this question more seriously, we might look to Paul Mattick's thorough critique of Mandel's work, published as the final chapter of his 1974 book *Economic Crisis and Crisis Theory*. In my view, Mattick convincingly shows that Mandel's analysis is riddled with inconsistencies due to misapplications of Marxist categories, a theory of crisis that over-emphasises relations of supply and demand, and a failure to consistently ground his periodising scheme upon the long-term structural tendencies of capitalist accumulation, rather than a cyclical theory of long-waves and an accompanying stagist logic. In Mattick's technically refined view (the meticulous articulation of which is perhaps what Jameson dismisses as 'scholastic' or 'theological'), Mandel's book does not offer a usably Marxist perspective. Far from viewing it as a foundation for further theoretical construction, Mattick finds that 'it would take a new book to trace Mandel's inanities in detail if one wanted to show that his work represents not dialectics but ordinary inconsistencies. Perceptive readers of his book will see this for themselves.'[22] What are the stakes of this divergent assessment, wherein one of the most theoretically perspicuous Marxists of the twentieth century views the same text Jameson hails as a 'great book' as an inconsistent compendium of 'inanities'?

What is at issue in Mattick's stringent critique is the importance of a theoretical framework that consistently approaches relations between secular and cyclical tendencies in the movement of capitalist accumulation by granting explanatory priority to the former, thus grounding an account of the history of modernity in the secular dynamics of capital's totalising structural contradictions rather than in the expansion of markets, technological revolutions, cyclical fluctuations of profitability or periodic shifts in the relation between supply and demand. The basic point of Mattick's critique is that Mandel's stagist theory of the history of capitalism fluctuates inconsistently between orders of explanation while frequently prioritising cyclical over secular dynamics, and this is what allows him to posit three stages characterised by the relation between market dynamics and phases of machine production: first, an era of 'free competition', characterised by a 'relative international immobility of capital' and correlated with the 'machine production of steam driven motors'; second, 'the classical era of imperialism', characterised by increasingly international concentration of capital and correlated with the 'machine production of electric and combustion motors'; and, third, 'late capitalism', characterised by multinational corporations as a dominant organisational form and correlated with 'machine production of electronic and nuclear-powered apparatuses'.[23] Rather than a theory of capitalist stages prioritising cyclical dynamics and an order of explanation prioritising markets and technological innovations, what the work of periodisation requires is a unified framework for understanding capital's secular dynamics, within which the tendential contradictions of accumulation are granted clear explanatory priority and constitute a consistent referent for periodising transitions.

Marx's categories

In *Capital*, we already find four periodising terms with which to develop such a framework: primitive accumulation, formal subsumption, real subsumption and the tendency of the rate of profit to fall. In order to understand and to mobilise the relationship between these terms and their periodising logic, however, we have to relate them to distinctions Marx draws, within the process of valorisation, between two kinds of surplus value and two kinds of capital: absolute surplus value and relative surplus value; constant capital and variable capital. The utility of primitive accumulation, formal subsumption, real subsumption and the tendency of the rate of profit to fall as periodising categories is that they *cannot be understood* otherwise than through the relational integration of these Marxist categories. That is, to ground a periodising schema in these categories requires us to remain at all times within the framework of Marx's theory of valorisation and accumulation. It is through the interrelation of these categories, delineating the structure of capitalist accumulation as a moving contradiction, that one can explain the political-economic causes of the first and second industrial revolution, the integration of Taylorist management and assembly line labour into the process of production, the movement from the postwar manufacturing boom to tendential deindustrialisation and financialisation, the long downturn in profit rates since the 1970s, and the continuing stagnation of economic growth following the 2008 crash. The graph of my own periodisation accompanying this essay organises these phenomena according to their relation to overlapping phases of primitive accumulation, formal subsumption, real subsumption and tendentially declining profit rates. It is intended as a flexible guide and summation of the periodising structure for which I argue in what follows.

Let me approach an explanation of this periodising framework with two questions. What is Mandel talking about when he refers to 'the period in which all branches of the economy are fully industrialised for the first time'? And what is Jameson talking about when he describes the completion of the 'modernization' process? They are talking about the achievement of what Marx calls 'real subsumption': the achievement of a properly capitalist process of production through the subsumption not only of relations of production but also the process of production under capitalist social and productive relations. But what is 'a properly capitalist process of production'? It is one that is thoroughly reorganised through the exigencies of capitalist competition to produce the greatest volume of relative surplus value, in addition to absolute surplus value. Yet this fundamental Marxist distinction between relative and absolute surplus value – to which Marx's understanding of the history of capitalist accumulation and his periodising terminology is so intimately related – does not play a major role in Mandel's account and is nowhere to be found in Jameson.

Briefly, the expanded production of *absolute* surplus value is predicated upon lengthening the working day and lowering wages. There are obvious limits to these measures, since workers have to reproduce their labour power. These limits are addressed through the expanded production of *relative* surplus value, predicated upon the reduction of necessary labour time (the time required to reproduce the value of the worker's daily wage) in relation to the length of the working day. Such a reduction requires managerial and technological innovations: alterations of the process of production itself (real subsumption) in addition to the subsumption of pre-capitalist productive processes under capitalist social relations (formal subsumption). It is limits to the expanding production of absolute surplus value and competition over the maximal production of relative surplus value that drives capitalist technological innovation, the capitalist division of labour, the introduction of new management techniques, and the coordination of all of these through synthetic technical / managerial apparatuses like the assembly line. Moreover,

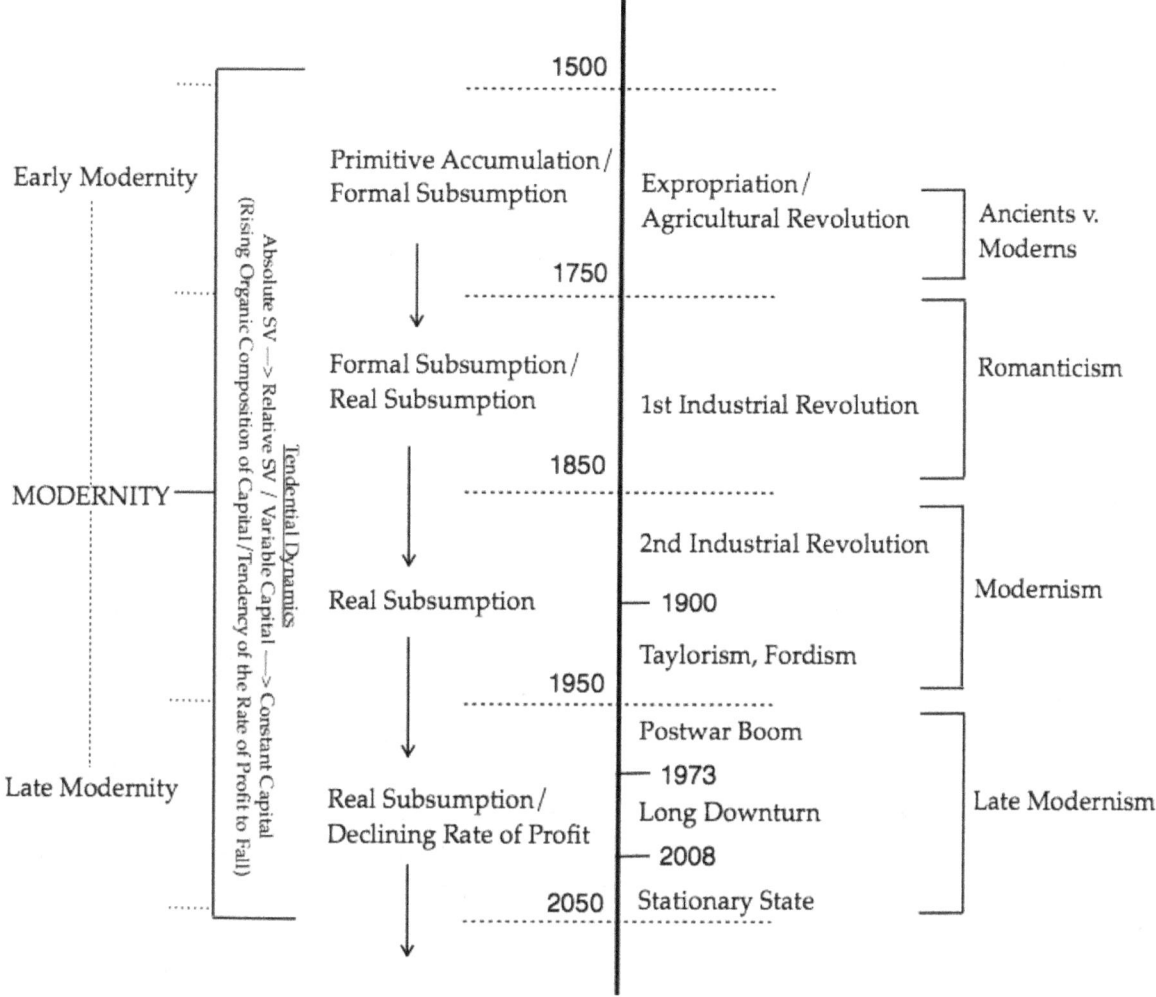

it is competition over the production of relative surplus value (in addition to absolute surplus value) that increases investment in constant capital (plant, equipment, materials) and decreases investment in variable capital (wages). As Marx shows, this pattern of relatively increasing investment in constant capital ('the rising organic composition of capital') entails two secular trends that are fundamental to understanding the historicity of capitalism: 1. the tendentially increasing production of surplus populations resulting from diminished access to the wage (variable capital); 2. the tendency of the rate of profit to fall, since surplus value is ultimately drawn *only* from investment in variable capital, which (relative to investment in constant capital) tendentially decreases according to the exigencies of capitalist competition, which require the maximal reduction of necessary labour time (increased productivity).

These are Marxist fundamentals; I certainly do not mean to imply that such thinkers as Mandel or Jameson are unaware of them. Nevertheless, there is something of a split between Marxist approaches to periodisation grounding their logic in the analytic of relations between absolute / relative surplus value and constant / variable capital and those which prioritise market dynamics, technological revolutions or supply and demand theories of periodic crises. For example, Robert Brenner and Mark Glick's important critique of the methodology of the French Regulation school is proximate to Mattick's critique of Mandel in criticising explanatory reliance upon underconsumptionist theory and the exaggerated imposition of phases of capitalist development that are insufficiently grounded in deep structural contradictions rather than local shifts in modalities of accumulation.[24] Thus, Brenner and Glick point out that the Regulationist distinction between 'extensive' and 'intensive' regimes of accumulation, situated at the rise of Taylorist scientific management and Fordist assembly line techniques, belies the massive dependence of capitalist accumulation upon relative surplus value throughout the nineteenth century.[25] Here we see the importance of understanding 'formal' and 'real' subsumption not as wholly discrete periods but rather as overlapping processes responsive to contradictions of accumulation whose movement is neither cyclical nor linear but rather tendential, and thus requiring an account fundamentally grounded in the secular dynamics of capitalism. Indeed, one might also extend Brenner and Glick's critique to, for example, the theoretical foundations of David Harvey's account of postmodernity, which relies upon the Regulationist periodisation of 'extensive' and 'intensive' phases of accumulation while adding a more recent regime of 'post-Fordist', 'flexible' accumulation characteristic of 'postmodernity'.[26]

Late capitalism as the long downturn

When Jameson wrote his foundational article on 'postmodernism', the conjunctural importance of Mandel's *Late Capitalism* as a critical intervention against theories of 'post-industrial society' made it indispensable for his effort to apply Marxist historiography to the postmodernism debates. Its conjunctural utility in those debates also made it opportune to dismiss Marxological critiques of Mandel as 'scholastic' or 'theological', since a thinker like Mattick, however acute, did not offer a ready periodising framework within which to situate cultural production since the 1960s. Today, however, we have at our disposal Robert Brenner's persuasive periodisation of the postwar and contemporary period, informed by decades of hindsight since Mandel's 1972 intervention. Mandel's book was poised on the brink of the crisis of 1973 and thus in no position to situate the postwar period with respect to the forty year decline in profit rates that would follow from it, as does Brenner's lucid account of the relationship between the manufacturing boom of 1945-1965 and the subsequent 'long downturn', continuing into the present.[27] We should note that, contra Jameson, the dynamics of continuing uneven development are central to Brenner's account. Moreover, we now also have, among other works, an important periodisation of the link between the changing structure of the class relation and cycles of communist struggle by *Théorie Communiste*, developed since the 1970s;[28] the work of the journal *Endnotes* on deindustrialisation, tendentially rising surplus populations and the logic of gender and racialisation during the long downturn;[29] and a suggestive speculative account of the prospective 'stationary state' of stagnating growth following from the crash of 2008 by Gopal Balakrishnan.[30] These are rigorously Marxist accounts of economic and political history that might help us to revise our periodisation of the late twentieth and early twenty-first century in accordance with what we know now, rather than what we knew in 1972 or 1984. Thus we can also situate Jameson's theory of 'postmodernism' within this revised context, placing it within its conjunctural limits rather than continuing to take it at face value as a theory determinate of our periodising horizons in the present.

What all of these accounts (Brenner, *Théorie Communiste*, *Endnotes*, Balakrishnan) have in common is a commitment to grounding periodisation first and foremost in the secular dynamics of accumulation, rather than in cyclical phenomena or technological ruptures. These accounts are already integrally related, as Balakrishnan relies upon Brenner's account of the long downturn, while *Endnotes* synthesises Brenner's account of economic history with *Théorie Communiste*'s periodisation of the class relation and cycles of struggle, developing a political-economic account of capitalist dynamics and contemporary struggles that is also broadly consistent with Balakrishnan's speculative prospectus on the 'stationary state'. I would argue that the high degree of relational consistency between these accounts can also be articulated through the periodising categories of primitive accumulation, formal subsumption, real subsumption and the secular tendency of the rate of profit to fall. Brenner's theory of agrarian class structure and economic development in early modern Europe gives us an account of primitive accumulation and formal subsumption upon which his later work is grounded, while this later work gives us a history of structural contradictions that follow from the achievement of real subsumption. *Théorie Communiste* gives us a periodisation of formal and real subsumption in relation to the structure of the class relation, and we can read and adjust their periodisation in relation to recent work on this question within the communisation current.[31] *Endnotes* gives us an account of the effect of the long downturn upon class composition and the tendentially increasing exteriority of proletarians to the wage, while attending to the relationship between real subsumption and unwaged reproductive labour, as well as to links between racialisation, carceral labour and state violence in a time of declining industrial profitability. Balakrishnan diagnoses the limits upon future growth imposed by the structural impossibility of returning to the tendentially rising production of relative surplus value after the accomplishment of real subsumption in the nineteenth and twentieth century.

I want to emphasise that these accounts, reconstructed and related in these terms, offer us a contemporary understanding not only of the structure of capitalist contradictions but of their *history*. They offer us the framework for understanding the continuing history of modernity as the history of capitalism: of transformations of the class relation, of the process of production, of gender and racialisation as social relations, of the changing horizons of class struggle. Most importantly, they allow us to see that, although the process of real subsumption is accomplished by the 1960s (as is evident from globally tendential deindustrialisation[32]), the history of modernity continues as the movement of the *same* structural contradictions that necessitate the accomplishment of real subsumption in the first place. One sign that the accomplishment of real subsumption does not signal a radical break with the history of modernity is that the period of declining profitability following from it is attended by profit-seeking through the renewed expansion of absolute surplus value production, through the offshoring of manufacturing labour to zones where labour regulations do not prohibit longer working days and lower wages. We do not exit modernity into a fully modernised world in which uneven development is eliminated, but we do enter into a late phase of modernity, correlated with a late phase of capitalism, during which the social and political consequences of real subsumption play out. Modernity is structured as the history of the contradictions of capitalist accumulation, and as long as those contradictions persist across and through discrepant phases, so, too, does the history of modernity continue to unfold as the history of capital. It is crucial, to note a particularly pressing contemporary example, not to understand global warming in terms of the 'disappearance' of nature but rather in terms of the *persistence* of its unpredictable relation to the history of accumulation and the class relation (i.e., *not* 'everything is now organized and planned').[33] It is politically important to understand the neo-slavery of the American carceral state as *part* of the history of modernity, included within its social logic, rather than as posterior to it. It matters that we recognise the tendentially increasing production of surplus populations as every bit as fundamental to the socio-historical dynamics of modernity as the initial subsumption of the peasantry under the wage and the concomitant process of urbanisation. We can only grasp the history of modernity through the moving contradiction of capitalist accumulation if we are willing to think the structural determinations of that history through to the end of capital's tumultuous dynamics, rather than cancelling the history of modernity as it moves into a late phase characterised by the achievement of real subsumption: a phase which, we must note, Marx had already predicted within the same historical conjuncture in which he identified modernity with capitalism. The consequences of real subsumption are as much a part of modernity as the process of real subsumption itself, precisely because both result from and inhere within the history of capitalism.

While taking seriously the importance of Mattick's critique of Mandel, I will thus retain 'late capitalism' as a periodising term, correlating it with 'late modernity' in order to mark the achievement of the process of real subsumption during the postwar period and the movement thereafter into the long period of declining profitability theorised by Brenner. This is indeed a 'late' phase of capitalism, during which the dynamic accumulation enabled by the expanded production of relative surplus value tendentially declines. This is also a 'late' phase of modernity, during which the modern growth of the industrial proletariat and the technological dynamism of a transformed process of production traverses the arc of real subsumption and passes into a period of relative decline and stagnation, thus transforming the social dynamics and lived class structure of recent history without thereby breaking its continuity with the structural determinations that brought us to this point. Indeed, the continuing legibility of those structural determinations depends upon our capacity to situate them within the continuing history of modernity, rather than as a radical break with or termination of the latter.[34] Just as the long period we refer to as 'early modern' involved a gradual movement toward the onset of real subsumption, 'late modernity' is characterised by the unfolding of the consequences of real subsumption, grasped as the deepening of capitalist contradictions and their irreversible dynamics. Again, in order to think modernity *as* the history of capital – and not as a process of modernisation abstracted from capital's contradictions – we have to continue to think modernity as the history of capitalism as long as the latter exists.

Modernism/Modernity

How then does this adjustment of our periodising terms bear upon the relation between modernism and modernity? Clearly, modernism is neither coeval nor coextensive with modernity. Whereas Jameson frequently equivocates between 'modernism' and 'modernity' and 'the modern', we must clearly distinguish the former as a discrete period of cultural production within the larger history of modernity. What then distinguishes this period of cultural production according to the structural account offered here? Why does it become a cultural dominant at a particular moment in capitalist modernity? My answer aims not at originality, but rather specificity and consistency: modernism is the cultural logic of real subsumption. From the first cultural configurations reflexively addressed to modernity – the quarrel between the ancients and the moderns – we move through a romantic period characterised by a transitional subsumption of social relations and the process of production under capitalism: a transitional movement from formal to real subsumption that persists through the first industrial revolution. Modernism is then the apogee of culture's reflexive attunement to modernity, and it is proper to a period in which real subsumption is fully underway (ca. 1850-1950): in which the capitalist process of production is integrally transformed by the competitive necessity of expanded relative surplus value production. This involves all sorts of contradictory dynamics, such as the colonial extraction of raw materials for industrial production driving the nineteenth-century scramble for Africa. Thus futurism and primitivism flourish at the same time: the muddy water of the factory drain into which his racing automobile plunges can recall for Marinetti the breast of his Sudanese nurse; Baudelaire, amid his reflections upon the transformation of Paris, will 'think of the Negress, gaunt and consumptive / Trudging in sludge, and seeking, eyes haggard, / The absent palms of splendid Africa';[35] the Dadaists can style themselves as skyscraper primitives. Modernism takes its course when it does because it is not the cultural logic of primitive accumulation nor of formal subsumption but of their collision with and integration into full-blown real subsumption, the cultural registration and inscription of modernity at the crest of its contradictions.

Jameson will eventually elaborate a category of 'late modernism' to designate cultural production from 1945 to the 1960s as 'a product of the Cold War'.[36] What I propose is that we disentangle the periodising reference of this term from its relatively superficial attachment to the Cold War and extend it to encompass cultural production into the present. What is at stake in this adjustment is the recognition that the constitutive relation of contemporary cultural production to modernism continues to structure the art market (perhaps most importantly), as well as the formal innovations of twenty-first century literature and architecture. Jameson characterises the cultural-historical situation of 'postmodernism' as one in which modernist styles have become postmodernist codes.[37] My sense is that this is now also true of the relation of twenty-first-century cultural production to the 'postmodern' codes gleaned from modernist styles: they too now serve as a system of referents for discrepant transformations. If this is so, it is because we have remained, throughout, within a late phase of modernism itself, a phase in which the new continues to have become old while the abolition of the economic and cultural imperative of novelty has not yet been traversed.

In 1983, Perry Anderson concluded his essay 'Modernity and Revolution' with what remains the best diagnosis of the relation of the prospective end of capitalism to our periodising categories:

> If we ask ourselves, what would revolution (understood as a punctual and irreparable break with the order of capital) have to do with modernism (understood as this flux of temporal vanities), the answer is: it would surely end it. For a genuine socialist culture would be one which did not insatiably seek the new, defined simply as what comes *later*, itself to be rapidly consigned to the detritus of the old, but rather one which multiplied the different, in a far greater *variety* of concurrent styles and practices than had ever existed before: a diversity founded on the far greater plurality and complexity of possible ways of living that any free community of equals, no longer divided by class, race or gender, would create. The axes of aesthetic life would, in other words, in this respect run horizontally, not vertically. The calendar would cease to tyrannise, or organise, consciousness of art. The vocation of a socialist revolution, in that sense, would be neither to prolong nor to fulfill modernity, but to abolish it.[38]

Clearly, we are not there yet. I concur entirely with Anderson's last sentence: the end of capitalism must also be the end of modernity, of the structural determination of history and culture by the contradictions of capitalism. Yet I do not agree with Anderson's assessment, just prior to this passage, of 'modernism' as 'the emptiest of all cultural categories'.[39] Modernism is a valuable category precisely *because* it is capable of including both the primacy of the new and its structural relation to 'what comes *later*': it names the structural contradiction between the new and the late that Anderson expounds and that he views as expressive of capitalism's 'temporal vanities'. Modernism does indeed name 'the axes of aesthetic life' which could now only be abolished by the abolition of capitalism – and these have not yet been abolished. To speak of 'late modernism' as the cultural logic of late capitalism, as the culture of late modernity, is to recognise that once we have passed over the crest of real subsumption its effects upon both capitalist economics and capitalist culture (and thus anti-capitalist culture) are irreversible, and we are still within them. The term 'late' designates this condition of being after-yet-within; it acknowledges the ambivalence of the *not yet*, and it demarcates the extension of a horizon that we still have to pass beyond.

'Postmodernism' and 'postmodernity' are among the dominant ideologies of late capitalism. In this sense, Jameson's diagnosis was correct. But when he extends his diagnosis to the affirmation of a veritable historical period designated by the term 'postmodernity' he goes awry. The desire to be postmodern, in history and in culture, expresses a desire to have *already* passed through the wrenching historical crux that, as Anderson notes (and it is still true today), we have *not yet* passed through. It is thus not *too late* to adjust Jameson's periodisation to bring it into line with the conjunctural demand he tried to meet: to align cultural production with the cultural logic of late capitalism, rather than with the presumption of a post-capitalist epoch.

Late Modernism/Late Modernity

Here I can only briefly elaborate some consequences of this realignment for our understanding and characterisation of cultural production.[40] My concern in this respect is not to quibble with the traits of what Jameson considered the cultural dominant of the late 1960s, '70s and '80s. Indeed, Jameson's empirical *description* of those aesthetic phenomena he called 'postmodernist' seems to me lucid enough. I have no particular quarrel with his assessment of Andy Warhol's *Diamond Dust Shoes* or its relation to Van Gogh's *A Pair of Boots* (though the selection of the latter as a representative of modernist painting indicates the strain of imposing a sharp enough periodising break to warrant the term 'postmodernism'). Likewise, Jameson's description of the Wells Fargo Centre and the Bonaventure Hotel in Los Angeles still seem plausible enough, even after thirty years of hindsight (although the former seems to me a late incarnation of suprematist architecture). These pages in his famous essay remain among the high points of cultural criticism in the 1980s. Rather, my concern is to ask after *what else* might come into view during that period from a revised periodising perspective, and to consider how the shift in perspective I have proposed might enable us to grasp the relationship between cultural production in that period and in the present.

Jameson highlights William Gibson's 1984 novel *Neuromancer* as a paradigmatic exemplar of the relationship between sci-fi and the structural conditioning of culture by capitalism during the upsurge of financialisation in the 1980s.[41] For Jameson, science fiction is the literary organon of our incapacity to imagine the breakdown of capitalism. His argument is that 'SF does not seriously attempt to imagine the "real" future of our social system. Rather, its multiple mock futures serve the quite different function of transforming our own present into the determinate past of something yet to come.' What is authentic about science fiction, Jameson argues, 'is not at all its capacity to keep the future alive, even in imagination. On the contrary, its deepest vocation is over and over again to demonstrate and to dramatise our incapacity to image the future, to body forth, through apparently full representations which prove on closer inspection to be structurally and constitutively impoverished, the atrophy in our time of what Marcuse has called the *utopian imagination*.'[42] In this mode, *Neuromancer* involves a technological extrapolation of the late capitalist future from the late capitalist present, and also a re-entry of that imagined future into a displaced rendering of the present to which we cannot imagine an outside. To be sure, this operation makes a great deal of sense within the periodising lens of 'postmodernism', through which the world can only become *more and more* postmodern (as evidenced by the term 'post-postmodern' or by Jameson's use of the term 'full postmodernity' in the late 1990s).[43] Yet my sense is that the substitution of the term late modernity for postmodernity, and the shift in perspective this entails, opens a more lucid perspective upon Jameson's famous claim that 'it seems easier for us to imagine the thoroughgoing deterioration of the earth and of nature than the breakdown of late capitalism.' We can affirm that Jameson is correct – but this is because postmodernity is exactly what we do not yet know, not because we are already situated within it. What sort of grappling with the *lateness* of modernity might be obscured by the presumption that we are already beyond it?

Alongside the cyberpunk posthumanism of Gibson's novel, consider Cormac McCarthy's 1985 *Blood Meridian,* which situates the all-too-human degradation of Gold Rush-era western expansion within the sheer indifference of a non-human, cosmological time and space. Here the movement of modernity is recognised as already dead though it is not yet over: we are cast back from the late modernity of the 1980s (*The Evening Redness of the West*) and from the waning hegemony of the United States to its inception as a global economic power in the second half of the nineteenth century; from the structural accomplishment of real subsumption to a frontier that remains outside of yet contiguous with its development. In a late modernist style gleaned from Faulkner (at the level of the paragraph) and Hemingway (in his writing of dialogue), McCarthy narrates the terminus of western expansion from within an inability to imagine the end of 'the west'. The outside of modernity, which we do not yet know, presses in upon its movement as the slaughter of the Apache, as a cosmological void, as a geological prehistory of which we have no experience at all, though it surrounds us:

> They wandered the borderland for weeks seeking some sign of the Apache. Deployed upon that plain they moved in a constant elision, ordained agents of the actual dividing out the world which they encountered and leaving what had been and what would never be alike extinguished on the ground behind them. Spectre horsemen, pale with dust, anonymous in the crenellated heat. Above all else they appeared wholly at venture, primal, provisional, devoid of order. Like beings provoked out of the absolute rock and set nameless and at no remove from their own loomings to wander ravenous and doomed and mute as gorgons shambling the brutal wastes of Gondwanaland in a time before nomenclature was and each was all.[44]

Here, the lateness of modernity during which McCarthy writes is figured allegorically through the persistence of cultural exteriority and geological prehistory at the core of modernity itself. The historical torque of uneven development, of the non-identity of modernity to itself in its forward march, is displaced into the radical discrepancy between the history of modernity and that of the earth. The novel shows that the time in which it was composed still *bears* this non-identity of modernity within itself, through the figuration of its outside as geological prehistory. The outside of modernity is thus limned as the void ground of what it is, 'the absolute rock' prior to its venture, to its western movement. It is the persistence of this not-knowing from the mid nineteenth century into a lateness-not-yet-after that haunts the imaginary of late modernity, as the spectre of its own exteriority.[45]

Despite his evocation of the 'inverted millenarianism', the 'sense of an ending' proper to postmodernism,[46] it is difficult to make much sense of a novel like *Blood Meridian* through Jameson's characterisation of postmodernism as a cultural dominant. His pursuit of simulacra, leaning heavily upon Baudrillard, is oriented toward superficial depthlessness, the waning of affect, the complexity of the global system and network culture. Of course, all of this has its crucial place: precisely at the surface of late modern culture. But when and if we recognise that by the mid-1980s we are also already within the midst of the long downturn, that the development of information technology and the turn to financialisation are predicated upon the same dynamic as the tendency of the rate of profit to fall, upon the downward momentum of capital, then we might be more inclined to turn toward a novelist like McCarthy than to Gibson: that is, toward a novelist who narrates the nihilistic drift of *Evening Redness in the West*. But more precisely, what matters is to recognise the relationship between these two period styles, the tension between them, as crucial to the cultural logic of late capitalism, and to recognise that tension as indicative of a late (rather than post) modernity.

Consider, amid more recent fiction, Rachel Kushner's widely read 2013 novel *The Flamethrowers*. Here we have a narrative that moves between the speed culture of Italian futurism, Fiat industrialism and its harvesting of rubber from Latin America, the radical politics of the Italian movement of '77 and the Red Brigades, and the New York art world of the 1970s. We are immersed in the contradictions of real subsumption as we move from the technophilic, fascist aestheticisation of politics in the early twentieth century, to the development of 'Fordist' manufacturing, to the fallout of its declining profitability and rising class conflict in the 1960s and '70s, all the while shadowed by the abstractions and career moves of an art world that seems to double, displace and integrate both capitalist logics and anticapitalist energies. Kushner's book is of particular interest as a canny, implicit commentary on the upsurge of radical political movements during the period of its composition, following the 2008 economic crash and thus shadowing political movements after the crash of 1973. Thus we are drawn into a concatenated history of the twentieth century and the persistence of its contradictions into the twenty-first, absorbing and articulating the cultural resonance of real subsumption from its futurist moment to its results in the inception of the long downturn and the consequences of the latter in the present. We are invited to consider this as *one* trajectory, complex though it is, traversing the last one hundred years, following the movement of modernism, at the crux of modernity, to a present moment that is not yet beyond its structural and cultural exigencies.

Turning to Claudia Rankine's 2014 book *Citizen: An American Lyric*, a harrowing anthropology of quotidian white supremacy and anti-Black racism, we might ask ourselves how it is possible to understand such a text through a periodising lens situating us after modernity. Here we are grappling with the ongoing history of slavery in the United States, with 'the vexed genealogy of freedom' as 'burdened individuality' analysed by Saidiya Hartman in *Scenes of Subjection*, and thus with the *persistence* of the contradictory logic of modern liberalism in the present.[47] Does it not depoliticise the relation of this logic to the history of modernity to periodise in such a way that we situate ourselves after that history, rather than remaining within it? In Rankine's book, techniques of collage and documentary reportage we might associate with such modernist texts as Muriel Rukeyser's *Book of the Dead* or Charles Reznikoff's *Testimony* are inflected with a tone of belated exhaustion that amplifies, via the mood of the text's formal history, the ongoing burden and exasperation of Black positionality that the content of the book conveys. The cutting irony and accuracy of the book's subtitle, *An American Lyric*, relies upon the relationship of modernist anti-lyric to romantic lyric, and upon the contradiction between these, as *itself* a form of self-expression that is both thwarted and necessitated by the history of modernity and its cultural forms. This is a late modernist lyric, wherein modernist form persists as at once exhausted and renewed, and it belongs to a period of late modernity in which the political and social framework of anti-Black racism continues to play a constitutive role in regulating everyday life and policing the racialised inequalities of capitalist exploitation.

Finally, if I had to choose a single exemplar of the periodising congruence of late capitalism, late modernity and late modernism it would be Roberto Bolaño's *2666*. Returning us to the border lands of *Blood Meridian* from the other side of their history, and now some 150 years after the Mexican-American war and the western migration of the Gold Rush, Bolaño places at the center of his novel the brutal killings of women on the peripheral waste spaces of the *maquiladoras*, factories sprouting like flowers of evil from NAFTA's tariff-free manufacturing zones.[48] The *maquiladoras* are *there* because uneven development persists; yet both the possibility and necessity of relocating American manufacturing indicates that real subsumption has already happened. The novel's final section moves from 1902 through the Holocaust and back to Mexico, thus inscribing Mexico's recent history in the record of twentieth-century catastrophe. Yet the novel has already, before this final section, inscribed the longer history of modernity within the killing fields of 1990s Juarez, through its technically complex, tonally dispassionate, and thus all the more wrenching evocation of the structural causality of capitalist violence.

Formally, what is notable about Bolaño's book is its fusion of surrealist free indirect style and picaresque episode with social realism and documentary reportage. Like Pynchon, Bolaño has no trouble straddling the 'realism-modernism' debate that has been so central to Marxist literary criticism. One of the implications of my argument about the correspondence of modernism to the central phase of real subsumption during modernity (ca. 1850-1950) is that realism is not properly understood as a periodising category. With Courbet, we can say that realism is the death of romanticism, and that at the same stroke it is, in its self-recognition as an -ism, the birth of modernism, as in the pivotal case of *Madame Bovary*. Lukács can deploy Mann against Joyce because the realism-modernism debate is in fact a debate internal to modernism, a debate between modernist '-isms' that only makes sense on its original terms: expressionism versus realism or surrealism versus realism. The formal accomplishment of writers like Pynchon and Bolaño is to hold together, dialectically, the contradiction of these methods within a single form. In this respect they do not displace but rather carry on the legacy of modernism by holding together its contraries within an integral yet internally discrepant style of narration capable of making realism adequate to the contradictions of modernity, and thus of making modernism adequate to its own contradictions.

It is from Jameson's commentary upon the so-called 'realism-modernism' debate in the influential *Aesthetics and Politics* collection, originally published by New Left Books, that I have drawn my epigraph for this essay. There he tells us that 'in such extinct yet still virulent intellectual conflicts', the contradiction is between history and the conceptual apparatus that seeks to grasp it while actually reproducing the discord of those conflicts in the form an aporia, 'which contains within its structure the crux of a history beyond which we have not yet passed.'[49] It is in the spirit of attempting to hold to such an aporia that I have found it necessary to return to the now antiquated postmodernism debate, in order to reconfigure its conceptual apparatus on the basis of what has become structurally and historically legible since it took place. What's in a name, one might wonder? But it is a matter of no little consequence – politically, historically, and culturally – to decide whether or not modernity is over. If neither modernism nor modernity are behind us, if modernity remains the history of capitalism and if the belated reproduction, renewal and critique of modernist forms still characterises the present, such that the history of their contradictions has not yet passed, then it behoves us to hold our periodising categories accountable to their persistence.

Nathan Brown is Director of the Centre for Expanded Poetics at Concordia University and author of The Limits of Fabrication *(2017).*

Notes

1. William J.R. Curtis, *Modern Architecture Since 1900*, 3rd Edition (New York: Phaidon, 1996), 7.
2. Peter Osborne, 'Crisis as Form', Lecture at Kingston University, London (12 January 2017), http://backdoorbroadcasting.net/2017/01/peter-osborne-crisis-as-form/; Peter Osborne, 'The Postconceptual Condition: Or, the Cultural Logic of High Capitalism Today', *Radical Philosophy* 184 (March/April 2014), 19.
3. Jeffrey T. Nealon, *Post-Postmodernism, or, the Cultural Logic of Just-In-Time Capitalism* (Palo Alto: Stanford University Press, 2012), ix.
4. N. Katherine Hayles and Todd Gannon, 'Mood Swings: The Aesthetics of Ambient Emergence', in *The Mourning After: Attending the Wake of Postmodernism*, ed. Neil Brooks and Josh Toth (Rodopi: Amsterdam, 2007), 99. Hayles and Gannon argue that the everyday experience of surfing the World Wide Web has routinised 'the inconceivable complexities of the infosphere' that had previously occasioned 'shock, disorientation, and hyperbole at the meteoric rise of the information age' (99).
5. Tom Turner, *City as Landscape: A Post-Postmodern View of Design and Planning* (E&FN Spon: London, 1996), 8–9.
6. Ibid., 8.
7. Fredric Jameson, *Archaeologies of the Future: The Desire Called Utopia and Other Science Fictions* (Durham, NC: Duke University Press, 2005), 166.
8. Fredric Jameson, *A Singular Modernity: Essay on the Ontology of the Present* (London and New York: Verso, 2002), 80. See the review by David Cunningham, 'The Anxiety of Returns', *Radical Philosophy* 120 (July/August 2003), 41–43.
9. Fredric Jameson, *Postmodernism, or, The Cultural Logic of Late Capitalism* (Durham, NC: Duke University Press, 1991), 311.
10. Ibid., xix.
11. Jameson, *A Singular Modernity*, 215.
12. Rejecting the contemporary utility of the terms 'postmodernity' and 'postmodernism', Peter Osborne also rejects the term 'late capitalism' borrowed by Jameson from Mandel and Adorno. 'How very late, it now seems', he remarks in 2014, 'still to have been periodising capitalism as "late" in 1991, at the very moment of its most powerful renewal.' Osborne, 'The Postconceptual Condition', 19. Yet I would argue that we have also seen, since 2008, how pyrrhic that renewal was, and the fragility of its basis can be understood within a periodising framework consistent with usage of the term 'late capitalism' to name a period subsequent to the dynamic phase of what Marx called 'real subsumption'. Here I develop such a periodising framework through Robert Brenner's account of 'the long downturn' since the early 1970s and Gopal Balakrishnan's speculative account of a 'stationary state' of low growth in the wake of the 2008 crash. I use the term 'late capitalism' not necessarily to signify the imminent *end* of capitalism but rather to mark the prolonged extension of a historical period subsequent to the tendentially dynamic growth accompanying the process of real subsumption from the industrial revolution to the mid-twentieth century. I should note that by 'real subsumption' I refer strictly to the technical usage of this term in Marx: the development of a properly capitalist process of production on the basis of tendentially increasing investment in constant capital relative to variable capital, and tendentially increasing extraction of relative surplus value over absolute surplus value. I do not use the term to denote a generalised 'subsumption' of life or culture under capital.
13. Jameson, *Postmodernism*, ix.
14. Ibid., 309.
15. Ibid., 310. Note the slippage in Jameson's terminology in this passage between the categories of modernity, modernism and the modern. This remains a persistent feature of his rhetoric from his early essay to the present.

16. Ibid., 309–10.

17. Arno Mayer, *The Persistence of the Old Regime: Europe to the Great War* (London and New York: Verso, 2010). See Jameson's remarks on Mayer's book in *Postmodernism*, 365–66.

18. Ernest Mandel, *Late Capitalism*, trans. Joris De Bres (London: New Left Books, 1972), 191.

19. Jameson, *Postmodernism*, 400. See also Fredric Jameson, *The Cultural Turn: Selected Writings on the Postmodern, 1983-1998* (London and New York: Verso, 1998), 35 (where this passage is reproduced).

20. Jameson, *Postmodernism*, 53.

21. Ibid., xix.

22. Paul Mattick, 'Ernest Mandel's *Late Capitalism*' in *Economic Crisis and Crisis Theory* (1974), Marxists Internet Archive, https://www.marxists.org/archive/mattick-paul/1974/crisis/ch05.htm

23. See Mandel, *Late Capitalism*, 312–16, 118. Mandel also correlates these stages with the production of 'machine-made consumer goods', 'machine-made machines' and 'machine-made raw materials and foodstuffs', 190–191.

24. Robert Brenner and Mark Glick, 'The Regulation Approach: Theory and History', *New Left Review* I:188 (July-August, 1991), 45–119.

25. Brenner and Glick, 75.

26. David Harvey, *The Condition of Postmodernity: An Enquiry into the Origins of Cultural Change* (Oxford and Malden, MA: Blackwell, 1990).

27. See Robert Brenner, *The Economics of Global Turbulence: The Advanced Capitalist Economies from Long Boom to Long Downturn, 1945-2005* (London and New York: Verso, 2006). For an account focused on the 1980s and 1990s, see Robert Brenner, *The Boom and the Bubble: The U.S. in the World Economy* (London and New York: Verso, 2002). For an update of Brenner's history following the 2008 crash, see 'What's Good for Goldman Sachs is Good for America' (18 April 2009): http://www.sscnet.ucla.edu/issr/cstch/papers/BrennerCrisisTodayOctober2009.pdf

28. See Théorie Communiste, 'Communization in the Present Tense', in *Communization and Its Discontents*, ed. Benjamin Noys (New York: Minor Compositions, 2011), 41–58. See also 'The Present Moment', 'Théorie Communiste' and 'The Concept of the Cycle of Struggles', https://sites.google.com/site/theoriecommuniste/resources-in-english.

29. On deindustrialisation and surplus populations, see Aaron Benanav, 'Misery and Debt', *Endnotes* 2 (April 2010), 20–51. On gender and reproductive labour, see Maya Gonzalez 'Notes on the New Housing Question', *Endnotes* 2 (April 2010), 52-66; and Endnotes, 'The Logic of Gender', *Endnotes* 3 (September 2013), 56–90. On racialisation and capitalism, see Chris Chen 'The Limit Point of Capitalist Equality', *Endnotes* 3 (September 2013), 202-23; Endnotes, 'Brown v. Ferguson', *Endnotes* 4 (October 2015), 10–69.

30. Gopal Balakrishnan, 'Speculations on the Stationary State', *New Left Review* 59 (September-October 2009), 5–26.

31. For an account of tensions between periodisations offered by *Théorie Communiste* and *Endnotes*, see 'A History of Separation', *Endnotes* 4 (October 2015), 77–80. See also Screamin' Alice, 'On the periodisation of the capitalist class relation', *Sic* 1 (November 2011), http://sicjournal.org/on-the-periodisation-of-the-capitalist-class-relation/. The specific periodisation of formal and real subsumption offered in the graph presented in this essay is my own.

32. On deindustrialisation as a global tendency *relative to population*, see Benanav, 'Misery and Debt': 'It should thus be clear that de-industrialisation is not caused by the industrialisation of the "third world". Most of the world's industrial working-class now lives outside the "first world", but so does most of the world's population. The low-GDP countries have absolutely more workers in industry, but not relative to their populations. Relative industrial employment is falling even as agricultural employment collapses' (41).

33. See Andreas Malm, *Fossil Capital: The Rise of Steam Power and the Roots of Global Warming* (London and New York: Verso, 2016).

34. It is for this reason that I prefer 'late modernity' in correspondence with 'late capitalism' to the category of the 'contemporary' as the primary periodising category for the present and its recent history. I am sympathetic to Peter Osborne's persuasive account of contemporaneity as 'the temporal structure that articulates the unity of global modernity' or 'the temporality of globalisation: a new kind of totalising but immanently fractured constellation of temporal relations.' See Osborne, 'The Postconceptual Condition', 21, 23. Yet the category of the 'contemporary', while aptly connoting the fractured unity of globalisation as the economic and historical structure of the present, does not adequately mark the *history* of this form of temporality itself. That is, the temporality of the contemporary must itself be grasped and marked as proper to a 'late' phase of capitalist modernity emerging from the structural accomplishment of real subsumption, as a process devolving from the contradictory dynamics of capitalist accumulation. The very question begged by the categories of 'late capitalism' and 'late modernity' – 'late relative to what?' – offers an occasion for the elucidation of those contradictory dynamics: i.e., the manner in which it is possible to articulate a complex, overlapping and uneven, yet tendential history of capital moving from primitive accumulation through formal and real subsumption to tendentially declining profit rates. Insofar as that tendential history then poses the question of *when* capitalism will end, given the prolonged extension of its late phase, it is all the better suited for denaturalising the history of capitalism as that of the status quo. On the relevance of the category of the contemporary to recent developments in literary realism, see David Cunningham, 'Time, Modernism, and the Contemporaneity of Realism', in *The Contemporaneity of Modernism: Literature, Media, Culture*, ed. Michael D'Arcy and Mathias Nilges (London: Routledge, 2015), 49–62.

35. Charles Baudelaire, 'Le Cygne', in *Les Fleurs du Mal*.

Oeuvres Complètes I, ed. Claude Pichois (Paris: Gallimard, 1975), 87. My translation.

36. Jameson, *A Singular Modernity*, 165. For other accounts of 'late modernism' referenced by Jameson, see Charles Jencks, *The New Moderns* (New York: Rizzoli, 1990), and Tyrus Miller, *Late Modernism* (Berkeley: University of California Press, 1999).

37. Jameson, *Postmodernism*, 17.

38. Perry Anderson, 'Modernity and Revolution', *New Left Review* 144 (March-April 1984), 113.

39. Ibid., 112.

40. While my focus in this article is on historical periodisation, and thus theorising the contemporaneity of late modernity, a more capacious treatment of late *modernism* as the contemporary situation of cultural production will be undertaken in a subsequent piece. While this subsequent piece will work across the arts, here my focus is on contemporary literature.

41. See Fredric Jameson, 'A Global *Neuromancer*', in *The Ancients and the Postmoderns: On the Historicity of Forms* (London and New York: Verso, 2015), 221–237.

42. Fredric Jameson, 'Progress Versus Utopia, or, Can We Imagine the Future', in *Archaeologies of the Future*, 288–289.

43. See, for example, Jameson, *The Cultural Turn*, 87.

44. Cormac McCarthy, *Blood Meridian, or, The Evening Redness in the West* (New York: Vintage, 1985), 188.

45. On the relationship of McCarthy's fiction to elements of the so-called 'non-human turn' in contemporary theory and 'weird fiction', see Kate Marshall, 'The Old Weird', *Modernism/Modernity* 23:3 (September 2016), 631–649.

46. Jameson, *Postmodernity*, 1.

47. Saidiya Hartman, *Scenes of Subjection: Terror, Slavery, and Self-Making in Nineteenth Century America* (Oxford: Oxford University Press, 1997).

48. Sergio González Rodríguez's research on the structural relationship between NAFTA and the killings of women working at the *maquiladoras* directly influenced Bolaño. See Rodríguez, *The Femicide Machine*, trans. Michael Parker-Stainback (Cambridge: MIT Press, 2012).

49. Fredric Jameson, 'Reflections in Conclusion', in *Aesthetics and Politics* (London: Verso, 1977), 237.

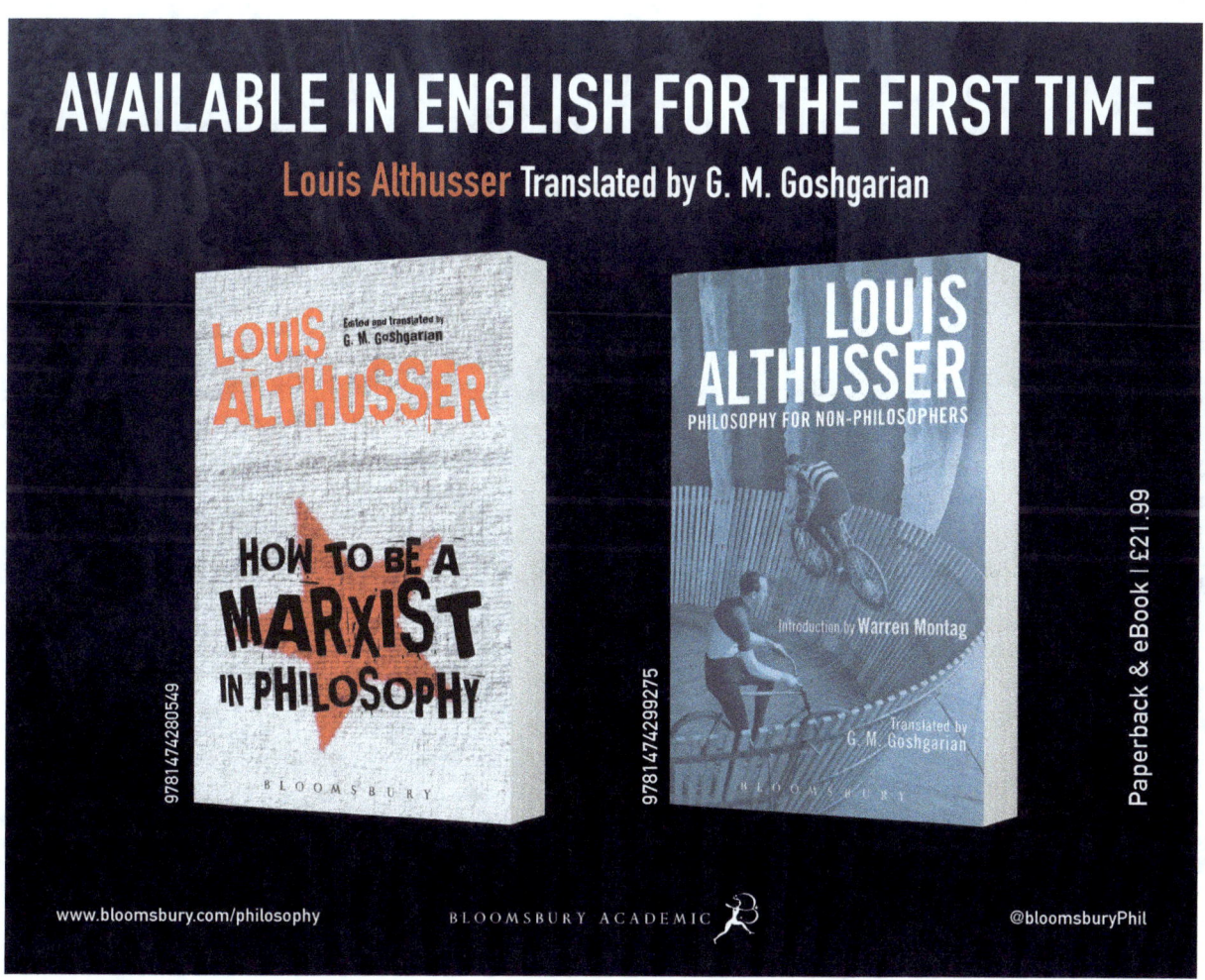

NEW FROM VERSO

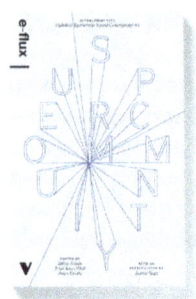

Supercommunity
Diabolical Togetherness Beyond Contemporary Art

e-flux

Introduction by Antonio Negri

Leading artists, theorists, and writers exhume the dystopian and utopian futures contained within the present.

Paperback / £19.99 / 9781786633590 / 480 pages
Hardback / £70 / 9781786633583 / November 2017

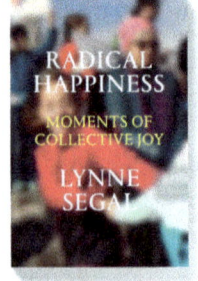

Radical Happiness
Moments of Collective Joy

Lynne Segal

"An engaging, enlightening read for anyone who wants to ponder the links between personal dissatisfaction and political disengagement – and possible remedies … Segal succeeds in inspiring on many levels" – Isabel Berwick, *Financial Times*

Hardback / £16.99 / 9781786631541
352 pages / November 2017

NEW EDITION

The New Spirit of Capitalism

Luc Boltanski and Eve Chiapello

"This massive book is an astonishing combination—an ideological and cultural analysis, a socio-historical narrative, an essay in political economy, and a bold piece of engaged advocacy … a dizzying theoretical tour." – *New Left Review*

Paperback / £20 / 9781786633255
688 pages / January 2018

The Right to Have Rights

Stephanie DeGooyer, Alastair Hunt, Lida Maxwell, and Samuel Moyn

Afterword by Astra Taylor

Five leading thinkers on the concept of 'rights' in an era of rightlessness.

Hardback / £14.99 / 9781784787547
160 pages / December 2017

NEW IN PAPERBACK

In the Flow

Boris Groys

The leading art theorist takes on art in the age of the Internet.

Paperback / £9.99 / 9781784783518
208 pages / December 2017

VERSO FUTURES

Psychopolitics
Neoliberalism and New Technologies of Power

Byung-Chul Han

Exploring how neoliberalism has discovered the productive force of the psyche.

Paperback / £9.99 / 9781784785772 / 96 pages
Hardback / £70 / 9781784785765 / December 2017

The Postconceptual Condition
Critical Essays

Peter Osborne

"Very little philosophical writing is inspiring enough to catalyse art and bring it into being. Peter Osborne's writing is consistently in this category." – Hito Steyerl, visual artist

Paperback / £19.99 / 9781786634207 / 240 pages
Hardback / £70 / 9781786634900 / January 2018

The Progress of This Storm
Nature and Society in a Warming World

Andreas Malm

An attack on the idea that nature and society are impossible to distinguish from each other.

Hardback / £16.99 / 9781786634153
256 pages / December 2017

Greece and the Reinvention of Politics

Alain Badiou

One of the world's leading radical philosophers analyses the failure of the Syriza experience in Greece.

Paperback / £12.99 / 9781786634177 / 112 pages
Hardback / £70 / 9781786634955 / January 2018

Duty Free Art
Art in the Age of Planetary Civil War

Hito Steyerl

"Steyerl's art is extremely rich, dense and rewarding … A pleasure in art can unhinge us in everyday life, where we are undone by falsehoods at every turn." – Adrian Searle, *Guardian*

Hardback / £16.99 / 9781786632432
256 pages / October 2017

Available at all good bookshops and through our website:

versobooks.com

Sign up to Verso's Twitter feed: **@versobooks**
Visit our Facebook page **facebook.com/VersoBks**

Hegel and the advent of modernity
A social ontology of abstraction
Jamila M. H. Mascat

> Abstraction is a bitter chalice but modernity must drain it to the dregs and reeling in simulated inebriation, proclaim it the ambrosia of the gods.
>
> Henri Lefebvre,
> *Introduction to Modernity*

> Bitter abstraction. In which the distance between cause and effect is developed with the aid of weaponry and mathematics to produce morbid symptoms in the economy, environment and the use of force.
>
> John Barker,
> *Dirty Secrets 8 / Bitter Abstraction*

In the third paragraph of his 1857 Introduction to the *Grundrisse*, 'On Method of Political Economy', Marx famously recalls the route 'historically followed by economics at the time of its origins': it started from the living whole of the state or of the population to ascend to 'a small number of determinant, abstract, general relations such as division of labour, money, value, etc.' While rejecting the analytical path embraced by seventeenth-century economists, Marx outlines his own method, which inversely begins with simple abstractions to finally attain the 'rich totality of many determinations and relations'. Such a concrete whole, which Marx defines in a manifest Hegelian fashion as 'the concentration of many determinations, hence unity of the diverse', is meant to appear 'in the process of thinking ... as a result, not as a point of departure, even though it is the point of departure in reality and hence also the point of departure for observation and conception.'[1] But precisely because on a methodological level 'abstract determinations lead towards a reproduction of the concrete by way of thought', and method makes concreteness appear as a result that merely belongs to thought (*Gedankenkonkretum*), illusions may arise. Indeed, Marx argues, 'Hegel fell into the illusion of conceiving the real as the product of thought concentrating itself, probing its own depths, and unfolding itself out of itself, by itself.' According to Marx, Hegel's illusion may have consisted in assuming the concept of the concrete as accountable for the concrete coming into being. '[T]his is characteristic of the philosophical consciousness', Marx observes, 'for which the conceptual world as such is thus the only reality, [and] the movement of the categories appears as the real act of production – which only, unfortunately, receives a jolt from the outside – whose product is the world.'[2] Yet, in fact, while focusing primarily on the dangers of Hegel's proverbial idealism, and warning against his perverted understanding of concreteness, Marx's stance misses the chance to engage with Hegel's own conception of abstraction and to ask, in Alfred Sohn-Rethel's words, whether there can be 'abstraction other than by thought' in Hegel's own philosophy?[3]

In the continuation of the same passage of the *Grundrisse*, Marx reflects on the very status of 'the simple abstract categories' that represent the starting point of his political economy. On the one hand, he observes that 'as a rule, the most general abstractions arise only in the midst of the richest possible concrete development, where one thing appears as common to many, to all'; on the other hand, he explicitly states that the abstraction of labour as such 'is not merely the mental product of a concrete totality of labours': such an abstract 'indifference towards any specific kind of labour' corresponds to the very specific form of capitalist society. Thus, Marx claims that in modern times, and more specifically since the advent of capitalism, abstraction does not only pertain to the category of labour, rather it belongs to 'labour in reality'.[4] Hence, he concludes that in bourgeois society 'for the first time, the point of departure of modern economics, namely the abstraction of the category "labour", "labour as such", labour pure and simple, becomes *true in practice*.'[5]

Not surprisingly, Hegel, for whom abstraction is synonymous with 'the system of all-round interdependence' that sustains the totality of the social whole, and for whom abstraction 'becomes also a *determination* of the mutual relations between individuals' in capitalism, would have completely agreed with Marx on this point.[6] Yet, Marx doesn't recognise Hegel as a precursor on the way to 'real abstraction', and the Marxist debate on the matter, with a few significant exceptions, seems to have overlooked the debt that Marx owes to Hegel regarding the notion of abstraction *qua* historically determined social form.[7] Within this field, many valuable researches have been conducted to trace and explore the multiple conceptual influences of Hegel's *Logic* on Marx's *Capital*, such as, for example, the writings of Chris Arthur, which stress with particular emphasis the structural homologies existing between the two seminal works.[8] Nevertheless, Hegel's own pivotal understanding of abstraction remains in the shadows, precisely because of the more relevant, radical and systematic use that Marx made of this notion. It is revealing that in delving into Marx's formulation of 'real abstraction', Sohn-Rethel's *Intellectual and Manual Labour* does not itself trace any comparison with Hegel's concept of abstraction; and Hegel is only recalled as 'the discoverer of dialectics',[9] never as 'the discoverer of abstraction', which in fact he was.

However, this paper's aim is neither 'to do justice' to Hegel nor to argue for the presence of proto-Marxian elements of political economy in Hegel's works that would have tacitly inspired his conception of modern society. Its purpose is rather to revisit Hegel's multifaceted 'theory' of abstraction, and to do it genetically so as to suggest that the notion of abstraction plays a pivotal role in the development of Hegel's *Gesamtsystem* as well as in the very structuring of his social and political thought.[10] Three main questions will frame the text that follows. First, what is abstraction in Hegel's terms and how does it operate in the distinct domains of his philosophy? Second, to what extent can abstraction be considered as a crucial cipher of Hegel's conception of social relations under modern capitalism? And, finally, what is the peculiar connection that Hegel establishes between the notion of abstraction and the advent of modernity?

To answer these questions, I will first provide an overview of the significant (though ambivalent) role played by the concept of abstraction in Hegel's early philosophy. Next, by looking more specifically at his Jena lectures and writings, I will distinguish the meaning and function of what I call Hegel's 'critique of theoretical abstraction' from his 'critique of social abstraction'. Third, by focusing on the former, I will illustrate logical abstraction's social relapses through the *Essay on Natural Law* (1802-03). As a fourth step, I will briefly consider three salient moments in the development of Hegel's theory of *Sittlichkeit* – the early *System of Ethical Life* (1802-03), the last *Lectures on the Philosophy of Spirit* (1805-06) and *Elements of the Philosophy of Right* (specifically, the section on 'Civil Society') – in order to expose how abstraction contributes essentially to the construction of social ties, becoming a *mode of social production*. Finally, I will argue that Hegel's 'practically true abstraction' should be understood as the core of his social ontology of modernity.

Who thinks concretely?

Heinrich Heine, a devoted pupil of Hegel, mentions him several times throughout his *Confessions* (1854). Among his memories, one is particularly telling with regard to the theme of this article: 'One beautiful starry-skied evening, we stood next to each other at a window, and I, a young man of about twenty-two who had just eaten well and had good coffee, enthused about the stars and called them the abode of the blessed. But the master grumbled to himself:

"The stars, hum! Hum! The stars are only a gleaming leprosy in the sky".'[11] In the addition to §341 of the *Encyclopaedia,* Hegel recalls this episode and somehow seeks to justify himself concerning his cynicism and his lack of enthusiasm for celestial bodies: 'It has been rumoured round the town that I have compared the stars to a rash on an organism where the skin erupts in an countless mass of red spots: or to an ant-heap in which, too, there is Understanding and necessity. In fact, I do rate what is *concrete* higher than what is *abstract*, and an animality that develops into no more than a slime, higher than the starry host.'[12]

Despite Hegel's candidly admitted preference for the concrete over the abstract, abstraction is not of mere secondary importance in his philosophy: on the one hand, 'real concreteness' includes abstraction as one of its necessary components; on the other hand, as we shall see, abstraction, so to speak, becomes concrete in modern society. Moreover, that a stubborn and acute upholder of the concept should express such a manifest inclination for concreteness may appear somewhat surprising. In a short essay that speculates on Hegel's famous reproach to Kant for having displayed in his antinomies too much 'tenderness for the things of the world',[13] Remo Bodei provocatively raises the question of why the 'starry heavens' and the 'moral law' – so important to the philosopher of Konigsberg – do not seem to interest Hegel, or perhaps even disappoint him.[14] Bodei convincingly interprets Hegel's lack of interest as the propensity to concentrate the efforts of reason on the sublunary world and its terrestrial matters, with respect to which the sky and the interiority of the moral commandment represent merely two lines of flight. To this extent, Hegel's *critique* of abstraction can be considered as one of the primary means by which he seeks to channel philosophical reason into the world.[15]

Although Hegel never explicitly tackles the theme of abstraction, except in his 1807 pamphlet *Who thinks abstractly?*, the concept often recurs in his writings. In fact, under the notion of abstraction Hegel labels a wide range of theoretical configurations and socio-historical phenomena: understanding is abstract, sensuous immediacy and intuition are abstract, labour in modern capitalism is abstract, as is 'right'. But also positivity, bad infinity, romantic irony, Fichte's theory of *Sollen,* the constitution of Germany, the Jacobin Terror, the German *Aufklärung*, Kant's morality, Jacobi's conception of faith, the empirical and formal sciences, can all be considered as *distinct* manifestations of abstraction. Indeed the concept of abstraction in Hegel's works is a *pollakòs legòmenon*, it can be said in many ways and must be 'handled with care' because of its constitutive ambivalences. Before *Hegel properly becomes Hegel*, the term 'abstraction' already appears in his youthful writings. In a fragment of 1792-93, the so-called *Tubingen Fragment*, where he distinguishes between subjective and objective religion, Hegel characterises the first as 'alive, having an efficacy that while abiding within one's being, is actively directed outward', while stating that 'objective religion is *abstraction*'. He illustrates the first metaphorically as the 'living book of nature', in which each element lives and reproduces itself in harmony with the whole, and the second as 'the cabinet of the naturalist' in which insects have been killed, plants desiccated and animals embalmed. Here abstraction coincides with the intellectual ratiocination that reduces the totality of life to a dead composition of parts in opposition to the much-hoped-for organic unity of reason and sensibility that inspired Hegel's early philosophical ideals.[16]

In the *Preface* to the second edition of his essay on *The Positivity of Christian Religion*, written in Frankfurt in 1800, Hegel calls 'abstract' those universal concepts used by reflection (*Reflexion* employed here as a synonym for *Verstand*, or understanding) to define the presumed essence of human nature. In an entirely arbitrary way, 'these simple concepts' by virtue of their universality become 'necessary concepts and characteristics of humanity as a whole', while 'the variations in national or individual manners, customs and opinions become accidents, prejudices and errors.' Such empty abstractions that foster the delusion of having embraced 'the infinite multiplicity of the manifestations of human nature' are opposed to the Living for which all that the concept treats as superfluous and contingent is 'the only thing which is natural and beautiful.'[17] Here abstraction stands for the vacuity of formalism.

Drawing on Hegel's early writings, a first appearance of abstraction can be discerned in the disintegrative and oppositional relation of abstract understanding to the whole – one that is accountable for obstructing the reconciliation (*Versohnung*) which the philosopher, working between Tubingen, Berne and Frankfurt (1788-1800), seeks to realise progressively through love, religion and in the immanence of life. However, from Jena (in 1801) onwards, Hegel distances himself from his previous Romantic denunciation of the ruinous consequences of abstraction to embrace a rigorous speculative criticism of abstract thinking as it is embodied in the philosophies of his contemporaries and predecessors.

Nonetheless, even in his mature works, Hegel never fully defines abstraction as such, nor does he explain unequivocally the significance of this polysemous notion, which appears in his writings in varying and sometimes even opposed senses. Etymologically, the abstract (*abs-tractum*) is the 'separate', the result of a reflective process that produces opposition and crystallises the terms of division. Hegel generally assigns abstraction a negative sense, but not always. For example, in §3 of the *Encyclopaedia* where 'the unintelligibility' of philosophy is connected to a general lack of training in the exercise of abstract thought – 'the inability (which in-itself is just a lack of practice) to *thinking abstractly*' – Hegel gives the faculty of *abstraktes Denken* a positive connotation.[18] Abstraction, which has the merit of elaborating pure thoughts unmixed with representations, is counterposed here to the phagocytising immediacy of intuition, and the philosopher acknowledges the superiority of the abstract thought that rises above sensory contingency and overcomes the accidental nature of the opinions of common sense.

In order to better grasp what abstraction is and, foremost, *what it does* in Hegel's philosophy, one needs to look at its antonym, concreteness. As has been noted, Hegel was the first to unsettle the historical divide between the abstract and the concrete traditionally identified with the speculative and the empirical, respectively.[19] His *Science of Logic*, which privileges the ascendant method – or the dialectical method – as a movement from the abstract to the concrete, considers the self-development of the Absolute Idea as the highest degree of concreteness. (This is why Marx in the *Grundrisse* actually attributes to Hegel the fallacious assumption that concreteness simply stems from thought, as noticed earlier.) For Hegel, indeed, the concrete occurs only in the form of totality and, in regard to this, he is careful to distinguish the concrete from the *immediate*: immediate intuition is by no means concrete; conversely, concrete knowledge is that which can acknowledge and articulate within itself the totality of the particulars, not in the form of a casual mirroring of the existent but in a *mediated*, speculative fashion.[20] Drawing on the etymology of *cum-crescere* (literally growing / expanding-together) which stands for a synthetic expansion of multiple determinations, Hegel argues that for the universal to be concrete it must shape an adequate relation between the form of totality and determinate matters. The universal 'taken formally, and put *side by side* with the particular', like Kant's universal law of moral reason emptied of all content, only reproduces the much-reviled frame of *bad infinity*, whereas the concrete universal consists of the speculative synthesis of speculation with worldly experience.[21] This presupposed result – the Absolute as a systemic 'organisation of propositions and intuitions' – which is 'the lost concept' that all Hegelian philosophy strives to restore, would be the paradigmatic embodiment of Hegel's concrete.[22] Thus the intimate connection between formalism, universality and abstraction can be deduced, *via negativa*, from Hegel's understanding of the concrete as opposed to the formal universal. At this point, the questions raised a few lines earlier – what is abstraction and, above all, what does abstraction do in Hegel's philosophy? – can be asked again and eventually answered.

The unbearable lightness of abstraction

'The abstract is finite; the concrete is truth', states Hegel in his *Lectures on the Philosophy of Religion,* meaningfully detaching finitude and abstraction from truth.[23] In fact, such an assumption doesn't do justice to finitude nor to abstraction, as both concepts, in Hegel's view, actually maintain a strong truth-value. Upon a closer examination of his texts, one could remark that for Hegel not all that is finite is abstract and not all that is abstract is false. As Herbert Marcuse points out in *Reason and Revolution* (1941), 'for Hegel all fixed forms reveal themselves to be mere abstractions',[24] i.e. not the finite forms per se, but the finite forms fixed as static ones or the unilateral self-positing of finitude. Along the same lines, Eric Weil argues: 'In Hegelian terms, that a notion is abstract does not in any way mean that it is false or that it can or must be abandoned. On the contrary, it indicates that it is indispensable – thought incomplete – in every respect. It is an essential element figuring in the comprehensive account of the development of the concept, and this account will have to, as Hegel says, *aufheben* the abstract quality, which means to abrogate it, but only in the sense of abrogating what is abstract in it in order to preserve it by sublimation and thereby give it its positive function in the organised totality of Reason.'[25] At a theoretical scale, abstraction consists, according to Hegel, in the surreptitious absolutisation of the particular that claims to raise itself to the level of the universal and instead plunges into the formalism of an empty concept. Once again the particular is not abstract because of its partiality, but only because of its ungrounded and accidental pretension to be universal.

The main consequence that arises from this unilateral self-positing of a particular determinacy is the necessity of its *reversal*. Theoretical abstraction, then, *doesn't hold up* and generates unstable settings generally doomed to be reversed. On the contrary, as we shall see, practical abstraction, which corresponds to abstraction originating in bourgeois society, gradually becomes, in the framework of Hegel's political theory, a crucial concrete instrument for reinforcing the social bond.

Looking at the evolution of Hegel's philosophy in Jena, and more specifically at the genealogy of the consecutive reconfigurations of his system drafts, one can trace a fundamental divide between two distinct schemes of functioning that belong to theoretical abstraction, on the one hand, and to social abstraction, on the other hand. Genealogical retrospection sheds light on the asymmetrical solutions that Hegel provides in order to overcome theoretical abstraction (or abstraction in thought) through the invention of the standpoint of consciousness in the *Phenomenology of Spirit* and to accommodate social abstraction (or abstraction in the socio-economic sphere) within the framework of his newly-emergent philosophy of Spirit (*Geist*). Following Hegel's critique of abstraction along these two separate paths, it is possible to distinguish his *critique of understanding* from his *critique of bourgeois society*. In this regard the Jena period is marked by a peculiar parabola whereby the two trajectories of Hegel's critique of abstraction have very different fates. Although both theoretical and social abstraction exhibit a peculiar *isomorphism* in relation to the abstracting mechanisms lying at their core – abstraction in both cases is premised on division, formalisation and universalisation – my claim is that an essential demarcation occurs between the two spheres, and that this demarcation appears to be irrefutable when one investigates the 'final destinations' reached by the two types of abstraction.

While for Marx theoretical abstraction represents a fruitful methodological option, for Hegel it constitutes a speculative obstacle to overcome; and, indeed, Hegel's effort to pursue this goal will induce an almost Copernican revolution in his early design of the *Gesamtsystem*. However, although from Hegel's early perspective, social abstraction represents an intrinsic threat to the unity of the ethical whole which he tries to secure and preserve, the later acknowledgement of the spiritual superiority of modernity over the simple political harmony of the Ancients allows Hegel to progressively make theoretical room for the constructive capacity of the abstract. As such, it becomes a vital ingredient for the consolidation of modern social relations. Finally, while the ontological character of the logic – or the intimate connection that the *Logic* establishes between thought and reality whereby the former constitutes the rational structure of the latter – allows Hegel to conceive of thought in terms of concreteness (the *Absolute idea* being the highest peak of concreteness), the peculiar nature of modern bourgeois society obliges him to give an account of the concrete power of social abstractions.

On the theoretical plane, the scope of the critique of abstraction corresponds to Hegel's challenge to the philosophies of reflection (*Reflexionsphilosophien*) that emerged through the Kantian turn. Despite their declared speculative ambitions, these philosophies (Kant's philosophy as well as those of his idealist successors like Fichte, Schelling and, to a different extent, Reinhold, Bardili, Schulze and Jacobi) eventually end up – some more crassly than others – grounding knowledge on the limited principle of finite understanding and deserting the philosophical task *par excellence*, namely the achievement of the *absolute*, i.e of *truth* that only exists in the shape of the *whole,* according to Hegel's famous statement from the Preface to the *Phenomenology.*[26] By condemning themselves to the horizon of finitude, the *Reflexionsphilosophien* manifest in philosophy that spirit of division (*Entzweiung*) that Hegel thought characteristic of modernity. Confronting himself with the panorama of contemporary German philosophy, he complains of what he would later (in the 1812 preface to the first edition of the *Science of Logic*) call the dishonourable spectacle of 'a cultivated people without metaphysics – like a temple richly ornamented in other respects but without a holy of holies.'[27] The philosophies of reflection constitute the sophisticated outcomes of *reflective understanding*, which 'insofar as it poses opposites' remains an 'abstract and therefore separating understanding, persisting in its separations.'[28] Therefore, according to Hegel, they are responsible for the reinforcement of metaphysical divisions, inasmuch as they work towards the reification of the finite at the expense of absolute.

Distancing his speculative endeavour from the modest and contradictory achievements attained by the *Reflexionsphilosophien*, Hegel sets his philosophy the task of overcoming the limits of finitude without getting caught in the vicious circle of *bad infinity* – an infinity thought of as opposed to, and isolated from, finitude – and accordingly conceives of the infinite as resulting from the very infinitisation of the finite. His critique of abstraction, in other words, consists in the rigorous effort conducted by reason to reconcile the abstract hypostases that reflective understanding can but fix apart. On the logical level, the elaboration of a dialectical notion of *negation* – namely the transition from *Vernichtung* (annihilation) to *Aufhebung* (sublation) – helps Hegel supersede the impasses reached by the abstract ratiocination of understanding for which not only does each position stands for an opposition, but also each opposition simply precipitates in the elimination of one of the opposites, i.e. in the crystallisation of a finite determinacy against the other, and hence in abstraction. *Aufhebung,* in Weil's words, is what allows Hegel to fight abstraction by 'abrogating what is abstract in it in order to preserve it ... and thereby give it its positive function in the organised totality of Reason.'[29]

However, in spite of Hegel's ruthless crusade against intellectual abstraction from his early writings onwards, the first variable sketches of his Jena speculative system – consisting of three parts: 1. *Logic and Metaphysics* followed by 2. *Philosophy of Nature* and 3. *Philosophy of Spirit* [30] – shows a significant remnant of abstract reasoning to be located precisely in the original division of Logic *and* Metaphysics. From Hegel's viewpoint, the complementarity of the two components of the entry-level of his *System of Science* results from the different functions respectively assigned to Logic and Metaphysics. Whilst the task of the first consists in displaying the successive unfolding of the categories of finite understanding in order to clear the way for the exposition of metaphysical principles, the task of the second consists in exposing its cognition (*Erkennen*) as separate and *abstract* from the logical path of understanding. However, the bipartition of Logic and Metaphysics perpetuates the exclusionary scheme of abstract thinking, by excluding the Logic (*qua* finite knowledge) from the perimeter of speculation (or Metaphysics *qua* infinite knowledge).[31] Indeed the bipartition of the first part of the system into Logic and Metaphysics that Hegel will abandon in his later Logic – where 'the metaphysical element falls completely within' – but still maintains in the system projects elaborated between 1801 and 1806, testifies to the difficulties that the philosopher encountered in dissipating the residual presence of abstraction which haunted his early *Gesamtsystem*. As the victim of a sort of philosophical retaliation, Hegel ends up stumbling on the *bad infinity* that his own speculative system produced by grounding infinite Metaphysics on the elimination of finite Logic.

At this stage, the problem of theoretical abstraction that inhabits Hegel's own philosophy will be truly solved and transcended only in the new emerging framework inaugurated by the *Phenomenology of Spirit* through the adoption of the standpoint of consciousness as the new organisational principle of the relationship between the finite and the absolute. It is in this sense that the *Phenomenology* signals the accomplishment of Hegel's critique of theoretical abstraction in at least two meaningful ways: first, by resetting the problem of the access to the Absolute – earlier entrusted to the Logic of understanding – and second, by re-determining the status, the forms and the scope of finitude inside speculation: no authentic speculative philosophy that aims at achieving the goal of the Absolute can disregard (or *abstract from*) the vital presence of the finite in it.[32]

To come full circle: the critique of abstraction, as critique of the *bad infinity* generated by abstract understanding, finally attains a vigorous requalification of the finite as the inescapable premise for the infinitisation of thought. Conversely, as we will see in the next sections, on the historical plane, abstraction survives, by converting Hegel's initial critique into a gradual acknowledgement of modern abstraction's social potentiality and unavoidability.

Abstract Impostures

Among the many theoretical configurations of abstraction, the one exposed in Hegel's *Essay on Natural Law* (1802) provides a good example of the practical consequences of abstract thinking. Here abstraction appears as the result of an incongruous mediation between intellectual form and empirical matter – a mixture of 'absolute form with conditioned matter', whereby 'the absoluteness of the form is *imperceptibly* smuggled into the unreal and conditioned character of the content.'[33] The main danger that occurs when an abstract universal concept proves to be incapable of mediating content – and properly articulating its relationship with the surrounding determinacies – is that it ends up gathering unmediated content that surreptitiously strives for universalisation. The outcome of this risky mismatch of form and content is the emergence of a universal imbued with one-sided obstinate particularity; hence, an illegitimate universal, an 'impostor'. It is remarkable that already in this early text Hegel does not describe abstraction according to classical parameters for which abstraction stands for conceptuality, and concreteness stands for sensitivity. At the same time, abstraction does not correspond either to the neutral intellectual mechanism of generalisation that arises from multiplicity so as to reach a formal unity through an abstract collection of particulars. Instead, abstraction has to do with the nexus between universality and particularity, and, more precisely, with the universalisation of particularity. But it specifically designates the accidental and ungrounded process of absolutisation of the particular into the universal. Metaphorically speaking, we can call abstraction a peculiar intellectual move triggered by an impulse of 'megalomania' on the side of determinacy, which strives to affirm its absolute claim to be universal.

The *Essay on Natural Law* investigates the material implications of such an intellectual megalomania. Hegel's declared aim here is to redefine – as is suggested by the title of the essay – Natural Law's 'Place in Moral Philosophy, and its Relation to the Positive Sciences of Law'. To this end he undertakes to demonstrate, on the one hand, the insufficiency of the formalist approach, and on the other, the limits of the empiricist tradition. While empirical science groups determinations in an accidental unity that does not correspond to organic totality, formalism, Hegel remarks, entrenches itself behind an empty universality, a universality devoid of contents, because its abstractness makes it unable to properly subsume and mediate the empirical. This is why as a pure and empty universal detached from and opposed to the empirical, Kant's moral law can only incarnate the 'non-substantial (*wesenlose*) abstraction of the one'.[34]

Hegel's critique of Kant's 'deposit example' is well known. How can a 'proper' moral maxim be distinguished from a non-moral one? Kant believes that the maxim 'I shall keep on a deposit entrusted to me whenever the opportunity presents' provides a good case for testing the criteria that would allow a maxim to be recognised as moral. Moral maxims are those that can be universalised, and actually not all maxims can become universal ones. According to Kant for example, the maxim of the deposit results in immorality because if generalised, Kant argues, it would come into conflict with the *concept* of deposit itself, thereby destroying the very possibility that deposit exists. To Kant's argument, Hegel objects that if no deposit exists any longer there would indeed be no contradiction. In fact, non-property simply as such does not contradict itself. Or, Hegel suggests, in order to prove the inconsistency / immorality of a maxim of this kind, one would have to admit that a particular content like property has taken on, contingently, a necessary and universal legitimacy such as to make its negation contradictory. The fact that 'property, *if property is*, must be property' constitutes the rigorous yet formal outcome of the legislating faculty of practical reason, but 'the interest at stake is precisely to prove that there must be property.'[35]

Hegel here addresses a double reproach to Kant: first, Kant has applied the mechanism of formal contradiction to a historical fact (the institution of property) whose negation cannot be contradictory in itself, in so doing projecting a contradiction where there is no ground for contradiction; and second, Kant has grounded the entire edifice of his morality on weak and inadequate foundations. Self-contradiction as a matter of fact is not enough, since it does not apply to empirical contents, hence the self-consistency of a maxim doesn't guarantee for its morality. A formal criterion cannot guarantee for moral validity concerning empirical matters, and in this sense the principle of non-contradiction can only be the ground of *abstract* morality which, in turn, precisely because of its abstract nature turns out to be immoral. Thus Hegel observes that when the moral law is pure, it is tautological, whereas when it has heteronomous contents, it is *false*, as it is imbued with a set of contingent background assumptions (such as, for example, the absolute value of property). At this point, where a contingent element imposes itself as an absolute content within an empty universal, the danger of formalism does not reside in its emptiness, but, rather, in the a-critical subsuming of particular determinacies that have not been adequately mediated in the form of a universal. Abstract forms, in other words, let themselves be filled with anything, and consequently end up being not too empty, but actually *too full*. This is why abstraction, which is constitutive of any formalist approach, becomes in Hegel's view accountable both for being a theoretical defect that falsifies knowledge and for having significant socio-cultural relapses.

Create two, three, many abstractions, or, the cunning of bourgeois society

In order to illustrate what I shall describe as Hegel's 'social ontology of abstraction', I will first consider three salient moments in the development of his theory of ethical life: the *System of Ethical Life* (1802-03), the last *Lectures on the Philosophy of Spirit* (1805-06) and the *Elements of the Philosophy of Right* (1821). The trajectory of Hegel's social theory from the early *System der Sittlichkeit* to the Berlin's *Grundlinien* reveals the occurrence of structural changes that concern primarily the status of so-called 'civil society', a concept that the young Hegel borrows from the Scottish Enlightenment and formally introduces only in 1817.[36] My suggestion is that we need to interpret this remarkable trajectory, which runs parallel to Hegel's redesigning of his speculative system, but follows a quite different rhythm, as a process of progressive *transvaluation* of social abstraction: from being a disruptive force susceptible to being contained and eliminated, abstraction, in Hegel's practical philosophy, ends up being upgraded to the rank of an inescapable ingredient in the formation of the ethical world.

The *System of Ethical Life* can be seen as the ground-zero of such a trajectory, the initial stage in which Hegel still subordinates the new instances that emerged with modernity and modern capitalism to the search for an organic synthesis with the structure of ancient ethical life. Drawing on Aristotle and still under the influence of Schelling's philosophy, Hegel's notion of ethical totality in the *System* implies an essentially negative conception of individuality, which, because of its tendency to abstract itself from and affirm itself against the ethical community, is accused of contributing to the disintegration of the social bond and must be overcome. The system testifies to Hegel's effort to work out a theoretical paradigm capable of accounting for the conditions of ruptured harmony that characterise modern bourgeois society, and at the same time capable of reconciling them. The result is a spurious anachronistic ensemble where the ferment and the antagonisms of the capitalist world are conveyed into a social arrangement largely patterned after premodern-precapitalist schemes. Hegel's approach to social abstraction as that which threatens to cause the modern ethical fabric to crumble, consists here in a resolute attempt to repress and limit the expansion of the economic sphere, which Hegel still understands only as a bubble of unlimited contingency to be domesticated and eventually circumscribed to a particular social group: the so-called 'class [*Stand*] of honesty' whose purpose 'lies in work for needs, in possessions, gain and property.'[37]

The lectures on the *Philosophy of Spirit* (in particular, the ones of 1805-06) distance themselves from the setting of the *System of Ethical Life* insofar as they abandon the conceptual constellation that Hegel previously borrowed from Schelling and substitute the immobile ethical substance with the new dynamic framework of 'Actual spirit'. In the *Geistesphilosophie*, in which the structure of Spirit becomes the ground on which individual consciousness manifests and realises itself, Hegel ceases to praise the unconditional superiority of the Greek world and to confine the status of the individual to 'the sense of his inner nullity'. Finally, he fully acknowledges the higher principles and prerogatives of modernity over the 'beautiful public life' of the Ancients, the 'immediate unity of the universal and the individual, [the polis as] a work of art wherein no part separates itself from the whole.'[38] The shift to the philosophy of Spirit represents the very condition of possibility for Hegel's *transvaluation of the abstract*, reaching the radical awareness that, to quote Henri Lefebvre, '[m]odernity is doomed to explore and to live through abstraction.'[39] Indeed, Spirit incarnates a subjective instance of mediation that allows abstraction to disseminate itself and become productive within it. In turn, the new spiritual texture of ethical life allows Hegel to recognise the social surplus value of abstraction. In the new spiritual framework set up in the 1805-06 lectures, the building of society takes shape differently, freeing ethical life from the incoherence of the earlier experiments. Since social abstraction is established as *the indelible mark of modernity*, the abstract forms of the economic and the juridical spheres now thoroughly pervade all strata of society.

On a closer and more accurate look, we can gauge to what extent the new social sphere delineated by Hegel ('Actual Spirit') appears totally permeated by abstract and impersonal infrastructures, such as the system of needs, the labour process, the market as well as abstract rights and civil and penal laws. Starting from the very basis of the economic sphere (the web of needs), abstraction triggers a domino effect that actually constrains the agents in a societal network and that creates socialisation by means of atomisation, separating individuals from one another and inserting between their labour and the satisfaction of their needs the long chain of produced and exchanged goods:

> In the element of being as such, the existence and range of natural needs is a multitude of needs. The things serving to satisfy those needs are worked up [*verarbeitet*] .... But in the element of universality, [this processing (*Verarbeiten*) of things] is such that it becomes an abstract labour. The needs are many. The incorporation of their multiplicity in the I, i.e., labour, is an abstraction of universal models [*Bilder*] .... The I, which is for-itself, is abstract I; but it does labour, hence its labour is abstract as well. ... Since work is performed only [to satisfy] the need as abstract being-for-itself, the working becomes abstract as well. But the more abstract [his labour] becomes, the more he himself is mere abstract activity.[40]

Hegel's remarkable merit consists not only in observing the proliferation of abstractions, but, first and foremost, in grasping how in modern capitalism such proliferation of parcelled needs, mechanised labour and multiple goods turns into a universally socialised totality, or, in other words, how abstraction generates concreteness:

> Among these diverse, abstract, processed needs, a certain movement must now take place, *whereby they once again become concrete need[s]*, i.e., become the needs of an individual, who in turn becomes a subject comprising many needs. The judgment which analysed them, placed them against itself as determinate abstractions. Their universality to which this judgment rises is [that of] the equality of these needs, or value. In this they are the same. This value itself, as a thing, is money. The *return to concretion*, to possession, is exchange.[41]

Abstract labour derived from the social division of labour lays the groundwork for the emergence of property and contract, the advent of crime and punishment and the enactment of coercive laws. (These are the progressive steps of the section on 'Actual Spirit' that provides a prelude to the last and third section of the lectures devoted to the 'Constitution' of the State.[42]) Thus the market and the law create an impersonal dominion that makes everyone horizontally dependent on everyone else and vertically dependent on the universality of the social bond. To cite Marx's statement in the *Grundrisse*, one can say that 'individuals are now ruled by *abstractions*, whereas earlier they depended on one another.'[43]

In the sphere of *law*, where possession becomes property, Hegel remarks that 'the highest abstraction of labour pervades that many more individual modes and thereby takes on an ever-widening scope'. This goes hand in hand with the increasing 'contrast [between] great wealth and great poverty…: the poverty for which it becomes impossible to do anything; [the] wealth [which], like any mass, makes itself into a force'. However, no structural solution can be provided to this phenomenon, only contingent remedies, insofar as the *cunning of government* precisely consists in 'indulging the self-interest of others [*laissez-faire*]', 'freeing individual selfishness … and managing it so that individual profit reverts [to government]'.[44] Yet, not even the *constitution* of the State, which incarnates the purpose and consummation of the ethical life of the people, can oppose the domination of the abstract, since, for Hegel, a state-run economy constitutes 'a pre-modern institution, incompatible with the modern principle of individual freedom'.[45] Instead, the reproduction of the body politic is premised on the State's capacity to balance 'state power over life and freedom to live', or in other words private interest and public ethos. Thus, the State finally culminates in the '*abstract system* of individual subsistence' that has 'many internal parts which [are complete in themselves and] develop in their abstractness contributing to the totality'.[46]

Since economic, juridical and political abstractions convert themselves into aggregating tools that account for the preservation and expansion of the *Sittlichkeit*, we can properly speak of a 'social ontology of abstraction' that from the Jena lectures onwards sustains Hegel's conception of ethical life, i.e Hegel's political theory *tout court*. Is there a further horizon beyond politics to which the issue of abstraction could be deferred? Hegel recognises the history of the Spirit (in its artistic, religious and speculative dimensions) as the overarching framework of his theory of ethical life. Yet, immediate history (Hegel's present) does not foresee any consistent response to the proliferation of abstraction, which as an enduring feature of capitalist modernity is merely consigned to the future advancement of the Spirit without being sublated or reconciled. Historical reconciliation, in other terms, must accept and comprehend abstraction as the non-transcendable *medium* of the modern age, as its ineliminable *constructive mediation*. Along with the modern emergence of 'a higher level of abstraction, a greater [degree of] contrast and cultivation', Hegel thus calls for 'a *deeper* spirit' equipped to come to grips with the necessity of that abstraction.[47]

The *Elements of the Philosophy of Right* (1821), almost two decades later, present us with an effective *mise en scène* of the *cunning of social abstraction*, by replacing the often obscure intricacies of Hegel's Jena lectures with a well-ordered systematic shape. Here we finally encounter Hegel's concept of civil society explicitly portrayed as the realm of the market economy and modern law and distinguished from both the private sphere of the family and from the State (although in Hegel's view civil society determines the political form of the modern state).[48] In Hegel's words, civil society designates 'a system of all-round interdependence, so that the subsistence and welfare of the individual and his rightful existence are *interwoven* with, and grounded on, the subsistence, welfare and rights of all, and have actuality and security only in this context'.[49] Such an *interweaving* is premised on principles of equivalence and indifference that represent the quintessential matrix of abstraction in modern capitalism. Because of the power of abstract indifference, the more the individuals 'make themselves links in the chain of this [social] *continuum* [*Zusammenhang*]', the more they attain their fulfillment; thanks to the value of abstract equivalence, the more abstract the right is, the more it is universal, since its abstract formalism precisely amounts to its universal capacity to guarantee the conditions for individual freedom to be realised.[50]

The domain of 'Civil Society' in the *Philosophy of Right* only partially coincides with the domain of 'Actual Spirit' in the Jena lectures, although many significant common threads (such as the system of needs, the division of labour, the administration of justice, among others) can be easily detected across the two texts. Interestingly, the term 'abstraction' and the attribute 'abstract' appear less frequently in the *Grundlinien* than in the lectures, and yet at § 192 Hegel formulates a concise definition of abstraction's *modus operandi* that epitomises its most meaningful characteristics: 'abstraction which becomes a quality of both needs and means also *becomes a determination of the mutual relations [Beziehung] between individuals*. This universality … is the moment which makes isolated and abstract needs, means, and modes of satisfaction *into concrete, i.e. social ones*.'[51] In these few lines, Hegel, on the one hand, acknowledges the determining function of abstraction in respect to the construction of social ties among individuals and, on the other hand, conceives of social concreteness as a direct outcome of the proliferation of social abstraction. Abstraction gets here a further upgrade and becomes a *mode of social production* that determines the very building of civil society as well as the shaping of the modern state. In fact, in spite of its all-encompassing normative function, the State doesn't eliminate abstraction but rather results from it, being the most suitable institutional configuration to contain the dissemination of abstract forms and relations. Marx significantly grasped this point in his *Critique of Hegel's Philosophy of Right* where he acknowledges 'the abstraction of the political State as such' which 'belongs only to modern times, because the abstraction of private life belongs only to modern times.'[52] Therefore, the transvaluation of social abstraction finds in Hegel's Philosophy of Right its full accomplishment.

Living abstractly in concrete capitalism

So far we have observed how, in the course of the evolution of Hegel's political theory, social abstraction becomes a founding moment of modern ethical life. As a consequence, we can see a structural enhancement of the economic inside the body politic that precisely occurs thanks to economy's characteristic traits of abstraction (and not in spite of them). The resulting ethical world, portrayed in the Jena lectures and more organically in the *Elements of the Philosophy of Right*, is a whole pervaded by abstraction throughout. Thus, in the Jena Philosophy of Spirit abstraction clearly spreads to all the levels of social formation: labour, exchange, law, administration of justice and state. Similarly, in the *Grundlinien*, civil society is produced and reproduced through the abstraction of needs and labour, whereas the foundations of the modern state are built on the abstractions of the law and of the economic sphere. Instead of constituting a factor of instability – as in the case of theoretical abstraction with respect to the logical grounding of Hegel's speculative system – abstraction in the historical world turns into a crucial tool for the production of social bonds. Moreover, abstraction does not simply represent a mere ingredient or component of civil society; rather, it operates as a dynamic factor that accounts through its own intensification and expansion for the actual construction of the social whole.

In examining Hegel's notion of abstraction and comparing it to Marx's – 'the most original element of Marx's social theory' – Roberto Finelli argues that, in the final instance, Hegel thought of social abstraction in a merely intellectualistic fashion, projecting onto his civil society the same logical scheme of intellectual abstraction.[53] Finelli claims, in fact, that the problem of 'how modern subjects, conceived as free and independent from each other, can join in sociality and at the same time maintain their autonomy' could be to some extent assimilated to the intellectualist problem of determining how many ones can generate the One, or, in other words, how to regain unity against division. Finally, Hegel's critique of abstraction still belongs to a 'predominantly humanistic horizon' that attempts to restore the lost immediate cohesion alienated from the social world. Only the late Marx, according to Finelli, actually managed through his labour theory of value to accomplish the process that Hegel could not bring to completion; namely, transforming logical abstraction into an abstraction that is 'true in practice' and behaves as the 'highest factor of reality and universalisation' in modern society.[54]

My claim is that actually Hegel already fulfilled this task (although manifestly Hegel is no Marx and *has no Capital*, i.e. he doesn't elaborate a critique of political economy).[55] I would argue, in this light, that Finelli's analysis hits the mark in attesting to a certain structural homology between the terrain of Hegel's theoretical and social abstraction. At the same time, however, Finelli ends up reducing social abstraction to an analytical function of understanding, precisely because he overlooks the most specific features that belong to abstraction in the social world and make it *really existing* in modern society. On the one hand, Finelli reasonably recognises that Hegel's social abstraction is real inasmuch as it concerns real praxis and resides in things rather than in thoughts, as he puts it. On the other hand, he emphasises that 'the quality of such abstraction ... remains intrinsically logico-analytical', where the 'analytical' refers to 'a function that remains a tool at man's disposal, that institutes an order which, though impersonal and alienating, is still at the measure of man'.[56] From this perspective, social abstraction incarnates an impersonal device of socialisation that nevertheless appears to be ruled by an intellectualist subject-predicate structure 'at the measure of man'. Social abstraction – like logical abstraction that reverses itself and results in the restoration of the concrete universal (the Absolute Idea) – is meant to revert to a cohesive social whole where unification is apparently gained through the removal of all determinacies. In both cases, for Finelli, the status of differences and determinacies would be inconsistent, being simply a 'moment' or the predicate of a subject it could be reabsorbed by, and, hence, merely 'intellectualistic'.

However, as noted by Peter Osborne, in Hegel 'this kind of practically "bad" abstraction – i.e. social abstraction as domination – has a different logical form to the "one-sided" bad abstractions of the understanding.'[57] Indeed, the most defining feature of social abstraction is precisely its *non-reversibility*. Unlike logical abstraction, which is doomed to be superseded by Hegel's re-foundation of a new speculative approach to the finite-infinite relation (through the *Phenomenology of Spirit*), social abstraction – modern capitalism's abstraction – *endures and remains*. As has been seen, through the detailed illustration above of Hegel's interweaving of atomisation and socialisation in civil society and his making the latter dependent on the former, social abstraction cannot be contained nor repaired: a long future of intense proliferation awaits abstraction in capitalist societies. Hegel makes do with this insight – the irreversible presence of social abstraction in the course of modern history – and does not engage in any criticism of modernity aimed at restoring the harmony of the social bond. Individual *alienation* that stems from the mechanisms of abstract socialisation underlying the economic, the juridical as well as the political spheres does not represent in Hegel's view a loss to recover. On the contrary, already in the Jena lectures, Hegel remarks that 'this alienation [i.e. the alienation of individuals' self-dependence into the magma of abstract sociality] is an acquiring (*Erwerben*)', inasmuch as it constitutes a peculiar form of *Bildung*, a deprivation that nevertheless guarantees a gain, which is precisely the surplus value of universal socialisation. Yet, universal socialisation does not correspond to universal cohesion, and for Hegel the *citoyen* remains an antagonist for the *bourgeois*, although both of them must be incarnated in the individual *Bürger* of *Bürgerliche Gesellschaft*.[58]

Accordingly, it seems that Hegel's notion of social abstraction operates in a way that cannot be simply assimilated, *pace* Finelli, to the proceeding of intellectual abstraction. The difference is primarily functional: intellectual abstractions are by definition susceptible to being reversed, since they prove through their one-sided partiality to be inconsistent and unable set up a solid theoretical order. On the contrary, social abstraction gives both firmness and concreteness to the asymmetrical and atomised relations around which it aggregates social objectivity. Further, if, as Moishe Postone argues with regard to Marx, 'what fundamentally characterises capitalism is a historically specific abstract form of social mediation – a form of social relations that is unique inasmuch as it is mediated by labour', one could argue that Hegel had already developed an identical insight, paving the way for Marx's understanding of bourgeois industrial capitalist society. Even more importantly, for Hegel as for Marx, 'this historically specific form of mediation ... becomes quasi-independent of the people engaged in those practices'. Indeed, in this sense, it is an *abstract* and *impersonal* form that becomes socially cohesive by means of its own abstraction and divisive power.[59]

Can abstraction ever end?

In the preceding, I have tried to provide a consistent framework for interpreting Hegel's social and political theory. Such a framework revolves around the pivotal notion of abstraction although abstraction itself is not a framework, nor a mere static component, but a dynamic device that in Hegel's philosophy accounts for the production and reproduction of social life.

In *Who Thinks Abstractly?*, Hegel connects abstract reasoning to the effects of *Denken abstrakt* on the plane of action and behaviour in order to explore the practical relapses of theoretical abstraction. Abstraction, Hegel argues, takes on an intrinsically practical significance because whoever thinks abstractly – and sees everything through the prism of a partial and distorted lens – *acts abstractly*. Or, in other words, whoever thinks abstractly conducts herself accordingly. This is the consenting crowd at the execution of a murderer, in whom they see nothing but 'the abstract fact that he is a murderer'. It is also the egg-seller who vilifies her customer for saying that her eggs are rotten and 'subsumes the other woman – scarf, hat, shirt etc., as well as ... her father and family too, solely under the "crime" that she has found the eggs rotten', never thinking past appearances. It is the master who thinks of the servant not as human but merely as servile, and 'clings to this one predicate'. Finally, it is the officer for whom the common soldier is no more than 'this *abstractum* of a beatable subject'.[60]

Thus, the answer to the original question of the pamphlet, 'Who thinks abstractly?', points to the *gemeiner Mensch* whose common sense is well rooted in accidental representations of all sorts, as well as to whoever understands and judges the world according to her obstinately limited and insufficient impressions. A different kind of abstraction, though, pertains to the *bourgeois* as a member of modern civil society; namely, an abstraction that cannot be reduced to single individual behaviours nor to the simple maxim 'I think abstractly, therefore I act abstractly', but, rather, a dynamic abstraction that *acts itself* as a driving force of social reproduction.

Insofar as, on a practical scale, abstraction constructs social bonds, builds up society and sustains the very structure of the body politic, a *social ontology of abstraction* would seem to be one of Hegel's most significant contributions to the understanding of modernity: the fact that modernity is unabashedly *made* of abstractions. Abstract thought is not a historical outcome produced by modernity, as it designates the proper mode of thinking that belongs to the ahistorical faculty of understanding. By contrast, social abstraction *qua really existing abstraction* constitutes a specific achievement of the modern era, an era torn apart by divisions and antagonisms unknown to the previous ages. Abstraction conceived as a historical phenomenon appears as the most truthful result of a time that has shattered the ancient ethical life, by opposing the individual and the community, by distancing the divine from the human and by substituting infinite reason for finite reflection. Abstraction is the fruit of this original rupture born of modernity through the emergence of the *higher principle* of subjectivity, 'a principle unknown to Plato and the ancients',[61] but it is also the intellectual instrument that perpetuates and perfects the current state of division (*Entzweyung*) on the cultural and philosophical plane.

However, abstraction not only defines modernity's *differentia specifica* with regard to previous eras; it also helps to trace a distinction within and through it. As is well known, several events temporally distant from one another mark in Hegel's historical overview the beginning of modernity (from the birth of the Roman Empire, to the origin of Christianity, to Descartes's philosophy). The hypothesis of interpreting the Roman Empire as the inaugural moment of modernity sounds very plausible, precisely because Rome is where abstraction makes its very first appearance though ancient abstract right whereby all individuals are equal to each other because all are equally deprived of political rights. The Roman Empire epitomises the corruption of the *Volk*'s ethical ideal, turning it into an infinite mass of atoms, a serial combination of individuals that have lost any attachment to the ethical whole.[62] Nevertheless, this kind of fragmentation does not resemble the peculiar fabric of modern abstraction, inasmuch as the seriality of the divisions remains fixed in itself and does not trigger the process of socialisation. To borrow once again from Osborne's argument, we are confronted here with empirical abstractions that must be distinguished from the actual (*wirklich*) abstractions of modern capitalist society.[63] Abstraction here remains static and, going back to Finelli's argument, seems to be subordinated to an intellectualist mechanism that conceives of the abstract merely as the result of separation and juxtaposition. Conversely, in the modern world, abstract atomisation succeeds in performing a synthetic function and implementing socialisation; thereby abstraction becomes *active* or rather *an actor* in the social world (i.e., the very impersonal protagonist of civil society's drama). Hence, social abstraction (properly speaking) coincides with modern capitalism's productive abstraction insofar as previous manifestations of abstraction do not amount to an organisation of concrete social reality. In this regard, Hegel's view echoes Marx's stance in the *Grundrisse*, according to which 'even the most abstract categories, despite their validity – precisely because of their abstractness – for all epochs, are nevertheless, in the specific character of this abstraction, themselves likewise a product of historic relations, and possess their full validity only for and within these relations.'[64]

Unlike Paolo Virno's interpretation of Marx's real abstraction as 'a thought becoming a thing', Hegel's conception of social abstraction can be recapitulated as 'division producing cohesion'.[65] In a similar sense, contrary to Sohn-Rethel's understanding of Marx's 'real abstraction' (derived from the division of labour as well as from the division between exchange and use) as a primary abstraction preceding and grounding the genesis of abstract conceptual thought, Hegel's notion of intellectual abstraction clearly does not derive from social abstraction: the first simply dates back to the history of civilisation, whereas the second specifically originates in modern times and remains intrinsically linked to the development of modern capitalism. However, although, unlike Sohn-Rethel, Hegel does not consider abstract thinking as a consequence of social abstraction, he nevertheless maintains an asymmetrical connection between the two, affirming that abstract thought contributes to reinforcing the material abstraction existing in society. At the same time, in Hegel's view neither abstract thought nor speculative thought can liberate modern society from abstraction. Precisely because of its irreversible status, capitalist abstraction cannot ever be reconciled – it endures and persists through the reproduction of capitalist societies. A concrete world (i.e. freed from social abstraction) would be a post-capitalist world, one that modernity could only achieve by reversing or exhausting its 'unfinished project', to borrow Habermas' notorious definition. Whether such a world – devoid of abstractions – is sustainable, and what kind of social device in this context could play the role that abstraction stemming from the value form plays in capitalist societies, are questions that cannot be answered only speculatively. Instead, what could be legitimately asked is to what extent some kind of 'practical' abstraction, conceived of as a strategy of generalisability and an experience of interconnectedness,[66] is actually needed for emancipatory anti-capitalist politics to counter the divisive and singularising instances that proliferate in the camp of the oppressed. In other words, to what extent can abstraction function as a strategic tool for mediation that would help to activate new senses of belonging and commonality among the dominated?

Jamila M.H. Mascat teaches at the University of Utrecht and is author of Hegel a Jena: La critica dell'astrazione *(2011).*

Notes

1. Karl Marx, *Grundrisse. Foundations of the Critique of Political Economy*, trans. Martin Nicolaus (London: Penguin, 2005), 100–1.
2. Ibid., 101.
3. Alfred Sohn-Rethel, *Intellectual and Manual Labour: A Critique of Epistemology*, trans. Martin Sohn-Rethel (Atlantic Highlands: Humanities Press, 1978), 17.
4. Marx, *Grundrisse*, 104. See also Theodor W. Adorno, *Introduction to Sociology*, trans. Edmund Jephcott (Stanford: Stanford University Press, 2000), 32: 'The abstraction, therefore, lies not in the thought of the sociologist, but in society itself'. Interestingly, in his *Drei Studien zu Hegel*, Adorno remarks that 'Because of his idealism, Hegel has been reproached with being abstract in comparison with the concreteness of the phenomenological, anthropological, and ontological schools. But he brought infinitely more concreteness into this philosophical idea than those approaches, and not because his speculative imagination was balanced by a sense of reality but by virtue of the approach his philosophy takes-by virtue, one might say, of the experiential character of his speculation itself.' See Theodor W. Adorno, *Hegel: Three Studies*, trans. Shierry Weber Nicholsen (Cambridge: MIT Press, 1993), 67.
5. Marx, *Grundrisse*, 105.
6. G.W.F. Hegel, *Elements of the Philosophy of Right*, trans. H.B. Nisbet (Cambridge: Cambridge University Press, 1991), 221 (§183), 229 §192).
7. Among the exceptions, Isaac Rubin in his 1927 lecture on 'Abstract Labour and Value in Marx's System', *Capital and Class* 2:2 (1978), 107–9, stresses the Hegelian derivation of Marx's notion of 'abstract universal' labour. See also Rubin's later *Essays on Marx's Theory of Value* [1928] (Montréal and New York: Black Rose Books, 1973). Roberto Finelli, *Astrazione e dialettica dal romanticismo al capitalismo* (Roma: Bulzoni, 1987) develops a comparison between Marx and Hegel on real vs. intellectual abstraction; see also Peter Osborne, 'The Reproach of Abstraction', *Radical Philosophy* 127 (2004), 21–28. For a synthetic reconstruction of the contemporary Marxist debate on 'real abstraction', see Alberto Toscano, 'The Open Secret of Real Abstraction', *Rethinking Marxism* 20:2 (2008), 273–87.
8. Chris Arthur interestingly analyses the abstract / absent nature of Marx's value form in the light of Hegel's dialectic of Being and Nothing in 'The Spectral Ontology of Value', *Radical Philosophy* 107 (2001), 32–42; see also *The New Dialectic and Marx's Capital* (Leiden: Brill, 2002), and Fred Moseley and Tony Smith, eds, *Marx's Capital and Hegel's Logic* (Leiden: Brill, 2014), which includes Arthur's chapter 'Marx, Hegel and the Value-Form', 269–291.
9. Sohn-Rethel, *Intellectual and Manual Labour*, 14.
10. To speak of a 'theory' of abstraction with regard to Hegel may be inappropriate precisely because Hegel never presents a consistent nor exhaustive account of the multiple meanings that the notion of abstraction covers in his work. Hence, the word 'theory' is placed here between inverted commas.
11. H. Heine, *Confessions* [1854], cited in Robert C. Solomon, *From Hegel to Existentialism* (Oxford: Oxford University Press, 1987), 58.
12. G.W.F. Hegel, *Hegel's Philosophy of Nature: Part Two of the Enclyclopaedia of the Philosophical Sciences*, trans. A.V. Miller (Oxford: Clarendon Press, 2004), 297.
13. Hegel blames Kant for considering the antinomies of pure reason as contradictions that do not belong to the essence of reality itself, but only to human reason: by doing so Kant proves to be excessively 'kind' to the things of the world. In the *Science of Logic*, Hegel refers to Kant's antinomies of the Pure Reason as follows: 'It is an excessive tenderness for the world to keep contradiction away from it, to transfer it to spirit instead, to reason, and to leave it there unresolved. In fact, spirit is the one which is strong enough that it can endure contradiction, but it is spirit again which knows how to resolve it. But nowhere does the so-called world – call it the objective, real world, or, in the manner of transcendental idealism, subjective intuition and sense content determined by the category of the understanding – nowhere, however you call it, does it escape contradiction; but it is not capable of enduring it and for that reason it is left to the mercy of the coming and ceasing to be'. See G.W.F. Hegel, *Science of Logic*, trans. A.V. Miller (Cambridge: Cambridge University Press, 2010), 201.
14. Remo Bodei, 'Tenerezza per le cose del mondo. Sublime, sproporzione econtraddizione in Kant e in Hegel', in *Hegel interprete di Kant*, ed. V. Verra (Napoli: Prismi, 1981), 179–218.
15. Jamila M. H. Mascat, *Hegel a Jena. La critica dell'astrazione* (Lecce: Pensa Multimedia, 2011).
16. G.W.F. Hegel, *Three Essays, 1793–1795: The Tübingen Essay, Berne Fragments and The Life of Jesus*, trans. Peter Fuss and John Dobbins (Notre Dame: Notre Dame Press, 1984), 34.
17. G.W.F. Hegel, *Early Theological Writings*, trans. T.M. Knox (Philadelphia: University of Pennsylvania Press, 1971), 167–9.
18. G.W.F. Hegel, *The Encyclopaedia Logic*, trans. T.F. Geraets, W.A. Suchting and H.S. Harris (Indianapolis: Hackett Publishing Company, 1991), 27.
19. Gérard Bensussan, 'Abstraction', in *Dictionnaire critique du marxisme*, eds. George Labica and Gérard Bensussan (Paris: PUF, 1982), 4–5.
20. Concerning the difficulty of reaching *concrete universality*, i.e. *Begriff*, Hegel remarks in the *Encyclopedia*'s *Logic*

(§163) that 'When people speak of the Concept, they ordinarily have only abstract universality in mind, and consequently the Concept is usually also defined as a general notion. We speak in this way of the "concept" of colour, or of a plant, or of an animal, and so on; and these concepts are supposed to arise by omitting the particularities through which the various colours, plants, animals, etc., are distinguished from one another, and holding fast to what they have in common. This is the way in which the understanding apprehends the Concept, and the feeling that such concepts are hollow and empty, that they are mere schemata and shadows, is justified. What is universal about the Concept is indeed not just something common against which the particular stands on its own; instead the universal is what particularises (specifies) itself, remaining at home with itself in its other, in unclouded clarity. It is of the greatest importance, both for cognition and for our practical behaviour, too, that we should not confuse what is merely communal with what is truly universal. All the reproaches that are habitually levelled against thinking in general, and, more specifically, against philosophical thinking, from the standpoint of feeling, and the oft-repeated assertion that it is dangerous to pursue thought to what are alleged to be too great lengths have their ground in this confusion. And in any case it must be said that in its true and comprehensive significance the universal is a thought that took millennia to enter into men's consciousness.' Hegel, *Encyclopaedia Logic*, 240.

21. Hegel, *Encyclopaedia Logic*, 38.

22. G.W.F. Hegel, *The Difference Between Fichte's and Schelling's System of Philosophy*, trans. Walter Cerf and H.S. Harris (Albany: SUNY Press, 1988), 113, 118.

23. In this passage Hegel is dealing with proofs of the existence of God. Against customary understanding, Hegel affirms that the ontological proof is not a movement from thought to existence that would derive a real object from a formal concept. Rather the proof coincides with what Hegel calls *comprehensive thinking* (*das begreifende Denken*) of a content: the unfolding of the concept that supersedes universality and difference to grasp itself as 'reality, infinitude, truth', the self-determination of the concept to objectivity. See Quentin Lauer, *Hegel's Concept of God* (Albany: SUNY Press, 1982), 230.

24. Herbert Marcuse, *Reason and Revolution: Hegel and the Rise of Social Theory* (New York and London: Routledge, 2000), 26.

25. Eric Weil, *Hegel and the State*, trans. Mark A. Cohen (Baltimore: The Johns Hopkins University Press, 1998), 42.

26. 'The True is the Whole' (*Das Wahre ist das Ganze*); see G.W.F. Hegel, *Phenomenology of Spirit*, trans. A.V. Miller (Oxford: Oxford University Press, 1977), 11.

27. Hegel, *Science of Logic*, 8.

28. Although abstraction is a product of reflective understanding, however, the intellectual function is not limited to the ability to abstract. According to a later definition in the *Encyclopaedia* (§79), 'With regard to its form, the logical has three sides: (a) the side of abstraction or of the understanding, (b) the dialectical or negatively rational side, [and] (c) the speculative or positively rational one' (125). Here, understanding and abstraction are synonyms representing the lowest grade of pre-dialectical philosophising generally associated with the negative characteristics of limitedness, separateness and speculative inconsistency. But in the course of the Jena writings, understanding is not limited to the exercise of abstract thought and actually carries out a critical and anti-dogmatic function with regard to metaphysical hypostases and commonsensical certitudes, playing an indispensable role in the emergence of speculative thought. The *Phenomenology of Spirit* celebrates understanding for exercising the 'tremendous power of the negative', one that is crucial to both philosophy and life. See Hegel, *Phenomenology*, 19.

29. Weil, *Hegel and the State*, 42.

30. The theoretical framework of the new *Philosophy of Spirit* actually appears only from 1803–04 onwards. For a detailed reconstruction of Hegel's previous systematic drafts, see Heinz Kimmerle, *Das Problem der Abgeschlossenheit des Denkens Hegels 'System der Philosophie' in den Jahren 1800–1804* (Bouvier: Bonn, 1970).

31. G.W.F. Hegel, 'Fragmente aus Vorlesungsmanuskripten (1801–02)–(1803)', in *Gesammelte Werke*, Bd. 5, eds. M. Baum and K. Meist (Hamburg: F. Meiner, 1998), 255–75.

32. See Mascat, *Hegel a Jena*. As noted by Koyré in 'Hegel à Iéna', the main feature of finitude is precisely its *Unruhe* (*inquiétude*) that pushes it beyond its limits through the infinitisation of its own determinacies. See Alexandre Koyré, 'Hegel à Iéna', in *Études d'histoire de la pensée philosophique* (Paris: Gallimard, 1971), 147–90.

33. G.W.F. Hegel, *Natural Law: The Scientific Ways of Treating Natural Law, Its Place in Moral Philosophy, and Its Relation to the Positive Sciences of Law*, trans. T.M. Knox (Philadelphia: University of Pennsylvania Press, 1975), 79.

34. Ibid., 72.

35. Ibid., 70.

36. See Hegel's manuscripts of the lectures on the *Philosophy of Right* (1817–18), in G.W.F. Hegel, *Lectures on Natural Right and Political Science: The First Philosophy of Right*, trans. J. Michael Stewart and Peter C. Hodgson (Oxford: Oxford University Press, 2012).

37. G.W.F. Hegel, *Hegel's System of Ethical Life and First Philosophy of Spirit*, trans. H.S. Harris and T.M. Knox (Albany: SUNY Press, 1988), 153.

38. G.W.F. Hegel, *Hegel and the Human Spirit: A Translation of the Jena Lectures on the Philosophy of Spirit (1805–06) with a Commentary*, trans. Leo Rauch (Detroit: Wayne State University Press, 1983), 160.

39. Henri Lefebvre, *Introduction to Modernity: Twelve Preludes, September 1959-May 1961*, trans. John Moore (London and New York: Verso, 1995), 193.

40. Hegel, *Hegel and the Human Spirit / Jena Lectures (1805–06)*, 121.

41. Ibid., 122.

42. In this respect, Hegel's philosophy can be considered as a 'philosophy of labour'; see Myriam Bienenstock, 'La

première philosophie de l'esprit: essai d'interprétation génétique', in G.W.F. Hegel, *Le premier système: la philosophie de l'esprit (1803–1804)* (Paris: PUF, 1999), 169. Just as the individual consciousness does, the spirit labours too: spirit also externalises itself, works outside itself for others, because its labour is *Begeistung*, the spiritualisation of the world. With this analogy between modern industrial labour and spiritual labour, bourgeois *Arbeit* is installed as a founding principle of the human world. On Hegel's notion of *Arbeit*, cf. Franck Fischbach, 'La 'philosophie du travail' dans les esquisses de système à Iéna (1802–1806)', in *Hegel à Iéna*, eds. J.-M. Buéé and E. Renault (Lyon: Ens Éditions 2015), 179–94.

43. Marx, *Grundrisse*, 164.

44. Hegel, *Hegel and the Human Spirit / Jena Lectures (1805–06)*, 172.

45. Allen W. Wood, 'Editor's Introduction', in Hegel, *Elements of the Philosophy of Right*, xviii.

46. Hegel, *Hegel and the Human Spirit / Jena Lectures (1805–06)*, 161.

47. Ibid., 159.

48. Although the market economy has a tendency towards rationality, Hegel sees it as the locus of inevitable antagonisms, conflicts of interest and social imbalances between producers and consumers. See also Frank Ruda, *Hegel's Rabble: An Investigation into Hegel's Philosophy of Right* (London: Continuum 2011).

49. Hegel, *Philosophy of Right*, 220 (§182).

50. Ibid., 250–1 (§218). See Jean François Kervégan's note in G.W.F. Hegel, *Principes de la philosophie du droit* (Paris: PUF, 2013), 181.

51. Hegel, *Philosophy of Right*, 229 (§192).

52. Karl Marx, *Critique of Hegel's 'Philosophy of Right'*, trans. Annette Jolin and Joseph O'Malley (Cambridge: Cambridge University Press, 2009), 28.

53. See Finelli, *Astrazione e capitalismo*

54. Ibid.

55. On Hegel's contribution to Marx's theory of value, see the already mentioned Arthur, 'Marx, Hegel and the Value-Form', and Jean-Philippe Deranty, 'Théorie de la valeur, travail et reconnaissance', in *Hegel à Iéna*, eds. J.-M. Buéé and E. Renault (Lyon: Ens Éditions, 2015), 195–215.

56. Finelli, *Astrazione e capitalismo*.

57. Osborne, 'The Reproach of Abstraction', 27.

58. Consciousness is duplicated in turn 'in the extreme of the universal that is also individuality' as *citoyen* and in the opposed extreme of an individuality 'that cares for itself and its family, works and stipulates contracts' as *bourgeois* (21). In this way, the division penetrates inner consciousness. The *bourgeois*, embodying the abstraction of bourgeois individualism, is not overcome by the universal consciousness of the *citoyen*: on the contrary, they coexist alongside one another. *Bewusstsein* cannot be the means of overcoming abstraction, because abstraction participates in the *Bildung* of the individual consciousness.

59. Moishe Postone, *Time, Labour, and Social Domination: A Reinterpretation of Marx's Critical Theory* (Cambridge: Cambridge University Press, 1996), 59.

60. G.W.F. Hegel, 'Who thinks Abstractly?', in *Hegel: Texts and Commentary*, trans. Walter Kaufmann (Notre Dame: University of Notre Dame Press, 1977), 117–8.

61. Hegel, *Hegel and the Human Spirit / Jena Lectures (1805–06)*, 160.

62. Hegel, *Natural Law*, 41, 101.

63. Osborne, 'The Reproach of Abstraction', 27.

64. Marx, *Grundrisse*, 105.

65. Paolo Virno, *A Grammar of the Multitude*, trans. Isabella Bertoletti, James Cascaito and Andrea Casson (New York: Semiotext(e), 2004), 64.

66. See Osborne, 'The Reproach of Abstraction', 27.

Incitements
Series Editors:
Dimitris Vardoulakis
Peg Birmingham

 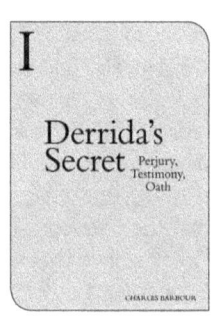

www.edinburghuniversitypress.com/incite
EDINBURGH
University Press

Dossier: On the 1917 commemorations

Revolutionary commemoration

Hannah Proctor

No more anniversaries!

Vsevolod Meyerhold[1]

Fire and ice

On 18th March 1921 the fiftieth anniversary of the foundation of the Paris Commune was marked in the Russian Soviet Federative Socialist Republic (RSFSR). Newspapers were emblazoned with headlines decrying the brutal suppression of the heroic Communards by bourgeois reactionary forces just seventy-two days after its foundation. In Petrograd, Emma Goldman awoke from an anxious night's sleep to hear people marching through the streets singing 'The Internationale'. She, however, experienced the city that day as a 'ghastly corpse' and to her mournful ears the song's 'strains, once jubilant … sounded like a funeral dirge for humanity's flaming hope.'[2] Her bitter reaction to this celebratory occasion was not a reflection on the fate of the Paris Commune itself but a response to more recent events. Just one day before, the guns of Kronstadt, the echoes of which had resounded across the streets of Petrograd for the past twelve days, abruptly stopped. Sailors from the Baltic Fleet based in the fortified city on the island of Kotlin had mutinied in solidarity with workers' demonstrations and strikes in the former capital. Many who had fought enthusiastically for the Revolution, and been recognised by the Bolsheviks for their loyalty, were now demanding reforms and accusing the Party of betrayal. The Politburo issued an ultimatum and a Red Army attack was launched over the still frozen waters. After ten days the rebels surrendered.[3] Brutal reprisals followed. As the Paris Commune anniversary banners moved past Goldman's window, the corpses of Red Army soldiers sent to quash the rebellion, in what Victor Serge described as a 'ghastly fraticide', still lay scattered across the blood-spattered melting ice.[4]

Admittedly Goldman and fellow American anarchist Alexander Berkman were unusual in how decisively they interpreted the events in Kronstadt.[5] Years later Leon Trotsky not only reiterated the necessity for crushing the revolt but characterised it as a counter-revolutionary 'armed reaction of the petty bourgeoisie against the hardships of social revolution' and remained unrepentant about the severity of the attack against it, branding Goldman and Berkman sentimental pacificides.[6] Nonetheless, the anniversary of the Commune and the suppression of the Kronstadt uprising clanged up against one another jarringly, creating an uneasy sense of (dis)analogy. In an ironic last gesture, the battleship 'Sevastapol', which had been taken over by rebellious sailors during the revolt, was renamed 'The Paris Commune' shortly after the mutiny was suppressed; a peculiar floating monument to the hypocrisy Goldman found so horrifying.[7]

Though framed as a lesson to improve upon rather than a model to replicate (the Parisian proletariat lacked a party; faux socialist 'petty bourgeois patriots' were too heavily involved; everything happened at the wrong time, etc., etc.), Trotsky, writing in 1921, like Lenin before him, placed the

October Revolution in a continuum with the Paris Commune.[8] The Commune became exemplary as a kind of Communist origin story, a tragic yet inspiring landmark in a fledgling canon of leftist struggle that would soon, it was assumed, ricochet around the world. Andy Willimott discusses how young activists experimenting with new domestic arrangements and modes of living in the aftermath of the October Revolution turned to the Paris Commune as 'a model of direct democracy, mutual cooperation, and collective reorganisation':[9] the Baku Commune of 1918 was framed as a 'reincarnation' of the Paris Commune, while a commune group based at the Stalingrad Tractor Factory a decade later proclaimed their explicit intention of emulating the martyred Communards. Though Willimott stresses that Soviet activists tended to rely on a romanticised image of the past, the example of the Paris Commune nonetheless inspired concrete quotidian practices in the present. Soviet babies were even named '*Parizhkommuna*':[10] newly born and future-oriented yet linked to a revolutionary inheritance.[11]

In the year preceding the fiftieth anniversary an enormous mass spectacle, 'Toward a World Commune', had been staged in Petrograd on the site of the former Stock Exchange, which enacted the history of the Third International, portraying the October Revolution as the last step before the 'apotheosis' of the proletarian struggles set in motion by the Paris Commune was reached. At the end of the scene depicting the defeat of the Communards: 'workers remove the bodies of their fallen comrades and hide the trampled red banner for future battles.'[12] The past was bequeathed to the future. Similarly, the final intertitle of Grigori Kozintsev and Leonid Trauberg's 1929 film *New Babylon,* a tragic love story set on the Parisian barricades of 1871, proclaims 'Long live the Commune!'; its final shots show the words 'Vive La Commune!' scrawled on a wall, implying that the dreams of the Commune outlive the slaughtered Communards.

The 18th March, commemorating the Paris Commune, was an official day of rest or *prazdnik* until 1929.[13] If Paris between 18 March and 28 May 1871 functioned (for a time at least) as a legitimation of, and kind of prototype for, the October Revolution, ritualised and increasingly formalised commemorations of the October Revolution itself soon became central to the regime's shifting master narrative.[14] In Trotsky's article on the lessons to be drawn from the Paris Commune, he concluded with a volcanic metaphor, noting that the 'temperament of the French proletariat is a revolutionary lava. But this lava is now covered with the ashes of skepticism.'[15] This contrast between the hot flowing lava of an original eruption and the dull grey ash that subsequently smothers it captures a contradiction common to revolutionary commemorations, one starkly evident in the coincidence of the crushing of the Kronstadt rebellion with the fiftieth anniversary celebrations of the Paris Commune, but one which rousing future-oriented spectacles like 'Toward a World Commune' sought to avoid. By 1927 Trotsky would be participating in demonstrations against the official commemorations of the tenth anniversary of the October Revolution, which was used to help justify his expulsion from the Party.[16] In the wake of the centenary year of the October Revolution (which was marked by little in the way of rousing future-oriented spectacles), and as we approach the fiftieth anniversary of May '68, can historic examples of revolutionary commemoration point towards an appropriate form for revolutionaries hoping to transform the present to reflect on revolutionary pasts? Or is the very notion of commemorating revolution a contradiction in terms?

October in Novembers

In his introduction to *October*, published to mark the centenary of the October Revolution, which follows the upheavals of 1917 month-by-month, China Miéville includes a short 'Note on Dates'. Although he observes that some historians of the Revolution have opted to use the Gregorian calendar and thus date the Storming of the Winter Palace to November, he justifies his decision to follow the Julian calendar, then still in use in Russia, by stating his desire to remain in sync with the 'the story of the actors immersed in their moment.'[17] The Gregorian calendar was adopted in the RSFSR in 1918. Unlike Miéville, Soviet officials retroactively plotted revolutionary time on the newly introduced calendar, synchronised with, yet hostile to, the capitalist world. Hence, 7th November became the official holiday for celebrating the anniversary of the October Revolution. (Today it remains an official public holiday in Belarus, Kyrgyzstan and the *de facto* state of Transnistria.)

In 1918, with the Civil War ongoing, the occasion of the first anniversary of the October Revolution was marked by a mass feeding of the population of Moscow, with children given priority, and an emphasis placed on providing women with a break from domestic labour. Prisoners' food rations were raised for a day and factory committees promised their workers extra cigarettes.[18] Cafes and restaurants stayed open, serving free meals.[19] Elaborate spectacles were organised in multiple locations. The Moscow Organising Committee of the anniversary celebrations announced that at 9pm on 7th November a ritual burning of the 'Old Imperial Order' should be organised in every region with a symbol of the 'New System', 'to be decided by local regional comrades', taking its place.[20] Richard Stites contrasts the exuberant, flamboyant, carnivalesque May Day celebrations that took place in Petrograd that year with the stiff solemnity of the heavily orchestrated anniversary commemorations in Moscow, in which, he claims, playful and vividly coloured artistic contributions were 'lost in the forest of mass-produced discs emblazoned with the new hammer and sickle.'[21] Stites imagines Lenin's opprobrious frown scowling over and eventually displacing the lively and chaotic celebrations of frolicsome utopians, like ash settling over lava.[22] Focusing more on the formal than the informal, Frederick C. Corney traces how the anniversary celebrations shifted over the decade following 1917, describing the emergence and stabilisation of a revolutionary narrative, script and set of rituals overseen by 'official arbiters.'[23]

The twentieth anniversary celebrations of 7th November 1937 coincided with the height of the purges and a period, in the aftermath of the First Five Year Plan (1928-1932), in which many people in the Soviet Union were materially worse off than they had been in the 1920s. A new narrative of the Revolution emerged positioning Stalin as Lenin's heir at the moment many who had participated in the Revolution were being arrested, imprisoned and killed, including the very cadres who had heretofore been relied upon to create and organise celebratory mass spectacles and commemorative exhibitions. The October Revolution was no longer positioned between the Paris Commune and the victorious global proletarian revolution; the anniversary reflected a major reappraisal of Soviet history that plotted a less internationalist historical trajectory, instead valorising aspects of the imperial past and lauding heroic individuals, including Peter the Great and Ivan the Terrible.[24] Tsarist ceremonies were even resuscitated as part of the celebrations, such as the distribution of keepsakes to children.[25] A shift away from the masses in favour of the elite was demonstrated by the decision to pay for a lavish anniversary curtain at the Bolshoi theatre rather than provide funding to build clubs and theatres in peasant villages.[26] But the repudiation of Stalinism under Nikita Khrushchev involved a return, revalorisation and re(re)conceptualisation of the October Revolution, even if the militaristic form of the main 7th November parade remained relatively consistent. The fortieth anniversary celebrations in 1957, a year after Khrushchev's 'secret speech', saw Mao Zedong join the First Secretary of the Communist Party atop Lenin's Mausoleum with replica Sputniks featuring heavily in the civilian parade. Such snapshots provide insights into official Soviet culture in each anniversary year, and indicate the malleable meaning of 'October', but a more meaningful question would be to ask what these rituals meant to the people who participated in them.

An uneasy relationship between transformation and stability, routine and rupture, the interruptive and the habitual, the spontaneous and the conscious in revolutionary anniversary celebrations coursed through Soviet life and thought. It might be tempting to casually characterise the former as revolutionary and the latter as reactionary or to plot a linear shift from one mode to another, but the conflict was evident from the very beginning.[27] As early as 1919 a newspaper article spoke anxiously of the 'initial revolutionary upsurge' giving way to 'the revolutionary quotidian.'[28] It is, however, also possible to find exceptions to narratives of ever-increasing hierarchy and regimentation. As Lynn Mally observes in her analysis of Soviet amateur theatre, in a mass spectacle organised in 1927 for the tenth anniversary celebrations called 'Ten Octobers', amateur performers took a far more active and vocal role than they had in the famous mass spectacles of 1920, indicating that history never flowed intractably in one direction.[29] Katerina Clark sees this paradox between the new and the extant at work within the mass spectacles of 1920, which she notes functioned simultaneously as a 'celebration of iconoclasm *and* a ritual legitimisation of the status quo.'[30] Although the latter may not conform to the ruptural logic of revolution, legitimation of an existing social order is only politically dubious if the order being affirmed is oppressive and the legitimising process is coerced. It is one thing to condemn the concrete example of the 1937 anniversary celebrations as a chilling spectacle (invoking a feeling similar to that experienced by Goldman in 1921), but it is quite another to argue that marking an occasion like an anniversary is inherently antithetical to communist politics in the abstract.

Furthermore, anniversary commemorations were not confined to the Soviet Union but also played an international role. Invitations to foreign Communist Party leaders and members were extended and delegations of revolutionaries and Soviet allies, including women's and youth delegations, travelled from across the world to the USSR to attend the annual Red Square parades. (Although, the famous 1963 photographs of lava-like Fidel Castro surrounded by ash-like members of the Politburo on Lenin's mausoleum were taken on a May Day celebration rather than on November 7th.)[31] Official and unofficial commemorative events were also hosted abroad. Images of the African American singer and actor Paul Robeson attending an October Revolution anniversary celebration at the Soviet embassy in Washington DC in 1950 circulated in the US Press as part of a campaign by the State Department to brand him a dangerous 'black Stalin' figure, whose radical influence might act as a 'deadly contagion' encouraging the spread of decolonisation.[32]

Anniversary rituals may have ossified into routine affirmations of an oppressive society in one context, but elsewhere they were still charged with a disruptive energy. Writing on the occasion of the twenty-second anniversary of the Revolution, in the immediate aftermath of the purges, C.L.R. James recalled how its example had reverberated globally, 'across the oceans and mountains from continent to continent.'[33] James acknowledged the 'monstrosity of Stalinism', but despite the contemporary situation

in the Soviet Union declared that the October Revolution remained an inspiration to oppressed people across the world, specifically to black people fighting colonialism and the afterlives of slavery:

> Broken and besmirched, attacked from without and betrayed from within, yet it lives. From the great peaks scaled in its early years, it has fallen far. But it remains a basis and a banner, a banner torn and bedraggled, stained with crimes and blood, carried by treacherous hands, but still a symbol of the greatest effort yet made by downtrodden humanity to rid the world of economic exploitation and political tyranny. To rid the world, not only Russia. Today Negroes, weighed down by still heavier burdens than those they carried on November 7, 1917, must celebrate that never-to-be forgotten anniversary, must reflect on what the Russian Revolution has meant, and still means, to them and to all mankind.[34]

Commemoration can function as a form of resistance, remembering what the ruling class wants forgotten.[35]

In capitalist countries outside the Soviet Union commemorations of the October Revolution were animated by a distinct temporality; oriented as much to the future as to the past, and intent on asserting the necessity to break with the prevailing society. Often taking the form of pageants or performances inspired by Soviet mass spectacles, theatricality functioned more as a rehearsal for revolutionary praxis rather than a reproduction of historical events.[36] As Larne Abse Gogarty observes in her analyses of Edith Segal's work with the Needle Trades Workers' Industrial Union Dance Group in the USA, dance became a 'weapon in class struggle' preparing workers for the antagonisms of the picket line.[37] In New York City the eleventh anniversary of the October Revolution was marked by 'The Giant Pageant of Class Struggle', which saw 25,000 people descend on Madison Square Garden. A year later, for the 1930 anniversary celebrations, the Workers' Laboratory Theatre performed a pageant called 'Turn the Guns' at the Bronx Coliseum.[38] In 1937, on the occasion of the twentieth anniversary, Lillian Shapero choreographed a dance inspired by Dziga Vertov's film *One Sixth of the World*, which included a ballet celebrating electrification performed to Marc Blitzstein's 'Moscow Metro'.[39] Mobile, malleable and detached from the historic and geographical specificities of the events that unfolded in Petrograd in 1917, commemorations of the October Revolution could be experienced as politically meaningful events of their own.

Counterfeit Lenins

In Gustave Flaubert's *Sentimental Education* (1869), the events of the revolution of 1848 are experienced by the novel's protagonist as though they are happening on stage:

> The drums beat the charge. Shrill cries arose… Frederic was fascinated and enjoying himself tremendously. The wounded falling to the ground, and the deadlying stretched out did not look as if they were really wounded or dead. He felt as if he were watching a play.[40]

This passage functions both to emphasise the superficiality of the character and to characterise the historical events he is witnessing as phony and inauthentic. In the case of commemorations of the October Revolution, however, forms of fictionalisation, symbolism and theatricality were not necessarily deemed antithetical to authentic experience. Indeed, re-enactments, reproductions and representations often sought to improve upon, intensify or heighten the original historical events in the hope of inspiring genuine surges of emotion in audiences or participants. As Corney discusses, the emphasis of the early mass spectacles was on physical attendance that would stir 'a primarily sensory experience in the individual.'[41] The events were 'vivid but ephemeral', like revolutions themselves.[42] Similarly, Clark notes that the directors of spectacles sought to 'revive the pathos of revolution, its élan, and its collectivist, iconoclastic spirit' through forms of re-enactment.[43] The emphasis was not on passively recalling the past through accurate reconstruction, but on actively and creatively conjuring revolutionary feeling through a interweaving of the past with the present. Corney traces how relatively subdued aspects of the events of 1917 became more dramatic in their re-telling, dating the 'storming' [*shturm*] of the Winter Palace to 1920 rather than 1917, when that term became established and the location was retroactively enshrined in the official narrative as an equivalent to the French Revolution's Bastille.[44] Similarly, a Soviet state television broadcast of the seventieth anniversary celebrations in 1987 traces its legacy back to the first anniversary parades of 1918 before mentioning the actual revolutions of 1917, as if the former were the historic event being commemorated.[45]

On May Day 1927 Sergei Eisenstein's film crew chose a parade across the Nikolaevsky bridge in Leningrad (as Petrograd had been renamed following Lenin's death in 1924) to act as a stand-in for the February Revolution of 1917 in his film *October*, which had been commissioned to mark the tenth anniversary of the October Revolution (although, due to Stalin's complaint at the prominence of Trotsky, the film was not finished in time for the 7th November celebrations). Demonstrators were enjoined to carry banners to help with a mass shot. Confused by the bourgeois slogans on display at the May Day demonstration, 'two men in leather coats' approached co-director Grigori Aleksandrov and he was taken away for questioning.[46] Aleksandrov's story highlights that processes of re-enacting the past unfold in a present of their own and exist as historical experiences in their own right with potentially serious repercussions. Aleksandrov notes that in casting the film they had given preference to people who had been involved in the revolutionary events over actors, in an attempt to come as close as possible to recreating the experience of the Revolution itself. Yet, without wanting to wade too deep into the intricacies Soviet aesthetic debates of the late 1920s, Eisenstein's film was criticised by many of his contemporaries, particularly those involved in LEF (Left Front of the Arts), for deviating too far from, or overly embellishing, historical events – the sailors smashing the Palace's wine cellars were too smartly dressed; they seemed too heroic; they were insufficiently engaged in drunken carousing, etc.[47] *October* featured the first cinematic portrayal of Lenin by an actor, which also met with strong objections. Vladimir Mayakovsky wrote to Eisenstein to express his outrage at the idea of a 'counterfeit Lenin',[48] while Osip Brik referred to it as a 'forgery'.[49] (Although it would not be long before cinematic Lenin replicas proliferated, Soviet theatres inserted 'Lenin plays' into their repertoires and Lenin busts and statuettes rolled off assembly lines.[50]) Esfir Shub, whose 'compilation film' *The Fall of the Romanov Dynasty*, edited together from vast swathes of archival footage, was also commissioned as part of the tenth anniversary commemorations, objected to the triumph of metaphor-laden theatricality over documentary and newsreel in Eisenstein's film.[51] But Eisenstein defended his approach. He was concerned with revolutionary mythology and insisted that romanticised rumours, even if apocryphal, had a historical weight and truth content of their own. As Yuri Tsivian notes, he preferred 'the popular legend to the true story.'[52] Anne Nesbet observes scrupulously that Aleksandrov's anecdote may also be apocryphal. The question is: does it matter? The answer would necessarily be different today than it was to critics of Eisenstein's film in 1927.

Nesbet reads *October* as an attempt to make the experiences of history, which have a tendency to slip past in the lower-case blur of routine existence, properly 'Historical' through aestheticisation. But in contrast to Eisenstein's own pronouncements on the conceptual clarity of 'intellectual montage', Nesbet insists persuasively on the strange effects produced by the various doubles, copies and replicas that appear in *October*, on the queasy, slippery and unsettled relationships between past and present that the film depicts.[53] *October,* itself a kind of maquette of history with an animated model of Lenin at its centre, constantly contrasts real people and statues. Kerensky is juxtaposed with a statue of Napoleon, the revolutionary masses with a statue of Alexander III, a Bolshevik woman with a Rodin sculpture signifying springtime. Although the meanings of these juxtapositions might seem clear, Nesbet argues the film nonetheless expresses an anxiety that 'the gulf separating flesh from marble'[54] might not be as definitive as it seems; the situation might reverse, like the famous shot depicting the destroyed statue of the Tsar reassembling. The problem of the museum, framed as a troubling paradox for revolutionaries, is central to her reading of the film, which argues that *October* poses an uneasy question: 'How does one prevent these unreliable, fickle images of the past from infecting the present?'[55] The Winter Palace and the bourgeois objects within it, Nesbet insists, seem disarmingly easy to repurpose; little seems to prevent them from returning just as swiftly to their former uses: 'The lesson of *October* seems to be that objects and images can never be entirely tamed ... Eisenstein's very interest in them argues that they are still too alluring to be considered harmless.'[56] But could the same be said of formerly revolutionary objects today? Does an object like *October* retain a threatening force or has it been rendered harmless by subsequent history?

Ruined dreams

In Miéville's *October* everything seems to unfold in the present tense. The strength of this approach is its refusal to view 1917 through the prism of, say, 1937. (This is a temptation the curators of the Royal Academy's centenary exhibition *Revolution: Russian Art 1917-1932* could not resist, even though it covered an earlier period.[57]) Miéville does not take for granted that any particular outcome was assured and his avoidance of discussing subsequent Soviet history is a convenient, although perhaps too convenient, way to avoid sinking into melancholy or despair. The reader is submerged in the chaotic events as they are unfolding, which rush along giddily and unpredictably. Miéville is also adept at the telling detail, as in his amusing account of the almost farcical murder of Rasputin or his evocative description of the wandering Tsar's lavishly decorated, opulent railway carriage, rattling incongruously around in the vast snowy landscapes.[58] His approach is closer to Shub's 'compilation film' than it is to the intellectual montage and symbolism of Eisenstein. It is nonetheless significant that the most prominent English-language account of the October Revolution published to mark the centenary was written by a novelist rather than a historian: 'it is precisely as a *story* that I have tried to tell it.'[59] This is not to accuse Miéville of falsifying or embellishing history, but to note that his approach advocates an aestheticised, emotion-stirring approach to the recounting of revolutionary events, similar in intent to the mass spectacles; a revolutionary commemoration that wants to reach beyond the confines of past.

Despite the rousing effect produced by Miéville's pacey prose, however, the book's resolute confinement to a linear narrative of 1917 ultimately strains to make a claim on the present. After the excitement of the events of 1917, the book concludes underwhelmingly with a limp Epilogue. The mood is sombre; the light is dim. At least, Miéville ventures weakly, it is not completely dark. Miéville glosses over what happened next with the jarringly abrupt statement: 'We know where this is going: purges, gulags, starvation, mass murder.'[60] Ultimately *October* tows a fairly standard Trotskyist line, repeating a narrative of progressive ossification that barely mentions the post-Stalin period at all. Although Miéville's account lacks the undergirding and guiding teleology of an orthodox Marxist-Leninist account of history, there is a kind of submerged telos in the assumption that 'catastrophe' simply followed 'dreamworld' (to borrow Susan Buck-Morss's terms), while a more uncomfortable and contradictory account would attend to overlaps, retreats and resurgences of both poles over time. Surely contending with Soviet history (which, after all, included a lot besides 'purges, gulags, starvation, mass murder', especially after Stalin's death in 1953), must form part of any attempt to explore the potential significance of the October Revolution in the present, when we no longer know where anything is going at all. Doing so might not involve imagining ourselves as being in sync with revolutionaries of the past, but instead demand that we reckon with our distance and difference from them.

A far bleaker vision of the present underpins Enzo Traverso's *Left-Wing Melancholia* (2016), which repeatedly reminds the reader that 'the history of revolutions is a history of defeats.'[61] Traverso treats communism as a dead object, a finished experience. He speaks of the paralysis of the utopian imagination, and observes the discursive displacement of the heroic 'vanquished' by the pitiable and passive figure of the 'victim'. According to his narrative, radical political possibility disappeared with the Berlin wall. 1989 figures as an 'internalised shipwreck that produced a blooming of memories'[62] and the twenty-first century emerges as a 'landscape of fragmented sufferings.'⁶³ Unlike the revolutionary defeats of the past, which spurred on future radical movements, he sees 1989 as a kind of final capitulation after which past struggles have no longer been understood as part of a future-orientated revolutionary continuum in which the October Revolution, Spanish Civil War, Cuban Revolution, May '68 etc., were strung together by a single red thread: 'the eclipse of utopias engendered by our "presentist" time has almost extinguished Marxist memory.'⁶⁴ One of the book's major contentions is that an obsession with 'memory', with its attendant discipline, 'Memory Studies', emerged with the collapse of 'actually existing socialism'. For Traverso 'left-wing melancholia' is a repressed strain in Marxist thought, which retains a commitment to honouring the 'vanquished' of history absent from dominant liberal understandings of memory (and one which seems to demand an overbearing tone of ponderous solemnity⁶⁵), but he nonetheless seems to take for granted that the future is dead. In a rubble-strewn book dominated by ghosts, shipwrecks and ruins under an unchanging crepuscular light (which unlike in Miéville's *October* never threatens to break into the hopeful glimmers of dawn), Traverso's occasional references to possible redemption feel tepid and unconvincing, even to himself: 'the loss appears irreparable.'⁶⁶ In this bleak landscape of endless ash and no lava, revolutionary commemoration is fixated on the past and severs all ties to political action in the present.⁶⁷

Traverso's vision of the contemporary world as a landscape of ruins is a familiar one. After 1989 the archaeological metaphor emerges as a common motif, particularly in the work of those on the Anglophone left seeking to rescue something of the optimistic utopianism of the early twentieth century for the present, evincing nostalgia for a past that could still imagine the possibility of a radically different future.⁶⁸ Critiques of 'Ostalgia' and 'ruin porn' are well-rehearsed by now. The anxiety is that scrubbed and aestheticised fragments of the revolutionary past circulate shorn of historical context, drained of political meaning, reduced to nothing more than diverting relics, which pose no threat to the existing state of things. As Traverso writes:

> We cannot exclude the possibility that our descendants will remember the historical experience of twentieth-century socialism as an isolated monument in an empty square, a vestige of the past whose charm will lie in its 'age value'.⁶⁹

Images circulate online as kitsch distractions: disinterred Lenin in the long grass, underwater Lenin encrusted with barnacles, Arctic Lenin submerged in snow up to his shoulders, desert Lenin among palm trees, mossy Lenin in parks full of other Lenins. The left-wing historian as archaeologist hopes that another kind of excavation might be possible; one that could reignite past hopes in the present and that would insist that the remnants of the past, like the threatening bourgeois objects in *October*, retain something of their original meaning. But this seems to imply that the excavated objects could be pulled whole from the rubble, that the cracks and holes caused by subsequent history could be erased or fixed. Revolutionary commemoration as a practice, as opposed to a scholarly theory or mode of curation, is less concerned with meticulous reconstruction, preservation or the placid cataloguing of remains than it is with looting the past for contingent political ends.

Contemporary, immediate, up-to-the-minute

> The statues are already defaced. Stripped of paint through centuries of erosion, they are beyond further damage. They've been torn out of context, inventoried, allegorised, eclipsed by their own exegetical apparatus. They can't see, their eyes are vacant, they leave us cold – they can't threaten or entice us. Blankly staring, their gaze has no more power to seduce. But let's turn them sideways, just in case.
>
> Rebecca Comay⁷⁰

Following the defeat of the Paris Commune, tourists visited Paris to see its ruins, but the status of those charred remains was ambiguous. Scott McCracken remarks of the ruins of the Palais des Tuileries:

> The afterlife of the palace, a symbol of monarchy whose ruins became a symbol of its overthrow, corresponds to a recognisably modernist set of cultural responses to the reaction that follows a revolution's defeat. The erasure of the event is never total. Traces

both material and textual are always left over, and the collection and rearrangement of these vestiges offers the same three possibilities as for the palace: restoration, the making of a lost connection with the past; reconstruction, a re-engagement with the past and an anticipation of the future; obliteration, the cutting off from the past to make a new future.[71]

In *Communal Luxury*, her recent book on the political imaginary of the Paris Commune, Kristin Ross cites a *New York Times* article that interviews an Occupy Oakland activist who gives her name as Louise Michel, a reference to the infamous Communard that the journalist failed to pick up on.[72] 'We call for a general strike around the country, and around the world', the activist is quoted as saying just days before the blockade of the port of Oakland in 2011.[73] Unlike Traverso, who is dismissive of the disparate political movements that erupted at that time, Ross explicitly addresses her book to the possibility of political transformation in the present. She is not melancholic and resigned, but hopeful and engaged. It is these kinds of echoes, resonances and returns in which she is interested, not solemn, organised commemorative occasions, but improvised citations in which the past momentarily collides with and inspires revolutionary movements now.

The death of a teleological conception of history is nothing to mourn, its disappearance might create space for struggles from the past that have been historically marginalised by the orthodox left to fray the taut narratives of familiar red threads to weave something new. In contrast to Emma Goldman's sorrowful account of the official commemoration of the Paris Commune in Petrograd, Ross describes the furtive and impromptu ways historical memory can form part of revolutionary praxis; fleeting dreamworlds constructed within and against the on-going catastrophe of life under capitalism. Ross suggests that revolutionary commemorations need not take the form of static statues to soberly contemplate in a dusty and unchanging museum of left-wing hagiography, but can be ephemeral, darting and disruptive acts. As Vladimir Mayakovsky wrote in the 1921 preface to his play *Mystery-Bouffe*, originally written to commemorate the first anniversary of the October Revolution in 1918:

> Mystery Bouffe is a high road – the high road of the Revolution. No one can predict with certainty how many more mountains will have to be blasted away by those of us who are travelling that high road. Today the name of Lloyd George rings harshly in our ears; but tomorrow he will have been forgotten even by the English. Today the will of millions is surging toward the Commune; in another fifty years the airborne battleships of the Commune may be rushing to the attack of distant planets ... Therefore, all persons performing, presenting, reading, or publishing Mystery-Bouffe should change the content, making it contemporary, immediate, up-to-the-minute.[74]

Perhaps it is only possible to access counterfeit versions of October, but revolutionary commemoration could involve re-reading the scripts of the past as inspiration for new improvisations; returning to history not as archaeologists or curators but as actors.

Hannah Proctor is an editor of Radical Philosophy.

Notes

1. Cited by Daniel Gerould in 'Eisenstein's "Wiseman"', *The Drama Review: TDR*, 18:1 (1974), 71–76, 73.
2. Emma Goldman, *Living my Life* (1931), https://theanarchistlibrary.org/library/emma-goldman-living-my-life.
3. Alexander Berkman's *The Kronstadt Rebellion* (1922) ends by noting the coincidence of the anniversary of the beginning of the Paris Commune and the supposed 'victory' over Kronstadt, https://www.marxists.org/reference/archive/berkman/1922/kronstadt-rebellion/ch7.htm.
4. Victor Serge, *Memoirs of a Revolutionary*, trans. Peter Sedgwick with George Paizis (New York, NY: New York Review Books, 2012), 152. Serge provides an explanation of why he and his Communist comrades, 'after many hesitations, and with unutterable anguish', ultimately chose to side with the Party despite their sympathy with the uprising (*Memoirs*, 150). Paul Avrich's historical account takes a similar view: 'Kronstadt presents a situation in which the historian can sympathise with the rebels and still concede the Bolsheviks were justified in subduing them. To recognise this, indeed, is to grasp the full tragedy of Kronstadt.' Paul Avrich, *Kronstadt, 1921* (Princeton, NJ: Princeton University Press, 1970), 6.
5. Avrich makes this point and argues that it was only in hindsight that this event acquired a more intense symbolic status, *Kronstadt, 1921*, 228.
6. Leon Trotsky, 'Hue and Cry over Kronstadt', *The New International* 4:4 (April 1938), 103–106, https://www.marxists.org/archive/trotsky/1938/01/kronstadt.htm.
7. Avrich, *Kronstadt, 1921*, 213.

8. Leon Trotsky, 'Lessons of the Paris Commune' (February 1921), https://www.marxists.org/archive/trotsky/1921/02/commune.htm. Lenin discusses the Paris Commune at length in the third chapter of *The State and Revolution* (1917). He is said to have danced in the snow on the day the Bolsheviks' time in power outlasted the Paris Commune.

9. Andy Willimott, *Living the Revolution: Urban Communes and Soviet Socialism, 1917-1932* (Oxford: Oxford University Press, 2017), 42.

10. Richard Stites, *Revolutionary Dreams: Utopian Vision and Experimental Life in the Russian Revolution* (Oxford: Oxford University Press, 1989), 111. Stites lists numerous new baby names that came into use after the October Revolution, some more conceptual (Joy, Spark, Electric, Rebel), some based on revolutionary figures (Marx, Engels, Robespierre, Rosa Luxemburg).

11. On the 'happy child as icon of Soviet transformation' see Lisa A. Kirschenbaum, *Small Comrades: Revolutionising Childhood in Soviet Russia, 1917-1932* (London: RoutledgeFalmer, 2001), 163.

12. James von Geldern, *Bolshevik Festivals, 1917-1920* (Berkeley, CA: University of California Press, 1993), 186.

13. Irina Shilova, 'Building the Bolshevik Calendar through Pravda and Izvestiia', *Toronto Slavic Quarterly*, 14 (2007), http://sites.utoronto.ca/tsq/19/shilova19.shtml.

14. See, Jay Bergman, 'The Paris Commune in Bolshevik Mythology', *English Historical Review*, 129:541 (2014), 1412-1441. On the Paris Commune's shifting status as prototype for the 1905 Revolution and both the February and October Revolutions of 1917, see Casey Harison, 'The Paris Commune of 1871, the Russian Revolution of 1905, and the Shifting of the Revolutionary Tradition', *History and Memory*, 19:2 (2007), 5–42. Harison notes that the annual anniversary marches to Père Lachaise in Paris were reinvigorated following the October Revolution; revolutionary inspiration did not only flow in one direction (24).

15. Trotsky, 'Lessons of the Paris Commune'.

16. Michael David Fox, *Revolution of the Mind: Higher Learning Among the Bolsheviks, 1918-1929* (Ithaca, NY: Cornell University Press, 1997), 116, 231.

17. China Miéville, *October: The Story of the Russian Revolution* (London: Verso, 2017), 3.

18. Frederick C. Corney, *Telling October: Memory and the Making of the Bolshevik Revolution* (Ithaca, NY: Cornell University Press, 2004) 52-56.

19. Von Geldern, *Bolshevik Festivals*, 95.

20. Corney, *Telling October*, 58.

21. Stites, *Revolutionary Dreams*, 91.

22. Von Geldern similarly describes a tension in the anniversary celebrations between 'artists' iconoclastic exuberance and the organisers who wanted to tame that exuberance', Bolshevik Festivals, 93.

23. Corney, Telling October, 104.

24. On the 1937 anniversary, see Karen Petrone, *Life Has Become More Joyous Comrades: Celebrations in the Time of Stalin* (Bloomington, IN: University of Indiana Press, 2000), 149–174. On the centrality of artistic debates in that year (which was also the centenary of Pushkin's death), see Katerina Clark, *Moscow, The Fourth Rome: Stalinism, Cosmopolitanism, and the Evolution of Soviet Culture, 1931-1941* (Cambridge, MA: Harvard University Press, 2011), 79–80. On shifts in historiography that attended the fiftieth anniversary celebrations another thirty years later, see Robert V. Daniels, 'Soviet Historians Prepare for the Fiftieth', *Slavic Review*, 26:1 (1967), 113–118.

25. Petrone, *Life Has Become More Joyous Comrades*, 158.

26. Petrone, *Life Has Become More Joyous Comrades*, 153.

27. For a discussion of the 'dialectic of permanence and transformation' in Soviet thought considered in the *longue duree*, see Galin Tihanov, 'Continuities in the Soviet Period', in *A History of Russian Thought*, ed. William Leatherbarrow and Derek Offord (Cambridge: Cambridge University Press, 2010) 311–339, 331.

28. *Ural'skii rabochii*, 81, 7 November 1919, 6, cited in Corney, *Telling October*, 92.

29. Lynn Mally, *Revolutionary Acts: Amateur Theater and the Soviet State, 1917-1938* (Ithaca, NY: Cornell University Press, 2016), 106.

30. Clark, *Petrograd*, 130 (my emphasis).

31. A forthcoming collection edited by Jean-François Fayet, Valérie Gorin and Stefanie Prezioso will explore international commemorations of the October Revolution: https://www.lwbooks.co.uk/book/echoes-of-october. For a typical itinerary of a foreign politician, culminating in attendance at the anniversary celebrations, see AS Kochetov, *The Guest from Ethiopia* (1980). Synopsis here: https://www.net-film.eu/film-8452/.

32. Kate Baldwin, *Beyond the Color Line and the Iron Curtain: Reading Encounters Between Black and Red, 1922–1963* (Durham, NC: Duke University Press, 2009), 250.

33. C.L.R. James (under the pseudonym J.R. Johnson), 'The Negro Question: The Greatest Event in History,' (1939) https://www.marxists.org/archive/james-clr/works/1939/11/greatest.html. Originally published in *Socialist Appeal*, 3, 87, 14 November 1939, 3.

34. Ibid.

35. On how the French state repressed the popular memory of the Paris Commune, for example, see Colette E. Wilson, *Paris and the Commune, 1871–78: the Politics of Forgetting* (Manchester, Manchester University Press, 2007).

36. Clark notes this was also the purpose of 'Toward a World Commune' which was performed before a military audience and intended as inspiration for the army's upcoming operations against the Polish. Clark, *Petrograd*, 131.

37. Larne Abse Gogarty, 'Cells in Organisms/Cogs in Machines: 1930s Proletarian Performance and Jazz', *Cesura/Acceso* 2 (2017), 20–39, 22.

38. Ellen Graff, *Stepping Left: Dance and Politics in New York City, 1928-1942* (Durham, NC: Duke University Press, 1999), 34–35.

39. Julia L. Mickenberg, *American Girls in Red Russia: Chasing the Soviet Dream* (Chicago, IL: University of Chicago Press, 2017), 224.

40. Gustave Flaubert, *Sentimental Education*, trans. Robert Baldick (London: Penguin, 1964), 286.
41. Corney, *Telling October*, 91.
42. Corney, *Telling October*, 93.
43. Clark, *Petrograd*, 132–133.
44. Corney, *Telling October*, 90.
45. 'Soviet October Revolution Parade, 1987 Part I', https://www.youtube.com/watch?v=1SmuBMANFKw.
46. GV Aleksandrov, *Epokha i kino* [*Epoch and Cinema*] (Moscow: Izdatel'stvo politicheskoi literaturi, 1983), 104.
47. The first objection was voiced by Sergei Tret'iakov, the second and third by Osip Brik, see Yuri Tsivian, 'Eisenstein and Russian Symbolist Culture: an Unknown Script of October' in *Eisenstein Rediscovered*, ed. Ian Christie and Richard Taylor (New York, NY: Routledge, 2005), 75–104, 89. Thanks to Alex Fletcher for recommending this essay.
48. Anne Nesbet, *Savage Junctures: Sergei Eisenstein and the Shape of Thinking* (London: IB Taurus, 2003), 78.
49. Jeremy Hicks, *Dziga Vertov: Defining Documentary Film* (New York, NY: IB Tauris, 2007), 102.
50. On Lenin plays in the 1930s see Petrone, *Life Has Become More Joyous Comrades*, 166. On the deification of Lenin, see Nina Tumarkin, *Lenin Lives! the Lenin Cult in Soviet Russia* (Cambridge, MA: Harvard University Press, 1997).
51. See, Esfir Shub, 'We Do not Deny the Element of Mastery', *Film Factory: Russian and Soviet Cinema in Documents*, ed. by Ian Christie and Richard Taylor (New York, NY: Routledge, 2015), 185–186. On Shub see, Esther Leslie, 'Art, Documentary and the Essay Film', *Radical Philosophy*, 192 (2015), 7–14.
52. Tsivian, 'Eisenstein and Russian Symbolist Culture', 92.
53. Nesbet, *Savage Junctures*, 77. Corney also discusses *October*, specifically the antagonisms between people who had been involved in the revolution in the film's development, *Telling October*, 205–208.
54. Nesbet, *Savage Junctures*, 87.
55. Nesbet, *Savage Junctures*, 89.
56. Nesbet, *Savage Junctures*, 89.
57. The exhibition ended with a 'Room of Memory', devoted not to artworks but to photographs of people arrested or killed in the Stalinist purges.
58. Miéville, *October*, 37, 64.
59. Miéville, *October*, 2.
60. Miéville, *October*, 307.
61. Enzo Traverso, *Left Wing Melancholia: Marxism, History, and Memory* (New York, NY: Columbia University Press, 2016), 32.
62. Traverso, *Left-Wing Melancholia*, 232.
63. Traverso, *Left-Wing Melancholia*, 18.
64. Traverso, *Left-Wing Melancholia*, xiv.
65. See also: TJ Clark, 'For a Left with No Future', *New Left Review*, 74 (2012) or Walter Schivelbusch, *The Culture of Defeat: on National Trauma, Mourning and Recovery* (New York, NY: Henry Holt and Company, 2013). In his review of exhibitions in London commemorating the centenary of the Revolution, Clark, like Traverso, privileges 1989 over 1917 as the key landmark with which the contemporary left must reckon. Unlike the sure-footed sombre tone of his earlier piece on the supposedly moribund left, however, this review strikes a more anxious and uncertain note (eight of the ten sentences in the opening paragraph end with a question mark). Clark seems less concerned with the status of revolutionary history today than he does with his fraught relationship to his past political commitments. See, TJ Clark, 'Reinstall the Footlights', *London Review of Books*, 39, 22, 16 November 2017.
66. Traverso, *Left-Wing Melancholia*, 48.
67. Walter Benjamin's 'Left-Wing Melancholy', a scathing review of a book by poet Erich Kästner, which Traverso skims over briefly, addresses a very specific phenomenon that he identifies in the supposedly radical literature of Weimar Germany. Despite proclaiming themselves sympathetic to the working class, poets like Kästner, Benjamin claims, address themselves to a 'middle stratum' of society; these self-proclaimed left-wing intellectuals 'are the decayed bourgeoisie's mimicry of the proletariat.' Distant from political action, these writers render forms of political struggle as pleasant objects to consume for the titillation and amusement of a bourgeois public. The left-wing melancholic is a reactionary figure, politically complacent and nihilistic, who reifies political struggles in which they have no direct involvement. (See Walter Benjamin, 'Left-Wing Melancholy', *Screen* 15:2 (1974), 28–32, 28.) Wendy Brown's analysis of 'left-wing melancholia' is a clear critique of the tendency although her characterisation of the post-89 left elsewhere is ultimately not so dissimilar from Traverso's.
68. See, for example: Svetlana Boym, *The Future of Nostalgia* (New York, NY: Basic Books, 2001), 78; Susan Buck-Morss, *Dreamworld and Catastrophe: the Passing of Mass Utopia in East and West* (Cambridge, MA: MIT Press, 2000), 68; T.J. Clark, *Farewell to an Idea: Episodes in the History of Modernism*, (New Haven, CT: Yale University Press, 1999), 1; Mike Davis, *City of Quartz: Excavating the Future in Los Angeles* (London: Verso, 1990), 12; and Owen Hatherley, *Militant Modernism* (Winchester: Zero Books, 2009), 8 (with apologies to Owen Hatherley who I know would probably not make the same arguments now). Traverso also sets out to 'excavate', *Left-Wing Melancholia*, xv.
69. Traverso, *Left-Wing Melancholia*, 43. Obviously such observations do not account for the status of that past *within* the former Soviet Union (especially in former Soviet Republics other than Russia) or in other parts of the former Eastern bloc, as policies pertaining to the removal of literal monuments from the Communist era clearly demonstrate, indicating the limits of Traverso's 'we'.
70. Rebecca Comay, 'Defaced Statues: Idealism and Iconoclasm in Hegel's *Aesthetics*', *October* 149 (2014), 123–142, 124.
71. Scott McCracken, 'The Author as Arsonist', *Modernity/Modernism* 21:1 (2014), 71–87, 80.
72. Kristin Ross, *Communal Luxury: the Political Imaginary of the Paris Commune* (London: Verso Books, 2016), 16 (epub).
73. http://www.nytimes.com/2011/11/02/us/oakland-activists-regroup-and-call-for-general-strike.html.
74. Vladimir Mayakovsky, *Plays*, trans. Guy Daniels (Evanston, IL: Northwestern University Press, 1995), 39.

Order in disorder
Revolution against the state becomes but a page in its history
Ilya Budraitskis

It would seem that the centenary of the Russian Revolution could not have come at a more inopportune moment for Russia. The colossal scale and universalist ambitions of that event are at odds with the apathetic state of Russian society today. Indeed, efforts to dispense with this inconvenient ghost appear to provide the sole point of consensus. The policy of 'Reconciliation' [*Primirenie*] that has become central to official discourse on the centenary is a case in point: resolving a conflict that has split society is not on the agenda; rather, it is asserted that there is no conflict. The only reconciliation offered serves to consolidate the present state of affairs as not only legitimate but the only possibility. The Revolution is both condemned as a violent and utopian experiment and embraced as a 'fact' in the history of the nation.

Sheila Fitzpatrick, in her recent review of new books on the Russian Revolution, expressed her concern about the change in its status. A few decades back the Revolution was widely perceived as a tipping point in the world history of the twentieth century. Today its significance is being rapidly marginalised. Historical studies as well as current politics increasingly see it as a local accident or one of history's dead ends.[1] Fitzpatrick raises the alarm: in the year of its centenary this dramatic chapter in history faced, like a rare species, the threat of extinction.

Eternal present: Russian version

The Kremlin's policy on history in general is based on the idea of a struggle to preserve a heritage that is under constant attack by external competitors and internal enemies. The only history that exists is the history of the forebears – of rulers and their faithful subjects. This is the history of a nation that is reproduced in every one of their heroic feats or crimes, a Russia that demands devotion to itself alone. Such devotion can justify any action and leaves no room for choice.

1917 is no exception to this schema. Here also we have the devious machinations of the neighbouring countries, the moral forces of internal resistance, a thousand-year-old state imperilled. It is from this complex that the genuine spiritual 'meaning' of the conflicts of the Revolution can and must be extracted, a meaning that would have been beyond the comprehension of the actual participants in the original events, but now familiar to every present-day government official: the Revolution is a legitimate part of our history that must never be repeated.

This is precisely the 'objective assessment' of the Russian Revolution that Vladimir Putin requested from the participants in the Congress of Russian Historians a year ago.[2] In January 2017, at the first meeting of the official agency charged by the President with arranging the centenary events, The Organising Committee for the Centenary of the 1917 Russian Revolution, Sergey Naryshkin, the former Chairman of the State Duma and one of the United Russia party leaders, unequivocally launched the following anti-revolutionary mission for contemporary Russia:

> A number of countries in recent years have been victim to the import of so-called revolutionary technologies and colour revolutions, which are always fraught with bloodshed, the death of citizens, destruction and hardship for the countries subject to such experiments. The Russian nation, however, has a vivid genetic memory of the price one has to pay for

the Revolution and therefore highly values stability.[3]

The Organising Committee for the Centenary of the 1917 Russian Revolution includes academics along with public figures from both liberal and patriotic camps. (Liberals such as journalists Nikolai Svanidze and Alexey Venedictov, and patriots such as film director Nikita Mikhalkov and writer Sergey Shargunov.) All of them presented the Committee as an agency of national reconciliation, assembled in commemoration of an event that no longer has any political significance. This stance was clearly articulated by Shargunov (who is also a Member of Parliament for the Communist Party):

> Let us all see our national history as dreadful, murderous, tragic and yet great. Let us all see that we do have a state and that it will develop further. This trust in Russia is what should be felt by us all while commemorating this important event.[4]

According to this scenario, the parties to the 'reconciliation' put aside their differences in order to swear allegiance to the country. In this respect, the fate of one of the hallmark projects of the centenary – the 'Monument to Reconciliation' [*Pamiatnik primirenyia*], which, according to the initial plan, should have been unveiled in Crimea in November 2017 – is very revealing. The design for the monument consisted of a column crowned with the figure of 'Russia', flanked by two kneeling soldiers symbolising the Red and the White armies in the civil war, now reconciled in genuflection before the nation. However, the mere depiction turned out to be too 'hot' for official politics: on the eve of the monument's installation local Stalinists in Sebastopol held a number of protests at this image of reconciliation, making the future of the project rather uncertain. The litigation between the city administration and activists remains unsettled, with the project's completion now scheduled for 2018, probably not before the presidential elections in March.[5] This exposure of political conflict over the historical representation of the Revolution is precisely what the official celebrations seek to conceal under the veil of patriotism.

The art exhibitions listed in the government's plan also promise to depoliticise the Revolution. The State Tretyakov Gallery held an emblematic exhibition, 'Someone 1917', which laid out a history of the Russian artistic avant-garde independent from the Revolution. The exhibition's curator, Irina Vakar, believes that 'in 1917 the artists didn't think about the Revolution at all. However, after it took place they started to use it … For Russian painting, 1917 became a sum total, a final point in concluding the decade of freedom.'[6]

On the way to 'Historical Russia'

These commemorations to reconciliation are, of course, merely epiphenomenal to the principal reconciliation between the Revolution and its opponents: the Russian state itself. According to Vladimir Medinsky, the Soviet state emerged from the revolutionary conflict as a 'third power', realising the continuum of 'historical Russia.' He argues that the Bolsheviks, despite their own anti-state attitudes, 'were obliged to deal with the restoration of the ruined institutions of the state and the struggle against regional separatism. … The unified Russian state became known as the USSR and maintained almost exactly the same borders. Moreover, 30 years after the demise of the Russian Empire, Russia unexpectedly found itself at the pinnacle of its military triumph in 1945.'[7]

This reproduces a conservative thesis first proclaimed about the French Revolution more than 200 years ago: the true significance of a revolution is not grasped by its revolutionaries. Conservative thinkers were convinced of their own ability to perceive the true content of a revolution, whether determined by divine providence, a metaphysical national destiny or historical inevitability. This was the ability, as Joseph de Maistre expressed it, 'to delight in the order in disorder.'[8] De Maistre wrote with satisfaction: 'All the monsters begotten by the Revolution have evidently only laboured for the sake of royal power.' Alexis de Tocqueville observed that the French Revolution completed the work of creating a centralised bureaucratic state that had been begun by Bourbon absolutism. Following de Tocqueville's logic, one could say that the French Republic existing today is heir to both the *ancien régime* and its revolution. Revolution is rendered

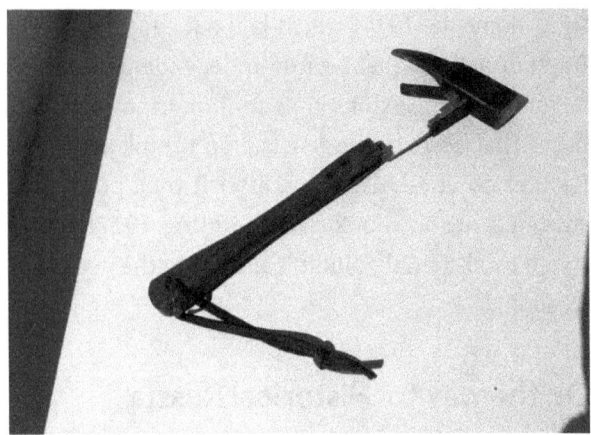

a myth, a quasi-religious faith in the ability of people to overthrow the old, sinful world through their own conscious effort and create a Kingdom of God on earth that lives according to completely different laws. A nation split apart by revolution can become aware of its continuing common history and overcome its own internal division only when it buries the destructive revolutionary religion conjointly. In this spirit, on the eve of the 200th anniversary of the French Revolution, the historian François Furet called for the completion of the Revolution by taking final leave of the illusions to which it gave rise. The history of the Revolution has not been completed as long as the political tradition that it created, based on myth, is still alive.[9]

This conservatism infuses the Kremlin's commemoration of the Russian Revolution: dismissing the revolutionary ambitions to create a new world reveals the true significance of the events that happened one hundred years ago, enabling us to see the contours of the millenary state organism in the obscurity of the period's self-awareness.

But the more direct precedent for Medinsky's conservative notion of 'historical Russia' is the 'Change of Signposts' movement of the 1920s. Its ideologues, such as Nikolai Ustryalov and Yury Kliuchnikov, saw Soviet Russia as the continuation and development of a thousand-years-old Russian state, the logic of which has proved more profound and more powerful than the internationalist perspective of the Bolsheviks. Sergei Chakhotkin, in his article 'To Canossa' from the programmatic compendium *A Change of Signposts*, published in Prague in 1921, wrote: 'history has forced the Russian "communistic" republic, contrary to its official dogma, to take up the national cause of gathering together a Russia that had almost fallen apart and at the same time restoring and increasing Russia's relative weight internationally.'[10] Furthermore, in the opinion of the 'signpost-changers', the very victory of the Revolution had realised an internal necessity of Russian history, by overcoming 'the gulf between the people and power.' In Ustryalov's opinion, the tragically high cost of the Revolution was the price 'paid for the rehabilitation of the state organism, for curing it of the prolonged, chronic malady that led the St. Petersburg period of our history to its grave.'[11]

Through the zig-zags of Bolshevik policy, determined by the contradiction between communist ideology and reality, Ustryalov glimpsed the triumph of the 'reason of the state', manifested outside the law. In effect approximating Carl Schmitt's concept of a 'state of emergency', Ustryalov regarded the Russian revolution as a triumph of the spirit of the state through the flouting of its letter.[12] Every step the Bolsheviks viewed as taken under compulsion – the limited recognition of the market through the New Economic Policy, or the temporary rejection of world revolution in the name of 'socialism in one country' – was regarded by the 'signpost-changers' as being legitimate and inevitable. The Bolsheviks, having assumed the burden of state power, even though they regarded it as a dangerous instrument from the moral point of view, started becoming transformed into its agents. Their revolutionary practice, undertaken from outside the state, had attempted to subordinate it to the goals of an anti-state and liberating moral order. But the dictatorship of the proletariat was gradually reduced to the condition of a dictatorship of the bureaucracy over the proletariat. Under the influence of circumstances, the means were victorious over the goal.

The Revolution as a moral problem

The course of events in 1917 was a challenge, not only to the old world, but also to the revolutionary social-democratic movement in its previous form – a movement which saw itself as no more and no less than an instrument for the realisation of the laws of history. From the moment it was established, the

Second International, which had proclaimed Marxism to be its official doctrine, based itself on a clear teleology of progress in which the socialist character of revolution was determined by necessary and inevitable preconditions. A social revolution had to be prepared by objective circumstances and it had to be the resolution of the contradictions that are inherent in the capitalist mode of production. The Russian Revolution was the direct and deadly negation of this entire tradition of Marxist politics: it was a revolution in an unexpected place, with an unexpected result. This aspect of 'defiance' runs through the entire history of 1917, engendering hope and surprise in European radical dissidents within social-democracy. Thus, in April of that year Rosa Luxembourg writes exultantly that the Revolution is taking place 'despite the treason and the universal decline of the working masses and the disintegration of the Socialist International.'[13] Six months later Antonio Gramsci hails the October coup in Russia, calling it a 'revolution against *Das Kapital*.'[14] For Gramsci, Russia became a place where 'events have defeated ideology', and the Bolsheviks had opted for events. The unique combination of these events, which preceded the coup, repudiated the absolute determinism of the 'laws of historical materialism' by giving the masses, who had liberated themselves from the dictatorship of external circumstances, an opportunity to make their own history. According to Gramsci, this liberating act also signified the beginning of the liberation of Marxism itself, which had previously been 'corrupted by the emptiness of positivism and naturalism.' He concluded with an open appeal to return to the sources of Marxist thought in German idealist philosophy.

Despite the fact that class-conscious workers, organised into Soviets, were the main driving force throughout 1917, the goals of the Revolution and its socialist character resulted from moral and political decisions taken by the Bolsheviks. Just as the Russian Revolution was not predetermined by a simple combination of circumstances that added up to a crisis, the goal of the transition to socialism did not in itself grow out of the dynamics of the class struggle. On the contrary, it was a kind of new, autonomous circumstance, a genuine moment of Kantian 'practice': a moral action that was based only on an inner conviction of the correctness of the decision taken. The party of Lenin accepted this moral burden of making the transition to socialism in a country which, according to all the definitions, was not ready for it. The dead weight of this decision would assert itself throughout the whole of Soviet history, and without any doubt the moral responsibility for all the events of that history runs back to the crucial decision taken by the Bolsheviks to seize power in October 1917. The Bolsheviks themselves were fully aware of this responsibility. The choice made by Lenin's supporters began as a tragic acceptance of the risks involved in the contradiction between goal and means, in the decision to seize state power.

This contradiction was expressed most precisely and profoundly by Georg Lukács in his 'Bolshevism as a Moral Problem', written at the very dawn of Soviet history in 1918.[15] According to Lukács, the goal of the Revolution is not determined by itself, but lies outside its specific social content. It is directed not simply towards the victory of the working class, but to surpassing class society as such. This is a path from the 'great disorder' of capitalism, alienation and the splintered condition of human life to universal good. Such a goal is universal, global and transcendental in relation to the circumstances of the specific historical situation in Russia. A little later, in his 1919 essay 'Tactics and Ethics', Lukács writes: 'The final goal of socialism is utopian is the same sense in which it transcends the economic, legal and social framework of present-day society and can only be realized by destroying this society.'[16] Lukács diagnosed the new moral decision as follows: either remain 'good people', autonomous in one's moral relation to immoral circumstances, and wait until the general good becomes real 'through the will of all', or seize power and impose your will on these unjust circumstances. Inevitably the state becomes the instrument of this volition towards the common good, although historically it was founded for a diametrically opposed goal. The state is acknowledged as an evil which is nonetheless necessary. To use the state, which was designed to assert inequality and injustice, for the triumph of equality and justice, entails consciously accepting the destruction of one's own moral integrity, deliberately attempting, as Lukács put it, 'to drive out Satan with the hands of Beelzebub.'

In effect, Lukács explains in the terms of Kant's moral philosophy the contradiction of a workers' state, which was formulated in the terms of Marxist theory by Lenin in *State and Revolution*. This text was written in August 1917 on the eve of the seizure of power. Lenin assumed that the state the revolutionaries were about to seize would cease to be a continuation of the old type, an instrument of one class's domination of the others. On the contrary, Lenin's 'dictatorship of the proletariat' is a dictatorship to end all dictatorships. For Lenin, the mission of the new proletarian state lay in proving itself unnecessary to a victorious class, the true class interest of which lay in dissolving both its own domination and itself in a consciously organised society. The task of the Bolsheviks should not be to reinforce the state apparatus they have inherited from previous overlords, but to 'smash and break it.' According to Lenin, such a state should not attempt to present itself as a moral force, an educator of the masses: on the contrary, it must convince these masses that they no longer need any educators.

However, while accepting responsibility for the creation of such a historically unprecedented, self-negating state, the Marxists were aware of the immense danger implicit in it. Having become the stewards of the proletarian state, the revolutionaries must not forget that it is evil. The moment this state starts believing in itself as the good, not only will it not 'disappear', it will consume society and be transformed into a totalitarian apparatus of oppression, exploiting the argument of the common good as the basis for its own monopoly on violence.

Not only do these conclusions, which follow directly from the reasoning of Lenin and Lukács, contain a prophecy of the Stalinist dictatorship, but also, and most importantly of all, they are founded on an awareness of responsibility for its very possibility. The Bolshevik coup was not therefore the consequence of that old, familiar, unreflecting political instinct to seize the power that has fallen out of the hands of the previous government, as the coup is often explained by banal anti-communists. On the contrary, it was a moral choice that opposed itself to the previous laws of power and politics; a choice which also recognised the terrible risks of failure. Stalinism – this victory of 'the ethical state' over the striving for an 'organised society', to use Gramsci's terms – was this failure.

However, even in the harshest conditions of totalitarian dictatorship, the moral basis of Bolshevism, its will to struggle against overwhelming circumstances, remained. This can be seen in the tragic struggle of the Left Opposition in 1920s and 30s, and in the interpretation of the experience of the gulag by writers such as Varlam Shalamov. Forty years after 'Bolshevism as a Moral Problem', Lukács, having himself endured the tribulations, if not the trials, of the times, wrote that Solzhenitsyn's *One Day in the Life of Ivan Denisovich* was the finest example of genuine 'socialist realism', since the true question of 'real socialism' was still the moral question.[17] However, it is Lenin's *State and Revolution* that must be regarded as the fundamental text of the Soviet age and the mystery of its origins. It was always something like the ghost of Hamlet's father, hovering over the Soviet state throughout its entire history. Packed into the canon of official ideology, this book was a constant reminder of the arbitrary nature of this ideology, placing in doubt over and over again the very right of the bureaucracy to hold power.

This dual nature of Bolshevism – as moral choice and actual historical experience, as conscious practice and the overwhelming force of circumstances – constitutes its heritage in an essential, undivided form. Historical Bolshevism was an attempted answer to an irresolvable moral contradiction: the question of correct action by the individual in an incorrect, distorted reality. Admittedly, this attempt was not conclusive and it ended in defeat, but it is perhaps the only such attempt in modern history to have been undertaken so seriously and on such a vast scale. Reflecting on the centenary of the Russian Revolution one can conclude that its fundamental moral question remains unanswered.

**Translated by Andrew Bromfield
and Anna Yegorova**

Ilya Budraitskis is a member of the editorial boards of Moscow Art Magazine *and* LeftEast.

Notes

1. Sheila Fitzpatrick, 'What's Left?' *London Review of Books*, 39:7 (March 2017), 13–5.
2. 'Putin: revolyutsii 1917 goda nuzhno dat "glubokuyu obyektivnuyu otsenku"' [Putin: The Revolution of 1917 should be given 'a profound objective assessment'], *Rossyia segonya*, https://ria.ru/politics/20141105/1031839813.html
3. 'Pervoe Zasedanie Organizatsionnogo Komiteta po Podgotovke i Provedeniyu Meropriyatij Posvyashchennykh 100-letiyu Revolyutsii 1917', Rossyiskoye Istoricheskoye Obchestvo ['The First Meeting of the Organising Committee for the Centenary of the 1917 Russian Revolution', Russian Historical Society], http://rushistory.org/proekty/100-letie-revolyutsii-1917-goda/pervoe-zasedanie-organizatsionnogo-komiteta-po-podgotovke-i-provedeniyu-meropriyatij-posvyashchennykh-100-letiyu-revolyutsii-1917-goda.html.

'Colour revolution' is a term widely used in Russia and internationally to describe political movements in several societies in the former Soviet Union and Balkans, including Georgia in 2003, Ukraine in 2004 and 2014, and Serbia in 1999. According to the view of the Russian government, which dominates the Russian media, these revolutions were not the product of internal political processes, but were organised from abroad (mostly from the USA).
4. Ibid.
5. On the disputes over the monument see Andrey Yalovetc, 'Memorial geroyev vmesto Pamyatnika primireniya. Putin postavil krest na prozhekte Ovsyannikova?' [Memorial instead of the Reconciliation Monument: Has Putin put paid to Ovsyannikov's project?], *Nakanune*, https://www.nakanune.ru/articles/113196; and 'Pamyatnik Primireniya ne smog primirit' storony v sude' [The Reconciliation Monument: No Resolution in Court], *Informer: Krymskij Novostnoj Portal*, http://ruinformer.com/page/pamjatnik-primirenija-ne-smog-primirit-storony-v-sude. On the still unresolved plans for the monument see 'Vladimir Medinsky v interview *Der Spiegel*: "Ya ne odobrau rezkih sujdenii o proshlom"' [Vladimir Medinsky in interview to *Der Spiegel*: 'I don't approve of harsh judgments about the past'], *Russia Today*, https://russian.rt.com/inotv/2017-11-04/Medinskij-v-intervyu-Der-Spiegel.
6. Olga Kabanova, 'Irina Vakar: idei umerli. iskusstvo ostalos' [Irina Vakar: Ideas Die, but Art Remains], *Vedomosti*, https://www.vedomosti.ru/lifestyle/characters/2017/08/17/729854-irina-vakar-idei-umerli. The exhibition ran from 28 September 2017 until 14 January 2018.
7. Vladimir Medinsky, 'Pobedila istoricheskaya Rossiya' [It is Historical Russia that Triumphed], Rossijskoye Voyenno-Istoricheskoye Obshchestvo, http://rvio.histrf.ru/activities/news/item-2170.
8. Joseph De Maistre, *Considerations on France*, edited by Richard A. Lebrun (Cambridge: Cambridge University Press, 2009).
9. François Furet, *Interpreting the French Revolution*, trans. Elborg Forster (Cambridge: Cambridge University Press, 1981).
10. Sergeev, Kiselev and Konstantinov, *V Kanossu. Politicheskaya istoriya russkoy emigratsii. 1920–1940 gg. Dokumenty i materialy* [To Canossa: A Political History of the Russian Emigration, 1920–1940. Documents and Materials] (Moscow, 1999), 190–195.
11. Nikolai Ustryalov, *Rossiya (iz okna vagona)* [Russia (At the Carriage Window)], Biblioteka Maksima Moshkova, http://lib.ru/POLITOLOG/USTRYALOV/rossia.txt_with-big-pictures.html.
12. Nikolai Ustryalov, *Ponyatiye gosudarstva* [The Concept of a State], Biblioteka Maksima Moshkova, http://www.lib.ru/POLITOLOG/USTRYALOV/ustrqlow-7.txt_with-big-pictures.html.
13. Rosa Luxemburg, *Selected Political Writings*, edited and introduced by Robert Looker (New York: Random House, 1972), 227.
14. David Forgacs and Eric J. Hobsbawm eds., *The Gramsci Reader: Selected Writings 1916–1935* (New York: New York University Press, 2000), 32.
15. Georg Lukács, 'Bolshevism as a Moral Problem', *Social Research* 44:3 (Autumn 1977), 416–424.
16. Georg Lukács, 'Tactics and Ethics', in *Tactics and Ethics, 1919–1929* (London: Verso, 2014), 5.
17. Georg Lukács, *Solzhenitsyn*, trans. W.D. Graf (London: Merlin Press, 1971).

All power to the soviets
Marx meets Hobbes
Lars T. Lih

'[M]en have no pleasure, but on the contrary a great deal of grief, in keeping company, where there is no power to over-awe them all.'

Thomas Hobbes, *Leviathan*[1]

The way we think about revolution is deeply involved with the great traditions of political theory, and conversely, our understanding of these traditions is strongly influenced by what we think we know about the great revolutions. The Russian Revolution of 1917–21 is an exemplary case in point. Beginning with the Revolution itself and continuing to our day, the Russian Revolution has been viewed primarily through the lens of two fundamental political theories. One can be called the Lockean tradition: revolutions are about the consent of the governed. The other is the Marxist tradition that focuses on the world-historical mission of a class – bourgeoisie or proletariat – to take political power and remake society.

A third fundamental theory, associated with the name of Thomas Hobbes, focuses on the presence or absence of a generally acknowledged sovereign authority, or what Hobbes termed the Leviathan. This political tradition plays a much smaller role in current evaluations of the Russian Revolution. And yet, as we shall see, a tacitly Hobbesian framework was adopted by many people who were directly caught up in events, including top Bolshevik leaders. An inquiry into this confluence of political theory and history illuminates both.

From the point of view of theory, the Russian case demonstrates with particular force that Hobbes' theory is not just an abstract account of an imaginary state of nature, but can help clarify the fundamental issues that animate a historical drama. Hobbes wrote in the context of the English Revolution and civil war, of course, but his theory usefully brings out some features of the Russian Revolution and civil war as well. Our discussion will also help make Hobbes' theory more concrete by thinking through *how* a new Leviathan might actually be created to take the place of one that has abdicated.

From the point of view of history, reference to Hobbes helps to highlight a perspective that was meaningful to many participants because it addressed crucial features of the situation that we ignore at our peril. I will give particular attention to arguments around the dispersal of the Constituent Assembly in early January 1918, because from that day to this, the episode of the Constituent Assembly remains a critical point of reference for each of the competing interpretations based on the traditions of Locke, Marx and, as I shall show, Hobbes.

Popular theorising

The Hobbesian perspective concentrates on the presence or absence of a country's *sovereign political authority*. The Russian word for this sovereign authority is *vlast* – a more useful item of vocabulary for exploring the Hobbesian perspective than any one English word. Russian observers and participants in the Revolution and civil war often employed the word with obsessive insistence. For these reasons, I have kept the Russian word *vlast* untranslated in what follows. *Vlast* has a more specific reference than the English word 'power,' and evokes more the sovereign authority in a particular country: in order to have the *vlast*, one has to have the right of making a final decision or command, to be capable of making the decisions and of seeing that they are carried out. 'Soviet power' or *sovetskaia vlast* points then to a *vlast* based on the soviets, their principles and social constituency.

All three political traditions were in play during the Revolution as ordinary people, trying to make sense of events, argued among themselves. In the novel *V tupike* [Dead End], for instance, published in Soviet Russia in 1922, Vikenty Veresaev gives us a nice example of popular theorizing in a way that accurately reflects the way people really talked. The following dialogue from the novel takes place in the Crimea in 1920, as the civil war is winding down. The speakers are Ivan Ilych Sartanov, a liberal reformer arrested under both the tsars and the soviets, his daughter Katya who defends an orthodox socialist outlook, and some young Bolshevik soldiers of worker origin.

> [Katya asked:] – Then you are yourselves Bolsheviks?
> The soldier looked at Katya with surprise.
> – Well, yes, of course!
> Ivan Ilych asked:
> – And what *is* Bolshevism?
> The soldier was ready with his explanation:
> – Bolshevism means that you are *for* a worker *vlast*, that the whole *vlast* should come from the workers and peasants, and that we build a just system that's based on labour.
> – You say the peasants as well should have the *vlast*? Then why are you against the Constituent Assembly? In Russia, the peasants and workers are an ocean and the bourgeoisie just a handful. What difference would it make to anybody if there were a dozen or so representatives from the bourgeoisie in the Constituent Assembly? And in that case, everybody would see that it represented the will of the people [*narod*] as a whole, and each and all would bow with respect toward it.
> The soldier smiled.
> – I'll explain all that to you right away with complete properness. The peasant [*muzhik*] is unlearned ['dark'], he's led astray by any priest or any kulak. And we, the working class, will not let him be pushed around, we won't allow him to be duped.
> – You're off base if you think our peasant is such a fool. And you're also off base if you think he doesn't have his own interests that are distinct from the interests of the working class …
> The soldier asked Katya with curiosity:
> – And who do you stand for?
> – I stand for socialism, for ending utterly the exploitation of the toilers by capital. But I simply don't believe that right now in Russia the workers are capable of taking the *vlast* into their hands. For that, they are too unprepared, and in economic terms Russia itself is completely unready for socialism. Marx proved that socialism is possible only in a country with a large-scale, developed, capitalist industrial base.
> The soldiers looked at her in bewilderment, and their expressions became more and more guarded. And more and more even Katya felt that, for them, right now, under the given circumstances, everything her words implied was even more lifeless than the utopian socialism that she had been talking about.
> The one with the white moustache raised his brows, thought a bit and said:
> – You say, you're for the workers? So what about right now? I mean to say, we took the *vlast* – but now we should give it back to the bourgeois [*burzhui*], so that they'll develop this industry you talked about?
> – Give it back, don't give it back, but all the same they'll grab the *vlast* for themselves – or Russia will completely fall to pieces.
> Another Red Army man – yellowish pale, with a black beard asked sharply:
> – So, tell me, this little dacha – is it yours, do you own it?
> – Well … well, yes, it's ours! But how does that change anything?
> He stood up, took his rifle from the corner and answered carelessly:
> – Nothing. Thanks for the snack.
> They left the kitchen. Katya accompanied them to the fence gate. The one with the black beard said:
> – Well, Alexa old pal, here's the way things are, eh? What do you say we go into town, hunt up some bourgeois – it could be that there's still some of them around. We'll give our rifles to them and say: we're so sorry, your gradualty, please, take the *vlast* back![2]

The older intellectual Ivan Ilych focuses on institutional procedures that provide a vehicle for consent of the governed, and so the Constituent Assembly – the product of universal suffrage and contested elections – assumes a central place for him. He is convinced that these procedures will ensure a *vlast* to which all will bow with respect. On the surface,

Katya and the Bolshevik soldiers situate themselves within the Marxist framework of class mission, and so they argue about the preconditions and the current prospects of using state power to build socialism.

Above and beyond this official and well-worn rhetoric, however, there are overtones of another way of defining the Revolution. This conversation takes place in 1920 in the Crimea. The question of the *vlast* in the Crimea was not settled by electoral procedures nor by an assessment of the proper conditions for socialism. The White Volunteer Army had held the *vlast* in this locality until recently, when it was forced out by a brutal clash between mass armies. Even Katya feels that there is something irrelevant and lifeless in her discourse as she speaks to these Bolshevik worker-soldiers who have just survived a fight to the death.

The workers are not as sophisticated as Katya and her father, but they put their finger on the nub of the matter. What is crucial for them is the existence of a *vlast* based on the popular classes – neither proper consent of the governed nor socialist transformation is of any real concern for them. After much travail, this new *vlast* has emerged victorious and is no longer contested. The soldiers feel that in some basic way, it is *their vlast*. Furthermore, they instinctively feel that to hand over the *vlast* to other social forces is simply an absurdity. What! – plunge the country into the horrors of another civil war?

A more detached perspective on the same problem comes from an earlier episode in the novel in which a peasant gives Katya a ride home and recounts a story about the lawless and brutal requisition of bread – or, rather, official looting – carried out by the White Volunteer Army. Katya remarks that the Bolsheviks are no better. The peasant answers: 'Who knows? It's all the same to us. Let it be the tsar, let it be Lenin – only let there be order, and peace and quiet. Just trying to live is becoming intolerable.'[3] For this peasant, there is nothing worse than a war of all against all in which life is nasty, brutish and short. He therefore believes that any *vlast* will do, as long as it is uncontested and imposes order.

The Hobbesian perspective

Hobbes brings out precisely those features of the situation that are left out by Locke and Marx, but central to those caught up in the Revolution, whether workers, peasants or party leaders. Let us quickly review some familiar themes of the Hobbesian approach to politics. First, Hobbes's theories are a reaction to extreme situations: civil war, breakdown, times when the routines of everyday life mean nothing and sheer existence is at stake. Hobbes zeroes in on precisely the situation most relevant to the people in Veresaev's novel, one in which there is no generally accepted and uncontested *vlast*, so that the creation of such a sovereign power becomes an overwhelming imperative.

Second, Hobbes sketches out the dynamics created by the absence of a *vlast*, summed up as 'the condition of a War of every man against every man.' Without reliable coordinating institutions in society at large, no one can really trust anyone else. The war of all against all is in this situation an objective necessity, regardless of human psychology. Hobbes argues that this is the worst possible state of affairs. Indeed, his most celebrated flight of rhetoric sounds like a drily factual description of the Russian civil war: 'no place for Industry… no Culture of the Earth; no Navigation… no Arts; no Letters, no Society; and which is worst of all, continual fear, and danger of violent death.'[4]

Third, a functioning sovereign authority must be unequivocally supreme, a Leviathan: it cannot tolerate rivals, it must 'overawe them all.' Hobbes thought that a state *vlast* had to be a 'Mortal God' in order to carry out its proper function; he gave this Mortal God the name of Leviathan because of a verse from the Book of Job that proclaims that Leviathan 'is made so as not to be afraid.' What might be called the Leviathan requirement does not necessarily imply a dictatorial or authoritarian state. If the existence of the Leviathan is not threatened, it too stands to benefit if it allows a great degree of freedom, decentralisation and citizen participation in decision-making. Nevertheless, the Leviathan can only remain unthreatened if everybody realises that no one can mess around with it.

Finally, the logic of the Hobbesian argument implies that there is a *moral* duty to support a functioning *vlast* and thus avoid the total disaster of the war of all against all. But this moral duty rests on Leviathan's ability *actually* to carry out its duty, namely, to overawe them all. When an existing *vlast* collapses or totters on the brink, when there are duelling rivals for sovereignty, individuals (we can no longer say citizens) are free, first, to look out for themselves, and second, to choose which Leviathan candidate to support – in fact, they are forced to make this choice. If 'the Commonwealth is dissolved', then 'every man is at liberty to protect himself by such courses as his own discretion shall suggest unto him.'[5] At some point in the choosing process, hard to define but real, one and only one plausible sovereign authority is left standing, and the normal moral duty of support imposes itself once again. In the conversations from the Veresaev novel, we see these individual choices playing out in real time.

If a revolution is defined as the establishment of democracy (consent of the governed) or as 'the conquest of power' by a new social group or class (class mission), then it is clear that the term 'revolution' does not really fit the Hobbesian paradigm of breakdown and reconstitution. The Russians have a good term for this paradigm: 'time of troubles' [*smutnoe vremia*]. The term was originally applied to the decade between 1603 (the death of Boris Godunov) and 1613 (the coronation of the first Romanov), during which Russia experienced civil war, invasion, widespread brigandage and famine. Many Russians have applied the term to the period from 1914 to 1921, and latterly to the 1990s.

The Hobbesian perspective allows us to confront and begin to answer some central questions about the Revolution. Why was it the Bolsheviks who successfully took power in October and held it against all comers in the civil war that followed? This was an astonishing outcome, one that few in 1917 ever even considered. I argue that the Bolsheviks were *preadapted* by their prewar outlook to respond effectively to the central challenge facing Russia after the February Revolution and the fall of the tsar: to create a new 'tough-minded *vlast*' [*tverdaia vlast*, a rallying cry across the political spectrum], to build up adequate state institutions from scratch, and to ensure that a new Leviathan 'overawed them all'.

The hegemony scenario: the Bolsheviks preadapt

In 1910, one of Lenin's top lieutenants, Lev Kamenev, asserted that the proletariat will always 'raise all issues and all struggles to the level of a struggle for the *vlast* …. The Russian Revolution – as opposed to liberalism – strives for its full completion: the transfer of the *vlast* into the hands of the revolutionary classes.'[6] This focus on the *vlast* reveals that the Bolsheviks were preadapted to respond effectively to the unexpected challenges of 1917.

'Preadaptation' is a concept taken from evolutionary biology. Sometimes a characteristic that evolved to meet a challenge in one environment turns out to be unexpectedly useful in another environment with different challenges. Feathers that evolved to regulate a dinosaur's body temperature later enable a bird to fly. The concept helps explain why it was the Bolsheviks and no other who could respond to the Hobbesian challenges of 1917 – even though these challenges were as novel and unprecedented for the Bolsheviks as they were for everyone else.

The focus on the *vlast* was an integral part of Bolshevism's *hegemony scenario*, that is, their map of the dynamic forces and the ultimate prospects of the upcoming Russian Revolution. This was the basis of their political strategy after assimilating the experience of the 1905 Revolution. I have described the hegemony scenario in detail elsewhere; here we need only a review of its basic Marxist logic.[7]

According to Marxism, the fundamental world-historical mission of the proletariat was to use state power to build socialism. The paradigmatic case of a class taking state power in order to remake society in its own image was the bourgeoisie in the French Revolution of 1789 and in other 'bourgeois revolutions'. Marx and Engels always considered the destruction of absolutism and the achievement of political freedom as an essential step in the emancipation of the proletariat, and in their first writings they were

more than willing to hand over this task to the bourgeoisie. But the major development in Marxist thinking between 1848 and the early years of the twentieth century was the realisation that the bourgeoisie was growing less and less capable of carrying out proper 'bourgeois revolutions' in countries like Germany and Russia, while the proletariat was growing more and more capable. As Engels claimed in 1892: 'If the German bourgeoisie have shown themselves lamentably deficient in political capacity, discipline, energy and perseverance, the German working class have given ample proof of all these qualities.'[8] Thus the historical mission of the bourgeoisie – replacing absolutism with democracy and full political freedom – was more and more assigned to the proletariat.

As Kamenev stated in the quotation above, the proletariat strived to 'transfer the *vlast* into the hands of the revolutionary classes.' The proletariat was to be the *hegemon* or leader in this process. The question then arises: lead whom? In Russia, the Bolshevik answer was clear: the peasants, who remained the great majority of the population. The class interest of the peasants (need for land, economic dependence on the landowners, inferior legal status) made them a potential ally in the complete democratisation of society, even though they required a better awareness of their interests as well as political leadership during revolutionary struggles. The Bolshevik strategy appointed the Russian proletariat and its party to play the role of leader. Thus the hegemony strategy as applied to Russia can be summed up as follows: in order to carry out a full democratisation of society and to clear the path to socialism of potentially fatal obstacles, the socialist party must strive to create a worker-peasant *vlast*, even if a temporary one. In 1917, this strategy was easily translated into the slogan 'All Power to the Soviets!'[9]

The hegemony strategy was thoroughly Marxist. Its orthodoxy is attested to by the overlooked but crucial fact that Karl Kautsky, the acknowledged spokesman of 'revolutionary Social Democracy' (the left wing of the Second International), penned a classic exposition of this strategy in his seminal article of 1906, 'Driving Forces and Prospects of the Russian Revolution.' Both Lenin and Trotsky enthusiastically endorsed this article as an authoritative statement of their own political views.[10] Yet with hindsight, we can see that this strategy could also be retrofitted to meet the Hobbesian challenge of creating a new *vlast* ex nihilo. The Bolsheviks were strongly attuned to thinking about the *vlast* and psychologically prepared to take responsibility for its actions. The wager of the 'revolutionary classes' gave them a potential social base for a new Leviathan. The programmatic goal of 'carrying the democratic revolution to the end' implied meeting the non-socialist challenges of national life, whatever they turned out to be.

The prewar Bolsheviks were focused on 'conquering the *vlast*,' but they certainly never contemplated a situation where there was no *vlast* to conquer. They did not foresee that building state institutions from scratch would become their primary programme. They would have been shocked to learn that their greatest achievement after the Revolution was the creation of the Red Army. They were indeed preadapted to meet these challenges – but there was no guarantee they would be able to turn preadaptation to effective adaption in an unprecedented and merciless political environment.

1917: The 'historic *vlast*' disappears

In February 1917, a dynasty that had recently celebrated its three-hundredth anniversary disappeared. Along with it disappeared any generally accepted principle of legitimacy. Hobbes seems to be talking about the February Revolution when he observes 'if a Monarch shall relinquish the Sovereignty, both for himself and his heirs; His Subjects return to the absolute Liberty of Nature.' In an instant, a whole new set of challenges arose, but the full scope of these challenges took some time to make itself manifest.

As Minister of Food Supply in the Provisional Government, Alexei Peshekhonov was in a good position to observe and reflect on these challenges. Food supply became a focal point for the tensions that more and more rapidly tore apart the economic, administrative and social fabric. A few years later he recalled 'how things were' in 1917, and we can hardly do better than quote his description extensively.

'On 27 February 1917', Peshekhonov remembered, 'the old state *vlast* was overthrown. The Provisional Government that replaced it was not a state *vlast* in the genuine sense of the word: it was only the symbol of *vlast*, the carrier of the idea of *vlast*, or at best its embryo.' The mechanism that supported the tsarist government also began to crumble. 'The machinery of state administration was thrown immediately out of kilter; those parts which were most vital from the point of view of the existence of a state *vlast* were completely destroyed. Courts, police, and other organs of state coercion were swept away without trace …. This process of destruction quickly spread to all local organs, down to the lowest, and to the army, in the rear and in the front.' New organs of local administration were tardy and ineffective. 'If any state order at all continued to maintain itself, this was for the most part by inertia. The forces needed to support it with compulsion were simply not there.'[11]

The full awareness of the absence of any effective *vlast* took a while to percolate to the population as a whole. According to Peshekhonov, the peasant population only grasped the new situation in May, while the ill-starred June offensive soon laid bare the ineffective combination of newly-elected soldier committees and an officer corps inherited from the past. Vladimir Stankevich, an assistant to Kerensky who was close to the Social Revolutionaries [SRs], reported from first-hand experience that military units pillaged the population, while the command staff felt unable to stop it because the military police were just as unreliable and often joined in.[12] In a recently published book, Tsuyoshi Hasegawa details how the dissolution of the much-hated yet efficient civilian police force and its replacement with a new municipal police led rapidly to the breakdown of order and an explosion of violent crime. The pushback came first from mob justice and then from the highly repressive and extra-legal actions of the Cheka.[13]

By Peshekhonov's reckoning, the culmination or rather nadir of the collapse of the *vlast* came in the months following the October Revolution. 'With their takeover, the Bolsheviks so to speak finished off any effective Russian state *vlast*: they decisively destroyed the army and swept off the face of the earth even those rudiments of a new state apparatus that the Provisional Government had tried to create. The country was thrown literally into anarchy.' During these months, very few people were afraid of ruthless Bolshevik tyranny – rather, they were afraid of a quick collapse into the sort of chaos that might lead directly to the triumph of counterrevolution. Peshekhonov recounts an anecdote that sums up the situation in the early months of the new revolutionary regime.

> In March or April 1918, that is, something like six months after the Bolshevik takeover, I happened to meet in Moscow the chauffeur who had driven me when I was a member of the Provisional Government. We greeted each other like old friends.
>
> 'Well,' I asked, 'how are you getting along? Once you drove the Tsar around, and now who?'
>
> 'There's no way around it,' he said, 'I have to work for the Bolsheviks ... But you know I don't submit to them all that much. Yesterday Comrade (and he named one of the People's Commissars) sent for an automobile, and I, as the secretary of our organisation, answered him in writing: there's a *vlast* up there, but there's also a *vlast* down here – we won't give you an automobile!'
>
> When the *vlast* at the bottom is no less strong than the *vlast* at the top, then one can say that there is no *vlast* at all.[14]

In Russia the state did not have to be smashed – it simply collapsed. Let us now look at the situation from another angle and ask: what forces in Russian society were ready, able and willing to take on the Hobbesian challenge of creating a new *vlast*? Among the forces that had the minimum qualification of a coherent national structure, we may list the state bureaucracy, the gentry (*dvorianstvo*), the Church, the 'voluntary organisations' recently created to aid in the war effort, the Army and the political parties.

We can quickly eliminate the first four. The state bureaucracy needed an external source of authority to set it running and to coordinate disputes. Without such an outside authority, it was capable only of negative and passive actions such as the widespread refusal to work that greeted the Bolshevik takeover. The gentry had long passed its expiry date as an effective source of either political leadership or even effective support for a national *vlast*. For a variety of reasons, the Orthodox Church was unable to launch a strong political intervention; in any event, it did not try. The wartime voluntary organisations managed to transfer some early prestige and legitimacy to the Provisional Government, but their lack of roots in the population soon became apparent.

The high command of the Army, with its control over unequalled means of coercion, seemed like a natural source of a new if counterrevolutionary *vlast*. What is striking in 1917 is the Russian Army's inability to play this role, either in February, in August during the Kornilov affair, or even in October. Ultimately the high command had less control over the loyalty of the troops than the soviets did – a striking fact that had its roots in the unpopularity of a war that the soldiers had long equated with meaningless butchery.

We are left, then, with the political parties. Three camps can be discerned: the liberal Kadets (short for Constitutional Democrats), with associated right-wing allies; the 'moderate socialists', that is, the majority factions of the Socialist Revolutionaries (SRs) and the Mensheviks; and the 'internationalists' opposed to any coalition or 'agreementism' with elite politicians. The latter were mainly Bolsheviks, but also including assorted small groups; some of these groups were independent, some were factions within the moderate socialist parties, and some directly joined the Bolsheviks.

We may quickly eliminate the liberal Kadets, who never had much in the way of mass social support. The legitimacy of the Provisional Government in its early days with a majority Kadet cabinet came more from the national and international prestige of the anti-tsarist reformers than from their ability to garner popular loyalty. The Kadets could only hope for power if allied either with the revolution (the moderate socialists) or, preferably, with the counter-revolution (the military). Both alternatives proved to be non-starters.

We can turn to Sergei Lukianov for a hostile but keen-eyed analysis of why neither of the two main rivals of the Bolsheviks were able to construct a new and effective *vlast*. Lukianov was a Russian nationalist who came from the right end of the political spectrum that was bitterly angry at the 'men of 1917', although very few of his erstwhile comrades went on to praise the Bolsheviks as he did. He summed up the reasoning of the moderate socialists as follows: 'Reforms are indispensable, but they mustn't weaken the economic, financial and military strength of the country, nor destroy cultural and legal values, even if these values are alien to the majority of the *narod* [the people, comprising peasants, workers, and urban "petty bourgeois"].' This reasoning reflected the inescapable double bind gripping the moderate socialists:

> This prudence [*ostorozhnost'*] of the political leaders of the first half of 1917 was their principal and unpardonable failure – their crime against the Revolution and, as a consequence, against Russia. [Yet] we cannot demand a prophetic clairvoyance from people, and none of the members of the Provisional Government could have committed themselves in an organic manner on the remaining alternative path: the belief that a worker-peasant *vlast* could be established immediately. More: to install such a *vlast* inevitably implied that one had to plunge for a time into the murkiness of the arbitrary of bloodshed and the destruction of material and cultural values.[15]

At this point, we seem to have eliminated all alternatives but one: the Bolsheviks.

All power to the Soviets! The path to a new *vlast*

In her book *Inside the Russian Revolution*, the American socialist, pioneering woman correspondent and fighter for women's rights, Rheta Childe Dorr, described her first impression in Russia:

> About the first thing I saw on the morning of my arrival in Petrograd ... was a group of young men, about twenty in number, I should think, marching through the street in front of my hotel, carrying a scarlet banner with an inscription in large white letters.
> 'What does that banner say?' I asked the hotel commissionaire who stood beside me.
> 'It says "All the Power to the Soviet",' was the answer.
> 'What is the soviet?' I asked, and he replied briefly:
> 'It is the only government we have in Russia now.'[16]

Judging from this passage, when did Dorr arrive in Russia? Most of us might naturally assume she arrived after the Bolshevik Revolution in October, since only then did the soviets overthrow the Provisional Government. But in actuality, Dorr came to Russia in late May 1917 and stayed in Russia only until the end of August. Her book was sent to press *before* the October Revolution and thus gives us an invaluable look at what was happening in 1917, free of hindsight.

Dorr's account brings home an essential fact: 'The soviets, or councils of soldiers' and workmen's delegates, which have spread like wildfire throughout the country, are the nearest thing to a government that Russia has known since the very early days of the revolution .... Petrograd is not the only city where the Council of Workmen's and Soldiers' Delegates has assumed control of the destinies of the Russian people. Every town has its council, and there is no question, civil or military, which they do not feel capable of settling.'[17] The soviets provided a framework for a viable *vlast*, but this framework could survive only if provided with effective political leadership.

The Bolshevik party attained the *vlast* after it won political leadership of the soviet system, an embryo *vlast* that arose in the course of the February Revolution. The soviet mass constituency – workers and soldiers – accepted Bolshevik leadership when it finally decided that the soviets must have *all* power – or, in Hobbesian terms, when it fully realised that there can exist only *one vlast*. The soviet constituency slowly came to believe that the soviets must overawe them all or else retire from the scene – and in the end only the Bolsheviks were prepared, at any cost, to defend the continued existence of the soviets.

From the beginning, there were Hobbesian overtones in the Bolshevik message to the soviet constituency. The heart of this message was precisely '*All* power to the soviets!' I emphasise 'all' because here the Bolsheviks were making a quasi-Hobbesian point – or rather, they were responding to a point first made by their opponents. The liberal Kadets complained that there could only be *one vlast*, so that 'dual power' [*dvoevlastie*] was equivalent to 'no power' [*bezvlastie*], that is to say, anarchy.[18] They therefore not so politely asked the soviets (at this point still led by the moderate socialists) to butt out. The Bolsheviks enthusiastically agreed with this basic logic, but inverted the conclusion: there indeed should be, there could be, only one *vlast* – and that *vlast* should be the soviets!

The Bolshevik case for soviet power in 1917 was powered much less by the praise of its democratism familiar to us from Lenin's *State and Revolution* (a book first published in 1918) than by a *negative* critique of 'agreementism' [*soglashatelstvo*], that is, of the insistence on some sort of compromise, deal or coalition with elite parties or politicians. The Bolsheviks presented themselves to the soviet constituency as the party that had the political will to *actually carry out* the programmatic promises of the other parties, without obfuscation, qualification or delay. The elite parties had no intention of carrying out these promises, and the moderate socialists were too afraid of breaking with the elites to push them through. More and more, the Bolsheviks argued, agreementism stood in the way even of accomplishing basic state functions such as national defence. A governmental coalition based on parties with totally different goals and class interests could only get lapse into flailing incoherence.

Agreementism, then, prevented the achievement of the goals of the Revolution. But what *were* these goals? Here we can discern a shift in the Bolshevik message over the course of the year or rather, various layers were gradually added on to earlier goals. In the beginning, the main revolutionary goals were the traditional 'three whales' inscribed on the prewar Bolshevik banner: democratic republic, land to the peasants, and the eight-hour day (synecdoche for worker protection legislation) – plus, of course, an end to the imperialist war. As the year proceeded, the current economic crisis came to the fore. Everyone agreed on the need for extensive state regulation of the economy, but a coherent and vigorous programme was made impossible by the conflicting interests that rendered any soviet/elite coalition impotent.

Gradually, a deeper and more urgently existential goal asserted itself: the creation of *any* sort of functional *vlast*. We may illustrate this final layer with comments made by Kamenev in September:

> If you want a coalition with the bourgeoisie, then conclude an 'honest coalition' with the Kadets but, if the Kornilov mutiny taught you what the party of the proletariat has been saying from the very beginning of the revolution, then you will say the following: the only salvation for revolutionary Russia, the only way to restore confidence [*doverie*] between soldiers and officers within the army, the only way to establish confidence on the part of the peasants that they will receive the land, the only way to give the workers the feeling that they live in a republic – the only method to do all this is to take the *vlast* into the hand of the worker, peasant, and soldier organisations themselves.[19]

This shift in the Bolshevik message brings us directly to the problem of the Constituent Assembly, an institution that was supposed to solve the problem of the *vlast* once and for all.

The Constituent Assembly: A case in point

The idea of a Constituent Assembly that would crown the Revolution and create a new political system had deep prewar roots in Russian politics. From the February Revolution on, all points on the political spectrum, Bolsheviks included, assumed that a Constituent Assembly should be elected as soon as possible under a system of universal suffrage. Theoretically, all crucial decisions would be made by the Assembly, and indeed the Provisional Government often evaded difficult choices by referring them forward to the coming Assembly. If it seemed necessary, however, Kerensky's government was prepared to anticipate the Assembly, for example, by officially declaring Russia a republic, in the autumn.

Elections to the long-awaited Assembly finally took place over the course of November. In early January 1918, however, the Bolsheviks and the Left SRs abruptly closed down the newly elected Constituent Assembly after a single one-day session. From that day to this, this action has been viewed as the moment when the Revolution lost genuine legitimacy, made civil war inevitable, and revealed the essentially tyrannical nature of the Bolsheviks. As such, it provides an excellent focal point for exploring our broader relationship between Locke, Marx and Hobbes.

The standard evocation of the Constituent Assembly rests precisely on a 'Locke meets Hobbes' approach. The Constituent Assembly was elected in November 1917 on the basis of universal adult suffrage (including women) and as such represented the consent of the governed. This consent gave the Assembly democratic legitimacy, and this legitimacy in turn was the only possible foundation for a stable *vlast* accepted by all (as affirmed by the spokesman for the intelligentsia in the Veresaev novel quoted above). By closing down the Assembly, the Bolsheviks and Lefts SRs thus made civil war inevitable, for everyone now realised that the Bolshevik government could not be removed peaceably.

The only well-known rationale for the Bolshevik action is the one proffered by Lenin at the time, and then given support by the widely-read *State and Revolution*, which appeared soon afterwards. Lenin argued that the soviets represented a *higher form of democracy*, as compared with 'bourgeois parliamentarianism'. This democratism made the soviets an ideal vehicle for 'the dictatorship of the proletariat', that is, the fulfilment of the class mission assigned by history to the proletariat. In the long run, however, the inadequacies of Lenin's argument have merely strengthened the standard anti-Bolshevik account.

The record of the Russian soviets as vehicles either for democratic consent of the governed or for genuine rule by the proletariat as a whole was hardly such as to convince anyone that they were preferable to parliamentary democracy. Furthermore, this argument immediately opened up the Bolsheviks to the charge of blatant hypocrisy. Throughout the year, the Bolsheviks – including Lenin – had vehemently rejected the charge that they were opposed to the Constituent Assembly. On the contrary: they insisted very loudly that only soviet power could guarantee that the Constituent Assembly would indeed be summoned and allowed to hold session.

In fact, Lenin's rationale did not reflect wider views among the Bolsheviks or the Left SRs (coalition partners with the Bolsheviks in the first months of the regime), or their constituency, but rather reflected his own personal theories about soviet democracy. In what follows, I will sketch out another rationale found in writings of prominent Bolsheviks at the time, such as Stalin, Zinoviev and Trotsky. Articles by these leaders contain no hint of the soviets as a higher form of democracy, but rather base their arguments on a more Hobbesian reasoning. Paying attention to this Hobbesian perspective allows us to uncover political arguments that have been hitherto overlooked. Conversely, these on-the-ground arguments allows us to see how the Hobbesian theoretical perspective might work out in practice. As a bonus, we will observe an issue in which Stalin, Zinoviev and Trotsky – usually seen as inveterate foes – are all pretty much on the same page.

No one in Russia had really thought through the coming unprecedented situation in which the Constituent Assembly might somehow coexist with the soviets. Some members of the elite certainly hoped that the soviets would just fold their tents and silently steal away. But even these people didn't think through the ways and means of removing 'the committees' now firmly established in army, factory and city, if by chance they refused to go gently into that good night. And who would fill the gap left by the soviets? The Provisional Government had not succeeded in setting up a structure for local administration to enforce the behests of the central *vlast*. The soviets, on the other hand, were already present everywhere except the villages, which had their own elected committees.

The resulting situation was apparent even before the formal assumption of the *vlast* by the national soviet structure. In articles written for *Pravda* in September 1917, Stalin argued that Russia was witnessing a struggle between the 'official' *vlast* and an 'unacknowledged' *vlast* that was based in 'the revolutionary committees and soviets in the rear and at the front.' This unacknowledged *vlast* was now moving from defence to offense; the task now was to turn the unofficial *vlast* into the official one [*oformlenie*]. If they wanted to avoid political bankruptcy, the agreementists had to choose sides in this life-and-death struggle between the two candidates for the *vlast*.[20]

The coming clash between the soviets and their possible replacement by the Constituent Assembly was already making itself felt in October, just prior to the Second Congress of Soviets, and surfaced in two popular arguments. First, why bother to even hold a Second Congress of Soviets, since the Constituent Assembly was almost upon us? Let's just muddle along with an admittedly unsatisfactory Provisional Government until then. Further, on a local level, were not democratically elected city councils now in place, ready to take over from local soviets? Zinoviev addressed these arguments in *Pravda* in early October.[21]

Zinoviev wrote at a time when the Bolsheviks still thought of themselves as the champions rather than the foes of the Constituent Assembly. He therefore insisted that the immediate declaration of soviet power was the only guarantee that the Constituent Assembly would even be summoned. In light of later events, these kinds of arguments sound highly ironic, not to say openly hypocritical. Nevertheless, there is no reason to suspect that Zinoviev was not speaking in good faith when he argued that the success of the Revolution would be manifested by a government that would be a 'combined type of Soviet and Constituent Assembly'. Looking back after the dispersal of the Constituent Assembly, this argument sounds moderate. But the real gravamen of Zinoviev's argument is that *soviets would continue to exist* – and this insistence provides continuity with later Bolshevik actions.

Zinoviev pointed to the wave of revolutionary action sweeping the country: the peasants taking land by their own means, the elemental [*stikhiinoe*] peasant movement, disorders in the cities caused by food shortages, and the lurking counterrevolutionaries left at liberty. Only soviet power could prevent this protest from degenerating into anarchy. The bourgeoisie would no doubt like nothing better than for the workers and peasants to let their strength dribble away in such elemental outbursts, rather than seeing their protests 'receive an organised political expression … leading the revolutionary classes to the *vlast*' (note the direct echo of Kamenev's words in 1910).

Zinoviev observed that the widespread assertion that the Second Congress of the Soviets was not needed cut both ways. If the voice of the national soviet constituency was unneeded *before* the Constituent Assembly, then presumably it was even more superfluous *after* the Constituent Assembly was summoned. But was it remotely possible to imagine a successful *vlast* without the soviets? First of all, who would defend a government that was really determined to confiscate gentry land, thus liquidating the existing elite?

Only a 'mystical view' of the Constituent Assembly would credit the mere prestige of electoral legitimacy with the actual ability to overcome determined opposition by an entrenched elite. (This is Zinoviev's answer in advance to Ivan Ilych Sartanov, the fictional representative of the intelligentsia in Veresaev's *V tupike*, who argued that 'all would bow with respect' to an Assembly elected with universal suffrage.) Since when did right-wing or even liberal politicians and generals show such reverence for the will of the *narod* [*narodnaia volia*]? Any new government must have its own apparatus of power to carry out decisions nationally and locally:

> The Constituent Assembly will be strong only insofar as the *real correlation of forces* speaks for it. If it does not have an apparatus in the localities, among the workers, among the peasants, you can be sure that the gentry landlords and the capitalists will not only laugh at it, but will openly disband it, as the tsar openly disbanded the first two dumas. And what other apparatus is available to the Constituent Assembly in the localities but the Soviets? The Soviets in the localities must remain the fundamental basis, the revolutionary cells of the *vlast*.

Unlike the existing soviets, newly-elected city councils 'are unable in the near future to carry out this assignment of providing local cells for a national *vlast* … Compare the significance, for example, of the Moscow City Duma to the Moscow Soviet of Worker and Soldier Deputies as militant revolutionary units, and it will become clearer to you why this is the case.'

Zinoviev's call for a 'combined type' of government envisioned a central authority that decreed the revolutionary programme of the soviets and then relied on the existing soviets to carry it out energetically. There can be little doubt how the person who made these arguments in early October would react if forced later on to make a choice between Constituent Assembly and the soviets.

We can now turn to Trotsky to hear why the Bolsheviks thought that making this choice did indeed become inevitable. Trotsky's discussion of the Constituent Assembly is found in one of the first narrative accounts of the Revolution written by a Bolshevik leader, or for that matter by anyone.[22] Trotsky's history was written in early 1918, hard on the heels of the Assembly's dispersal in early January. Trotsky reaffirmed that 'when we argued [in October] that the road to the Constituent Assembly lay ... through the seizure of power by the Soviets, we were absolutely sincere.' He is still willing to argue that, in fact, only the declaration of soviet power guaranteed the summoning of the Constituent Assembly.

Why, then, did soviet power also become the Assembly's executioner?

Trotsky does not deny that the Constituent Assembly had real democratic legitimacy and that, all things being equal, this legitimacy should have been respected. (Later on, he and other Bolsheviks would have been much more contemptuous of electoral democracy as such.) Certainly, there is no hint in his account of Lenin's argument that the soviets had intrinsically higher democratic legitimacy. Rather the problem was a straightforwardly political one. The Right SRs (the SR party after the schism with the Left SRs) held the majority in the Assembly and so it was the only candidate for forming a non-Bolshevik government – but it was also inherently barred from relying on the existing local and national soviet apparatus that was crucial for a truly effective *vlast*.

Trotsky makes the point that the votes received by the SR party are extremely hard to read, given that the Left SRs were in the process of splitting from the parent party, a fact not reflected in the party lists. Often the peasants voted for leaders who were openly opposed to policies supported by the peasants. 'The result of it all', Trotsky notes, 'was a most incredible political paradox: one of the two parties which were to dissolve the Constituent Assembly, viz. the Left Socialist Revolutionaries, was actually elected on the same lists as the party which had obtained the majority in the Constituent Assembly.'

The bigger problem remained the disconnect between any Right SR government and the only material apparatus available for an effective *vlast*, namely, the soviets – who, as Trotsky remarked in an earlier article, represented the majority of the 'population capable of political life.'[23] Thus Trotsky links up with Zinoviev's argument in October about the indispensability of the local soviets.

The Right SRs could have formed a government anytime during 1917 – in fact, up to September, the slogan 'All Power to the Soviets!' implied just such a government. But (Trotsky continued) they were unwilling to do so and instead happily remained a junior member in a hapless coalition with the elites. Whatever the reasons, they were profoundly unwilling to break with elite, educated society and the Allies. This circumstance cast doubt on their willingness or ability to form a non-coalition government now. More importantly, this earlier failure had thoroughly alienated the people who ran the essential soviet apparatus.

> The working class, together with the Red Guard, were deeply hostile to the Right Socialist Revolutionaries. The overwhelming majority of the army supported the Bolsheviks. The revolutionary elements in the villages divided their sympathies between the Left Socialist Revolutionaries and the Bolsheviks ... [Thus any government set up by the Constituent Assembly] would have been completely deprived of the material apparatus of power. In the centres of political life, such as Petrograd, such a government would have met at once with an uncompromising resistance.

If not the soviets, on whom could the new government rely? 'It would have had behind it the rich of the villages, the intelligentsia, and the old officialdom, and, from the right, it perhaps would have found support, for the time being, among the bourgeoisie.' (The mists of time have obscured the fact that industrial elites were on the whole hostile – and with good reason! – to the idea of an assembly elected during severe external and internal crises and then given the task of deciding all the crucial questions of national life, all while a war was raging.) None of these social elements were prepared, for reasons addressed earlier, to become an effective support for a new *vlast*.

Putting all these considerations together, Trotsky made his final plea for historical justification:

> If the Soviets had, in accordance with the formal logic of democratic institutions, handed over their power to the party of Kerensky and Chernov, the new government, discredited and impotent, would have only succeeded in temporarily confusing the political life of the country, and would have been overthrown by a new rising within a few weeks. The Soviets decided to reduce this belated historical experiment to a minimum, and dissolved the Constituent Assembly on the very day when it assembled ....
>
> The material class-contents of the Revolution came into an irreconcilable conflict with its democratic forms. Thereby the fate of the Constituent Assembly was decided in advance. Its dissolution appeared as the only conceivable surgical way out of the contradictory situation which was not of our making, but had been brought about by the preceding course of events.[24]

It has been asked, by Rosa Luxemburg among others: why didn't the Bolsheviks just hold another election? But they did – within the soviet system itself, whose Third Congress met just a few days after the Constituent Assembly, from 23–31 January 1918 (and whose contested Fourth and Fifth Congresses convened later in the year). The Bolshevik-Left SR government set up in October and based on the Second Congress of Soviets already had more electoral legitimacy than any other government of 1917. The electoral machinery of the soviet system only gradually lost effectiveness; for example, the Fifth Congress of Soviets in May 1918 remained the scene of genuinely fierce debates between socialist parties. Although elections still took place, they lost meaning amid the civil war repression of political life, and the Sixth Congress of Soviets at the end of 1918 contained no real opposition elements. The asphyxiation of political life in Soviet Russia was certainly a very real process, but very little explanatory power is gained by turning the dissolution of the Constituent Assembly into the fatal crossing of the historical Rubicon.

Conclusions

Hobbes's reasoning receives a strong confirmation by the experience of the Russian Revolution. He accurately outlined the dynamics of a situation in which a previously uncontested *vlast* disappears – uncontested, not in the sense that nobody was violently hostile to it, but in the sense that no one doubted that it *was* indeed the *vlast* and had the ability to see its decrees enforced. After the February Revolution, people immediately put 'the crisis of the *vlast*' at the centre of attention, and there arose what Plekhanov somewhere calls 'a fierce longing [*toska*] for a tough-minded *vlast*.' The Bolsheviks proved unexpectedly, even paradoxically, able to respond to that fierce longing.

Conversely, the Russian Revolution reveals a hidden limitation of the Locke and Marx traditions: although revolution is a central concern for both of them, they unconsciously assume the continued existence of a *vlast* recognised as such by the population (Marxist slogans about smashing the state notwithstanding). Historical class missions and struggles over consent of the governed explain much in non-extreme situations, but in the context of full-blown civil war, these theories begin to seem lifeless and abstract, as the liberal Ivan Ilych and his socialist daughter Katya discovered in the Veresaev novel.

Nevertheless, when we look at the way that the hegemony strategy preadapted the Bolsheviks to respond to a Hobbesian challenge, we recognise that the Marxist tradition does help answer a concrete question that Hobbes's theory leaves open: just *how* does a new Leviathan come to be a Mortal God? The Marxist tradition spoke of large-scale historical missions involving the use of state power in the name of the interests of large sections of the populace. The Bolsheviks – the self-described Russian branch of international 'revolutionary Social Democracy' – came out of this tradition with a confident sense that they *deserved* the *vlast* and also with a sharp idea of where to find mass support. Once in power they found themselves doing a lot of very unexpected things, but these features of their Marxist upbringing served as a rock-strong base.

Looking ahead, we note that twentieth-century Communist regimes, when not imposed from abroad, usually took shape as an authoritarian response to a breakdown of state authority and resulting civil war. This prompts a hard question: does the Hobbesian perspective predict or justify the subsequent excesses of the Stalin era? I think not. Hobbes is relevant for the extreme situation of breakdown and reconstitution of a functioning *vlast*. Outside the dynamics of that situation, he has much less to say about the probable actions of the ruler. Or rather, he would hope and assume that the Leviathan would act rationally, and not endanger its own rule and alienate the population by adventurist, reckless and brutal policies.

Still, the experience of the Russian time of troubles helps explain some of the support or at least tolerance shown to Stalin by both the party and the population at large. The horror of civil war meant that unity of the party and the country was a top priority – an obsession – for almost everybody, coupled with a sense of the fragility of the new Leviathan, no matter how fierce its public face. We may leave the last word to Hobbes, so long as we try to remember that for Russians of the civil war generation (and we should recall that the civil war is not the only time of troubles in Russian history), these would not be mere words on a page but an assertion with deep and existential resonance. 'The estate of Man can never be without some incommodity or other; the greatest, that in any form of Government can possibly happen to the people in general, is scarce sensible, in respect to the miseries, and horrible calamities, that accompany a Civil War.'[25]

Lars T. Lih is author of Bread and Authority in Russia, 1914-1921 *(1990) and* Lenin Rediscovered *(2006).*

Notes

1. Thomas Hobbes, *Leviathan* (with selected variants from the Latin edition of 1668), ed. Edwin Curley (Indianapolis: Hackett, 1994), ch. 13, §5.

2. Vikenty V. Veresaev, *V tupike; Sestry* (Moscow: Knizhnaia palata, 1990), my translation. An English edition was published in 1928 under the title *The Deadlock* (New York: Century Co.), trans. Nina Wissotzky and Camilla Coventry, and the passage cited here corresponds to pages 119–120. Although published officially in the Soviet Union, Veresaev's novel gives an unflinching firsthand look at the abuse of power by all contenders for power during the civil war.

3. Veresaev, *V tupike; Sestry*, 47

4. Hobbes, *Leviathan*, ch. 13, §9.

5. Hobbes, *Leviathan*, ch. 29, §23.

6. As cited in Lih, 'The Ironic Triumph of Old Bolshevism: The Debates of April 1917 in Context,' *Russian History* 38 (2011), 199–242.

7. Lih, 'The Proletariat and its Ally: The Logic of Bolshevik "Hegemony"', in John Riddell, *Marxist Essays and Commentary* [blog], 26 April 2017, https://johnriddell.wordpress.com/2017/04/26/the-proletariat-and-its-ally-the-logic-of-bolshevik-hegemony/

8. Engels, Introduction to the English edition of *Socialism Utopian and Scientific* (1892), at https://www.marxists.org/archive/marx/works/1880/soc-utop/int-hist.htm.

9. For more on the relation between the hegemony scenario and 'All Power to the Soviets!', see my ongoing series posted on John Riddell's blog, starting with https://johnriddell.wordpress.com/2017/03/23/all-power-to-the-soviets-part-1-biography-of-a-slogan/ (23 March 2017).

10. Kautsky's article and the endorsements by Lenin and Trotsky can be found in Richard Day and Daniel Gaido, eds., *Witnesses to Permanent Revolution: The Documentary Record* (Leiden: Brill, 2009).

11. Alexei Peshekhonov, 'The Bolsheviks and Effective State Authority' [*gosudarstvennost*'], in his *Pochemu ia ne emigriroval* [*Why I Did Not Emigrate*] (Berlin: Obelisk, 1923), 50–60. For a fuller translation of this chapter of Peshekhonov's pamphlet, see Lih, 'Bolshevism's "Services to the State": Three Russian Observers,' *Revolutionary Russia* 28:2 (2015), 120–125.

12. Vladimir B. Stankevich, 'Oktiabr'skoe vosstanie' in *Oktiabr'skaia revoliutsiia: memuary* [*October Revolution: Memoirs*] (Moscow: 1991), 207.

13. Tsuyoshi Hasegawa, *Crime and Punishment in the Russian Revolution: Mob Justice and Police in Petrograd* (Cambridge, MA: Harvard University Press, 2017).

14. Peshekhonov, *Pochemu*, as cited in Lih, 'Bolshevism's "Services to the State"', 122.

15. Sergei Lukianov, 'Revoliutsiia i vlast', in Kliuchnikov, *Smena Vekh* [*Change of Signposts*] (Prague: Politika, 1921), as cited in Lih, 'Bolshevism's "Services to the State"', 128.

16. Rheta Childe Dorr, *Inside the Russian Revolution* (New York: Macmillan, 1918), 10.

17. Dorr, *Inside the Russian Revolution*, 10, 19.

18. The early period of the Revolution is often labelled the era of 'dual power' between Petrograd Soviet and the Provisional Government. In actuality, no one defended the concept of 'dual power': the Kadets claimed that 'dual

power' existed while the moderate socialists claimed that it did not (except perhaps for a few moments of emergency), but both sides agreed that 'dual power' as such was harmful and incoherent. For further discussion, see Lih, 'From February to October,' *Jacobin Magazine* 25 (Spring 2017), https://jacobinmag.com/2017/05/russian-revolution-power-soviets-bolsheviks-lenin-provisional-government.

19. G. I. Zlokazov and G. Z. Ioffe, eds. *Iz istorii bor'by za vlast' v 1917 godu* [*From the History of the Struggle for the Vlast in 1917*] (Moscow: Institut rossisko istorii RAN, 2002), 155.

20. Stalin, *Sochineniia*, 3: 279–85, 289–95; one article is signed (9 September 1917) and the other unsigned (14 September).

21. Unsigned lead articles by Zinoviev on 3 and 4 October 1917 in *Rabochii put'* [*Worker's Path*] (*Pravda*'s temporary title for censorship reasons).

22. Trotsky's *History of the Russian Revolution to Brest-Litovsk* can be found at https://www.marxists.org/archive/trotsky/1918/hrr/index.htm; Nikolai Bukharin also published a narrative account of the Revolution in this same period.

23. A new translation of Trotsky's August 1917 article 'The Character of the Russian Revolution' will be published in a forthcoming entry in my ongoing series 'All Power to the Soviets!' (2017–18).

24. Trotsky's argument is of course self-serving, but so are most arguments about the Constituent Assembly. For an informed argument by a staunchly anti-Bolshevik historian that the Constituent Assembly was inherently unviable, see Oliver Radkey, *The Sickle under the Hammer: The Russian Socialist Revolutionaries in the Early Months of Soviet Rule* (New York: Columbia University Press, 1963).

25. Hobbes, *Leviathan*, ch. 18, §20.

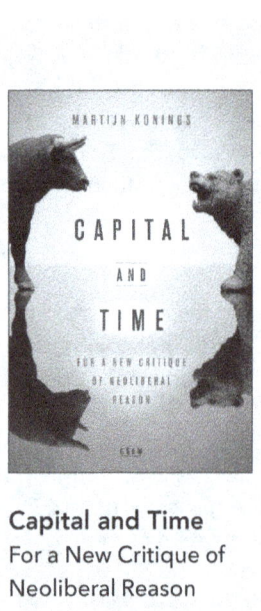

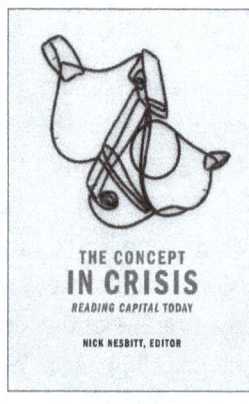

Capital and Time
For a New Critique of Neoliberal Reason
MARTIJN KONINGS

"This remarkable book offers a new perspective on speculation, neo-liberalism, and contemporary finance."
—Arjun Appadurai

STANFORD UNIVERSITY PRESS
978-1-5036-0443-8 PB £17.99

30% discount: CSA18RPHIL

Isonomia and the Origins of Philosophy
KOJIN KARATANI
TRANSLATED BY JOSEPH A. MURPHY

"Karatani's book makes you see the entire history of philosophy in a new way; it deserves to become an instant classic."
—Slavoj Žižek

DUKE UNIVERSITY PRESS
978-0-8223-6913-4 PB £18.99

www.combinedacademic.co.uk

The Concept in Crisis
Reading Capital Today
EDITED BY NICK NESBITT

"*Reading Capital* remains one of the most remarkable studies of Marx ever written, and this excellent collection... helps explain why its revolutionary inflection retains so much of its critical appeal to this day."
—Peter Hallward

DUKE UNIVERSITY PRESS
978-0-8223-6907-3 PB £20.99

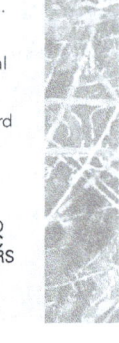

Marx in Algiers
Sandro Mezzadra

The following text is the last chapter of a book on Marx that will be published later this year in English under the title *In the Marxian Workshops: Producing Subjects*. Articulated in ten short chapters, the book combines a close reading of some of Marx's texts with a concern for the ways in which his work can be made productive in our present. I am not particularly interested here in reading Marx as part of a canon of 'classics'. At the same time, I am quite cautious with regard to any straightforward use of the theoretical framework of his critique of political economy to analyse contemporary capitalism and support its contestation. This is not only because capitalism, according to that 'revolutionary' nature pointed out so effectively by Marx himself, has changed so dramatically in the one hundred and fifty years separating us from the publication of *Capital*. It is also because these transformations have been driven by extraordinary social struggles and struggles of labour that have invented new languages of liberation and established new parameters of critique. This is not to say that the basic concepts of Marx's critique of political economy – labour power, abstract labour, living labour, to give just a few important examples – cannot be used today. I am convinced that the opposite is the case. Yet in order to be productively deployed, they first have to be understood theoretically (through close reading), and then plunged into the materiality of contemporary capitalism and into the history and present of class struggles after Marx (hence, my concern regarding the present).

In order to enable this dual move in the book, I track the emergence of, and mutations in, the problematic of a politics of liberation as well as its material rooting in a critique of the present in Marx's early philosophical writings, in the historical essays on the revolutions of 1848, and in what I regard as the open workshop of the critique of political economy. In doing so, I follow the thread provided by contemporary debates around the 'production of subjectivity'. My tenet is that such a consciously anachronistic reading of Marx's texts can open up new perspectives on the vexed question of subjectivity in his work. Shedding light on the interplay between Marx's analysis of the multiple forms of subjection that produce subjects, in addition to his emphasis on the productive power of (exploited and dominated) subjects, is intended to establish a renewed understanding of subjectivity as the privileged viewpoint for the articulation of a critique of capitalism which is attentive to the shifts, mutations and transitions constituting both its history and its present. This emphasis on subjectivity leads me to propose a reading of Marx that is quite different from the so-called *Neue Marx-Lektüre* (or 'new reading of Marx') and its focus on the value-form, although in my discussion of the notion of abstract labour I do try to take into critical account some aspects of this reading in the works of scholars such as Michael Heinrich and Moishe Postone. Rather, I understand my work on Marx as being in continuity with my own theoretical and political training in Italian 'autonomist' Marxism – although readers of the book (and of its last chapter) will also notice that I assume a critical distance from elements of that tradition, specifically in my interpretation of concepts such as the formal and real subsumption of labour under capital, the 'tendency' of capitalist development and even the question of the composition of the working class.

In a nutshell, my engagement with postcolonial criticism, as well as with theories and experiences external to what is traditionally considered as 'the West', has led me to be sceptical of any linear reading of the tendency of capitalist development and to be wary of related attempts to forge the image of the revolutionary subject according to its allegedly 'highest' point.

The last chapter of the book, which bears the title 'Marx in Algiers', and which is translated below, is of particular relevance from this perspective. The last station in the life of Marx, so shaped by persecution and mobility that Jacques Derrida memorably defines him as 'a glorious, sacred, accursed but still clandestine immigrant as he was all his life',[1] is taken here as symptomatic of a set of shifts and displacements characterising his thought after the publication of volume one of *Capital* in 1867. Taking stock of the work that I have done with Brett Neilson over the last decade on contemporary globalisation,[2] I focus here in particular on the concept of the 'world market' [*Weltmarkt*] and its relation with 'world history' [*Weltgeschichte*]: the space and time of capitalism, to put it simply, as well as of struggles for liberation. I am convinced that it is only by taking together 'world market' and 'world history' that we can forge an analytical and political framework that breaks free at once from any linearity and of the burden of a concept of 'progress' in understanding the temporality of capitalism. At the same time, this allows us to emphasise that the expansion of capital's frontiers within the global space does not result in a process of homogenisation. As I argue, such an analytical framework is consistent with Marx's search for a 'multilinear' approach to the investigation of capitalism in the last years of his life, recently highlighted by several scholars. Furthermore, it opens up new angles on the subjects exploited by capital, on the struggles and resistances that confront its expansion, and on the prospects of an anti-capitalist politics - not only historically, but most importantly in our present.

Marx in Algiers

> Capitalism arises and develops historically amidst a non-capitalist society... This is the setting for the accumulation of capital... Accumulation, with its spasmodic expansion, can no more wait for, and be content with, a natural internal disintegration of non-capitalist formations and their transition to commodity economy, than it can wait for, and be content with, the natural increase of the working population. Force is the only solution open to capital; the accumulation of capital, seen as an historical process, employs force as a permanent weapon, not only at its genesis, but further on down to the present day.
>
> Rosa Luxemburg (1913) [3]

Marx never went to Detroit and Adam Smith never went to Beijing. Marx did however actually stay in Algiers for a couple of months at the beginning of 1882, near the end of his life, hoping to find (in vain) some comfort from the harsh winter in London following his doctor's advice. As with the well-known works by Mario Tronti and Giovanni Arrighi just alluded to, the title of this article should not be taken literally.[4] Marx went to Algiers while harshly debilitated by poor health but also strained by the death of his wife Jenny in the previous year. The following will not reconstruct Marx's stay in Algiers, even though it admittedly presents more than a few elements of interest.[5] Instead, his passage to the 'South' and the 'East' will be used here as a (consciously allusive) metaphor for the set of displacements emerging in his thought after the publication of the first volume of *Capital* in 1867.

It is in this way that one could attempt to resolve the *enigma* of Marx's interruption of the plan to conclude his critique of political economy (he partially resumed it only in 1877). 'Illness', as Engels informs us, appears to have been among the major reasons for this interruption.[6] Yet, considering how passionately Marx supported the Commune, along with his active involvement in the International's internal disputes, it seems unlikely that he could not have found the energies necessary to order systematically the bulk of manuscript writing that he had prepared for the second and third volumes of *Capital*, even before the publication of Volume One. As such, solving this 'enigma' of Marx's interruption to his work means formulating the hypothesis that it was a series of theoretical blockages faced by Marx that halted the order of 'presentation' [*Darstellung*] of his critique of political economy, and so forced him to resume his 'enquiry' [*Forschung*].[7] In the last years of his life, Marx immersed himself in the study of the natural sciences of his time (from chemistry to geology), gathered materials for a 'critical history of technology' (influenced by Darwin) and filled up several notebooks with his commentaries upon the works of different anthropologists and ethnologists.[8] The latter is particularly important and indicates the need to take into account Marx's increasing interest in different realities and areas of the world, distinct from those around which he had hitherto constructed his theories of capitalism (England) and proletarian revolution (France).

As I have shown elsewhere, the concept of *Weltgeschichte* is particularly relevant to Marx's work in this respect.[9] In its standard English translation ('universal history'), the term loses its reference to the 'world'. This is not a mere terminological issue. The young Marx takes in earnest the spatial connotation of the syntagm *Weltgeschichte* – used in German philosophy from the eighteenth century – and consciously welds it to its temporal aspect. As we read, for instance, in *The German Ideology*: 'it is certainly ... an empirical fact that separate individuals have, with the broadening of their activity into world-historical activity [*mit der Ausdehnung der Tätigkeit zur Weltgeschichtlichen*], become more and more enslaved under a power alien to them ... a power which has become more and more enormous and, in the last instance, turns out to be the *world market* [*Weltmarkt*]'.[10] Evidently, the spatial connotation is unambiguously concrete in Marx's use of *Weltgeschichte,* and the spatial meaning goes so far as to point towards a historical time dominated by a power [*Macht*] that adopts the world as the field of its own action. The idea of proletarian internationalism stems from this intuition in Marx's work, which constitutes, at the same time, a formidable anticipation. As Jacques Derrida argues, 'No organised political movement in the history of humanity had ever yet presented itself as *geo-political*, thereby inaugurating the space that is now ours and that today is reaching its limits, the limits of the earth and the limits of the political'.[11]

One can notice here a further and markedly original aspect of Marx's thought that should also be emphasised from the standpoint of the production of subjectivity. His endeavour is aimed at sensing the action of forces whose constitution and efficacy is to be located within 'global' coordinates, in an epoch in which the process of the affirmation of national states and dissolution of 'local' affiliations in Europe was far from coming to an end. These forces determine the production and everyday experience of subjects who, for this reason, he defines as 'empirically universal individuals'.[12] With a certainty which cannot be found in any spokesperson of classical economics, Marx locates one of the distinctive characters of the modern capitalist mode of production in the intrinsic world dimension of its operations. Let us consider the following passage from one of Marx's economic manuscripts, posthumously published by Karl Kautsky between 1905 and 1910, under the title *Theories of Surplus Value*:

> It is only foreign trade, the development of the market to a world market, which causes money to develop into world money and *abstract labour* into social labour. Abstract wealth, value, money, hence *abstract labour*, develop in the measure that concrete labour becomes a totality of different modes of labour embracing the world market. Capitalist production rests on the *value* or the development of the labour embodied in the product as social labour. But this is only [possible] on the basis of foreign trade and of the world market. This is at once the precondition and the result of capitalist production.[13]

According to a formulation that Marx often repeated, particularly in the *Grundrisse*, the world market is thus 'the precondition and the result of capitalist production'. 'The tendency [*Tendenz*] to create the *world market* is directly given in the concept of capital itself. Every limit [*Grenze*] appears as a barrier [*Schranke*] to be overcome'.[14] While capital cannot exist outside of the horizon of the world market (which is indeed its 'precondition'), this very horizon needs nonetheless to be constantly fabricated and imposed (in this sense, the world market is 'the result of capitalist production').

The question of the specific production of space that characterises capital has been for some time the focus of Marxist geographers, most notably those whose analyses are based on the problem of the 'turnover of capital' – that is, of its cycle, 'when this is taken not as an isolated act but as a periodic process' and whose duration 'is given by the sum of its production time and its circulation time'[15] – so as to analyse the territorial hierarchisation resulting from it.[16] I wish here to draw attention to the ostensible circularity of Marx's argument whereby the world market – like the subjective figures of the capitalist and the worker – is both the precondition and the result of capitalist production. Such circularity is broken by the identification of a historical moment, the 'so-called primitive accumulation' analysed by Marx in Part Eight of the first volume of *Capital*, in which both the world scale of the capitalist mode of production and its subjects were *produced* through anomalous and exceptional procedures, in contrast to the description of commercial relationships advanced by classical economics. Amongst the 'violent means' of primitive accumulation,[17] Marx accords particular attention to colonialism and conquest because of their substantial role in the *opening* of the world market: 'The discovery of gold and silver in America, the extirpation, enslavement and entombment in mines of the indigenous population of that continent, the beginnings of the conquest and plunder of India, and the conversion of Africa into a preserve for the commercial hunting of blackskins, are all things which characterise the dawn of the era of capitalist production'.[18] The world market owes its existence to the violence of this 'opening'. However, it is important to stress that its space presents characteristics one can define as *formal* in that such space could be materially articulated and organised in substantially different ways, according to variable geometries of hegemony, domination and dependency. Where capital 'constantly revolutionises',[19] it does so also in relation to the production of those spaces in which its valorisation and accumulation on a global scale can come into being.

At the beginning of the twentieth century, the important debate about imperialism registered precisely this issue, which Marx himself had grasped when he distinguished the world market from 'international' intercourse.[20] What I would argue is that, initially, Marx was rather dazzled by what I termed above the 'formal' characteristics of the world market and, on this basis, he formulated a linear image of the *tendency* of capital in developing and imposing its own logic in a necessary way, and without any friction, according to an essentially unitary and homogenous model. Independently of their rhetorical efficacy (particularly in relation to the critique of utopian socialism), the celebratory tone that Marx adopts regarding the revolutionary role of the bourgeoisie in modern history in the *Manifesto*, together with the similar tone taken with regard to English colonialism in India in a dispatch written in 1853,[21] could also be seen as symptoms of an imbalance between the spatial and temporal aspects of Marx's understanding of *Weltgeschichte*. These pages, like others in Marx's texts, undoubtedly suggest a certain idea of progress as historical necessity which would disentangle the concept of *Weltgeschichte* from that concreteness potentially indicated by the spatial reference.

In fact, the same argument could be made for the section in the *Grundrisse* dedicated to 'Pre-Capitalist Economic Formations', which is generally guided by a retrospective reading aimed at bringing to the forefront the distinctive characteristics – and, ultimately, the 'superiority' – of the capitalist mode of production. Marx is working here with a concept of 'community' which is formulated, to a large extent, as the negative of those processes of 'dissolution' and 'separation' – chiefly of producers from the 'objective conditions' of their labour – constitutive of capitalist society, in ways that anticipate some of the most relevant developments in sociological theory over the following decades. However, Marx's interest in the development of the ethnology and anthropology of his time shows the extent to which, in the last years of his life, he felt the need to problematise this reading. At the same time, the immense collection of readings of and commentaries on societies other than the Western European which Marx accumulated from the 1850s on – mostly the result of his work as a journalist for the *New York Daily Tribune*, on India and China, slavery in the United States, Irish and Polish nationalisms – allowed him to fill out the concept of 'world market' with new material determinations.[22]

It would be best not to overestimate the amount of displacement and revision in Marx's thought that derived from this study and research, specifically after the publication of the first volume of *Capital*. Letters, drafts of letters and notebooks are to be read with some caution; at most they can support the formulation of hypotheses. What seems plausible, nonetheless, is that in his final years Marx shifted his perspective towards a multilinear approach to history and capitalist development. He did so by considering the possibility of a multiplicity of heterogeneous forms of the imposition and organisation of capital's social relations, adjusted to different geographical and historical scales.[23] Marx himself affirms this when he refers to his treatment of 'so-called primitive accumulation': 'the "historical inevitability" [of the transition to capitalism] is *expressly* limited to the *countries of Western Europe*', as he put it in a letter to Vera Zasulich in March 1881.[24] Furthermore, slightly more than three years earlier, Marx had warned the editorial board of a Russian magazine against transforming his 'historical sketch of the genesis of capitalism in Western Europe into a historico-philosophical theory of general development, imposed by fate on all peoples'.[25]

In theoretical terms, it is worth re-reading the short passage from the *Grundrisse* already cited above: 'The tendency to create the *world market* is directly given in the concept of capital itself. Every limit [*Grenze*] appears as a barrier to be overcome'.[26] There is an argument implied here which, if developed appropriately, would yield a productive intervention in the (often harshly polemical) debate around the evaluation of capital's 'universalism' and its relation with 'historical difference' – especially as this debate has occurred over the past few years in 'postcolonial studies'.[27] Stated differently, it could be argued that while, on the one hand, the 'tendency' of capital indicates the 'universal' moment concerning both the concept of capital and its action, on the other hand, the encounter with the 'limit' – defined at the same time from the point of view of its geographical extension and in relation to a set of historical, social and cultural conditions determining, amongst other things, the composition of 'living labour' – is also the basis for the profound heterogeneity of capitalism (as much with regard to its historical configurations as its contemporary one).[28] The limit Marx is referring to in this passage is geographical, signalled by the use of the term *Grenze* (border). Nevertheless, it is also social, as is evident in the following lines of the passage, in which Marx adds that the tendency of capital is 'to subjugate every moment of production itself to exchange and to suspend the production of direct use values not entering into exchange, i.e. precisely to posit production based on capital in place of earlier modes of production, which appear primitive [*naturwüchsig*] from its standpoint'.[29]

In this extract from the *Grundrisse*, capital confronts non-capitalist spaces, both in the limits to its geographical 'extension' and in the limits to its 'intensive' penetration into determined social formations. This is the problem of the transition to capitalism, central to Marx's analysis of the 'so-called primitive accumulation'. Marx was certainly convinced that in Western Europe such a process of transition was essentially over and that, if anything, it was itself repeating in the colonies. As he argues in the last chapter of Volume One ('The Modern Theory of Colonisation'): 'There the capitalist regime constantly comes up against the obstacle [*Hindernis*] presented by the producer, who, as owner of his own conditions of labour, employs that labour to enrich himself instead of the capitalist'.[30] In order to enrich the interpretative model of the relation between capital's 'universal' moment and the 'heterogeneity' of capitalism just outlined, it is essential, then, to qualify and articulate the reference to this 'obstacle' by including a set of historical conditions which go far beyond the existence of the figure of producer as 'owner of his own conditions of labour'. Furthermore, it is important to restate my conviction that the problems and the 'procedures' Marx studied in relation to 'so-called primitive accumulation' must be understood as characterising – while evidently taking into account that its forms transform over time – the entire historical development of the capitalist mode of production and, thus, cannot be confined solely to its 'prehistory'.[31] The generation of what appears at once as 'the precondition and the result of capitalist production' – the world market, of course, but also and more importantly the subjects circulating within it – is continuously posed anew as a problem that interrupts the historical linearity of development. This is particularly the case in those moments of crisis when capital must extend its essential need for 'constant revolution' to the highest degree when faced with specific *limits*.

In these moments, the problem of the limit re-emerges, in other words, as the problem of the transformation of a series of social relations, productive processes, forms of political organisation, of specific spatial arrangements into barriers to be overcome.[32] Our contemporary situation plainly illustrates the way in which these barriers are not necessarily non-capitalist environments, but can be constructed as 'external' to capital (from within, so to speak) in order to open new frontiers for its valorisation. For instance, one could look here at the attack upon the welfare state in the West or the dismantling of productive cycles belonging to past epochs of industrialisation in many parts of the world. It seems that this dynamic of 'opening', immediately guarded by specific mechanisms of 'closure' – that is, of the confining and hierarchisation of spaces, as well as the disciplining of subjects – is a structural trait of the capitalist mode of production, one of its indeed 'universal' moments to be critically understood in the particular circumstances in which it develops. However, ultimately, it is coupled with a specific production of subjectivity and of conflicts that are not reducible to the two fundamental images around which Marx's revolutionary imagination unfolds, the industrial working class and the rioting proletariat in the streets of Paris.

The different forms of communal property and communitarian relations cannot but assume a central role in these processes and conflicts, as they ultimately did in the scene of 'so-called primitive accumulation', both as a 'point of attack' for capital – by means of a wide spectrum of devices of enclosure and dispossession – and as a basis for resistance. If we were to accept the hypothesis whereby in the last years of his life Marx developed an acute awareness of the global significance of these issues, his encounter with the works of different anthropologists and ethnologists – as recorded in the notebooks of 1880-82 – becomes even more meaningful when compared to the ways in which Engels presents it in the preface to *The Origin of the Family, Private Property and the State* (1884). Put differently, Marx was not only looking for the historical origins of a series of criteria of social hierarchy, but had also been compiling an archive of diverse forms of the 'common' so that he could politically interpret some of the most important conflicts of his time as these were determined by the global expansion of capitalism.

Famously, in his final years Marx gave particular attention to the Russian case, and reflected on the possibility that the *obshchina*, the rural commune, could represent the basis for a direct passage to communism.[33] In this instance, the texts available to us are relatively fragmentary and recent attempts to shape a 'communitarian' version of Marx – principally in the United States – are definitely not very convincing.[34] I have no interest in extracting from the late Marx a complete theoretical revision of his work nor a solution to the aporias of his thought. Rather, it is necessary to bring to the fore Marx's unceasing requalification of the terms of a problem – that of *liberation* – which had been constant in his work since his first writings. It is certainly in the intensity of his theoretical engagement with forms of common property and communal relations that we can glimpse Marx's need to resume his enquiry, precisely on the topic of the production of subjectivity in capitalism in general and as materially conceptualised in its world dimension.

Perhaps this was Marx's concern while walking down the streets of Algiers at the beginning of 1882, gathering information about construction workers – who 'although healthy people and local residents they go down with fever after the first three days' of work and receive 'a daily dose of quinine' as part of their wages[35] – or sipping a coffee in a 'Moorish' tavern, fascinated by the spirit of 'absolute equality' he could perceive among its Arab regulars. However, in reporting his impressions to his daughter Laura on the 13th of April and to avoid any misunderstandings, Marx adds in his characteristic mixture of German and English: '*und dennoch gehen sie zum Teufel without a revolutionary movement*'. 'Nevertheless, they will go to rack and ruin without a revolutionary movement'.[36]

Translated by Yari Lanci

Sandro Mezzadra is Professor of Political Theory at the University of Bologna and co-author with Brett Neilson of Border as Method, or, the Multiplication of Labour *(2013).*

Notes

1. Jacques Derrida, *Spectres of Marx: The State of the Debt, the Work of Mourning and the New International*, trans. Peggy Kamuf (New York: Routledge, 2006), 219.
2. In particular, see Sandro Mezzadra and Brett Neilson, *Border as Method, or, the Multiplication of Labour* (Durham: Duke University Press, 2013); 'Extraction, Logistics, Finance: Global Crisis and the Politics of Operations', *Radical Philosophy* 178 (March/April 2013), 8–18; and 'On the Multiple Frontiers of Extraction: Excavating Contemporary Capitalism', *Cultural Studies* 31:2-3 (2017), 185–204.
3. Rosa Luxemburg, *The Accumulation of Capital*, trans. Agnes Schwarzschild (London and New York: Routledge, 2003), 348ff.
4. Mario Tronti, 'Marx a Detroit', in *Operai e Capitale* (Torino: Einaudi, 1966), 290–303; Giovanni Arrighi, *Adam Smith in Beijing: Lineages of the Twenty-First Century* (London and New York: Verso, 2007).
5. See Marlene Vesper, *Marx in Algier* (Bonn: Pahl-Rugenstein, 1995); and Marcello Musto, *L'ultimo Marx: 1881-1883* (Roma: Donzelli, 2016), 105–14.
6. Friedrich Engels, 'Preface', in Karl Marx, *Capital: A Critique of Political Economy, Volume 2*, trans. David Fernbach (London: Penguin Books, 1992), 85.
7. As Marx argues in the postface to the second edition of the first volume of *Capital* (1873): 'Of course the method of presentation must differ in form from that of inquiry. The latter has to appropriate the material in detail, to analyse its different forms of development and to track down their inner connection. Only after this work has been done can the real movement be appropriately presented. If this is done successfully, if the life of the subject-matter is now reflected back in the ideas, then it may appear as if we

have before us an *a priori* construction'. Karl Marx, *Capital: A Critique of Political Economy, Volume 1*, trans. Ben Fowkes (London: Penguin Books, 1990), 102. On the relation between *Darstellung* and *Forschung*, especially in relation to the *Grundrisse*, see Antonio Negri, *Marx Beyond Marx: Lessons on the* Grundrisse (London: Pluto Press, 1991), 12–13.

8. 'A critical history of technology', Marx contends in a note in Volume One, 'would show how little any of the inventions of the eighteenth century are the work of a single individual. As yet such a book does not exist. Darwin has directed attention to the history of natural technology, i.e. the formation of the organs of plants and animals, which serve as the instruments of production for sustaining their life. Does not the history of the productive organs of man in society, of organs that are the material basis of every particular organisation of society, deserve equal attention?'. Marx, *Capital, Vol. 1*, 493n4.

9. Sandro Mezzadra, *Nei Cantieri Marxiani: Il Soggetto e la Sua Produzione* (Castel San Pietro Romano, Roma: Manifestolibri, 2014), ch. 7. English translation by Yari Lanci, forthcoming from Rowman & Littlefield International.

10. Karl Marx and Friedrich Engels, *The German Ideology*, in *Collected Works, Volume 5, 1845-47* (London: Lawrence & Wishart, 1975), 51.

11. Derrida, *Spectres of Marx*, 47.

12. Marx and Engels, *Collected Works, Volume 5*, 49.

13. Marx and Engels, *Collected Works, Volume 32, 1861-63* (London: Lawrence & Wishart, 1989), 388.

14. Karl Marx, *Grundrisse: Foundations of the Critique of Political Economy*, trans. Martin Nicolaus (London and New York: Penguin Books, 1993), 408.

15. Marx, *Capital Vol. 2*, 235.

16. cf. David Harvey, *The Limits to Capital* (Oxford: Blackwell, 1982).

17. Marx, *Capital Vol. 1*, 883.

18. Ibid., 915.

19. Marx, *Grundrisse*, 410.

20. cf. Luciano Ferrari Bravo, 'Vecchie e nuove questioni nellla teoria dell'imperialismo', in *Imperialismo e classe operaia multinazionale*, ed. Luciano Ferrari Bravo (Milano: Feltrinelli, 1975).

21. Karl Marx, 'The British Rule in India', in Marx and Engels, *Collected Works, Volume 12, 1853-54* (London: Lawrence & Wishart, 1979), 125–33.

22. See, in particular, Kevin B. Anderson, *Marx at the Margins: On Nationalism, Ethnicity and Non-Western Societies* (Chicago ; London: University of Chicago Press, 2010).

23. See again Anderson, *Marx at the Margins*, but also Enrique Dussel, *El último Marx (1863-1882) y la liberación latinoamericana* (México D.F.: Siglo XXI, 1990), ch. 7.

24. Marx and Engels, *Collected Works, Volume 24, 1874-83* (London: Lawrence & Wishart, 1989), 370.

25. Ibid., 200.

26. Marx, *Grundrisse*, 408.

27. I am referring in particular to Vivek Chibber's *Postcolonial Theory and the Spectre of Capital* (London and New York: Verso, 2013). In his polemical book, Chibber accuses theorists of 'subaltern studies' – such as Guha, Chakrabarty, and Chatterjee – of not having fully recognised the 'universalising' tendencies of capital and ascribes to them an acritical celebration of historical and cultural differences, which would allegedly result in a new and paradoxical 'orientalism'. Even though Chibber grasps some of those aspects that are worthy of critical discussion within the project of 'subaltern studies' – and, more generally, in postcolonial theory – the overall tone of his argument leads him to fundamentally misunderstand not only that project, but also some of Marx's concepts that he deploys against it ('abstract labour', to begin with). This was well clarified by Partha Chatterjee in a debate with Chibber in New York, April 2013, available online at https://kafila.online/2013/05/07/partha-chatterjee-on-subaltern-studies-marxism-and-vivek-chhibber/. For a critical discussion of Chibber's book, see my review essay in *Interventions* 16:6 (2014), 916–25.

28. Although from a different perspective, see Thomas C. Patterson, *Karl Marx, Anthropologist* (Oxford and New York: Berg, 2009), ch. 5.

29. Marx, *Grundrisse*, 408.

30. Marx, *Capital Vol. 1*, 931.

31. I advanced this argument, which I share with many other scholars, in 'The Topicality of Prehistory: A New Reading of Marx's Analysis of "So-Called Primitive Accumulation"', *Rethinking Marxism* 23: 3 (July 2011), 302–21.

32. It is worth noting that in the *Grundrisse* Marx makes use of the pair 'limit' [*Grenze*] and 'barrier' [*Schranke*] to define capital in general, even in different contexts, as can be seen in the following extract: 'As representative of the general form of wealth – money – capital is the endless and limitless drive to go beyond its limiting barrier. Every boundary [*Grenze*] is and has to be a barrier [*Schranke*] for it. Else it would cease to be capital – money as self-reproductive. If ever it perceived a certain boundary not as a barrier, but became comfortable within it as a boundary, it would itself have declined from exchange value to use value, from the general form of wealth to a specific, substantial mode of the same'. Marx, *Grundrisse*, 334.

33. cf. Luca Basso, *Marx and the Common: From Capital to the Late Writings*, trans. David Broder, (Leiden and Boston: Brill, 2015), 85–99.

34. For an evaluation of this debate, see Anna Curcio, ed., *Comune, comunità, comunismo* (Verona: ombre corte, 2011).

35. 'Marx to Paul Lafargue, 20 March 1882', in Marx and Engels, *Collected Works, Volume 46, 1880-83* (London: Lawrence & Wishart, 1992), 220.

36. 'Marx to Paul Lafargue, 20 March 1882', 242.

The realism of our time
Interview with Kim Stanley Robinson

Kim Stanley Robinson and Helena Feder

Kim Stanley Robinson is the author of more than twenty works of fiction, including the celebrated Mars trilogy (*Red Mars, Green Mars* and *Blue Mars*), *Forty Signs of Rain, The Years of Rice and Salt, 2312* and, his latest novel, *New York 2140*. A former student of Fredric Jameson, Robinson's work is consistently anti-capitalist. His novels evince not only his deep interest in global economy and ecology, but also a belief that fiction may venture into spheres where theory fears to tread. For Robinson, science fiction is uniquely placed to do this, rooted both in what is and what could be. In the best tradition of the genre (H.G. Wells, Isaac Asimov, Ursula K. Le Guin), it can consider critically both the politics and possibilities of technology, and the social, ideological and ecological systems that give rise to it. Science fiction has, in this sense, a particular responsibility not only to imagine the future but to imagine *how we might change its direction*. In Robinson's *New York 2140*, a series of connected characters, centred around the MetLife tower in a future inter-tidal world, a financially and physically liquid city, come together to do just this. Sea levels have risen in two catastrophic 'pulses' of ten and forty feet, transforming planetary and human geography. In the midst of this ecological and refugee crisis, lower Manhattan becomes 'a veritable hotbed of theory and practice, like it always used to say it was, but this time for real.'

Robinson champions science fiction as 'the realism of our time.' And the reality, if not the realism, of our time is grim. The moment we inhabit has become inhospitable, terrifying and disorienting to contemplate. The Earth, 'the wholly enlightened', is, as Adorno and Horkheimer argued in *Dialectic of Enlightenment*, truly 'radiant with triumphant calamity.' Violence to humans and other animals seems to proliferate rhizomatically, slow and fast: the escalation of anthropogenic damage to the planet and its atmosphere, the Sixth Mass Extinction, the consolidation of wealth and power in the hands of fewer and fewer people, the waves of ideologically motivated attacks on the poor, people of colour, Jews, Muslims, women, democracy, secular thought and the secular world, all over the world.

Realism itself is a complex and disorienting category, multiply defined against other periods, genres, aesthetics and modes of thought; a kind of ideological palimpsest. As Jameson argues in *The Antimonies of Realism,* it is 'a hybrid concept, in which an epistemological claim (for knowledge or truth) masquerades as an aesthetic ideal, with fatal consequences for both of these incommensurable dimensions. If it is social truth or knowledge we want from realism, we will soon find that what we get is ideology; ... if it is history we are looking for ... then we are at once confronted with questions about the uses of the past and even the access to it which, as unanswerable as they may be, take us well beyond literature and theory and seem to demand an engagement with our own present' (London: Verso, 5–6). Robinson's work is such an engagement with the present.

Just as *New York 2140* reclaims pre-flood artefacts, narratives, and social forms, Robinson's vision of the future is archeological, uncovered from within the possibilities of our current moment and its manifold pasts. Building up or forward means also digging down. If we cannot dispense with realism, it is because we cannot dispense with another conceptual problem: that of *the real*. While the real may at times seem as fictive as Thoreau's 'Realometer', it is as necessary to us, as that 'hard bottom, rocks in place, which we can call reality, and say, This is, and no mistake; and then begin, having a *point d'appui*, below freshet and frost and fire … that future ages might know how deep a freshet of shams and appearances had gathered from time to time' (*Walden; or, Life in the Woods*). As the old radical intones, 'Be it life or death, we crave only reality.' Even in its most ethereal moments, Robinson's work conveys the truth of this craving. In the key image from his favourite of his own novels, *2312*, animals return to a post-climate change Earth from protective biomes (inside hollowed-out asteroids) in slow, giant bubbles. Elephants and orangutans, shimmering like dandelion seeds, drift home.

The interview with Robinson took place at his home in Davis, California in October 2016, a few months before the publication of *New York 2140*.

Helena Feder In a 1993 interview with Bud Foote, you said that 'science fiction proclaims more than it can do'; that, at its best, it is an 'enjambment of facts and values that our culture desperately needs right now because our culture develops and enacts change without much regard for underlying values.' *New York 2140* is just such an enjambment, in terms of form and content. Could you speak to this, to the novel's sections on history and ecology, your 'citizen' subchapters? At one point you warn the reader to skip ahead if she's the sort of person who cares only about smaller, human dramas.

Kim Stanley Robinson This is simplistic, but science is where we establish facts and fiction is where we establish values. The name 'science fiction' is very powerful because it seems to say we can bridge the fact/value conundrum. It's a question whether or not the genre can or does do that, but it seems set up for it. It tries. When you talk about the future you're always talking about history. A novel always does this, but science fiction does so explicitly, through thought experiments: 'If we do this we'll get here. If we do that we'll get there.' Also, whereas the nineteenth-century novel traditionally speaks to the individual's relationship to society and history, science fiction adds the nonhuman and the planet [to that list]. The content of science fiction helps to make biophysical systems and problems visible. Humans do not simply make their own history on a *tabula rasa*; [the world is] an actor network where nonhuman actors are important players too. We've hit the limits of carrying capacity, in some ways, on the planet. And what type of fiction that can tell this story best? I've been saying, for many years now, that science fiction is the realism of our time.

HF As you mentioned actor networks, do you like the work of Bruno Latour?

KSR I think *Laboratory Life* and *Science in Action* are crucial texts, and they taught me a lot. When people talk about the Latourisation of science studies, I see what they're talking about. He's an important thinker, but like a lot of European theorists, he seems to need to invent his own system, his own vocabulary. Theory thus continues to get harder to understand, weirder, more provocative. I read science studies with enormous interest. Science studies is now theory applied to the sciences, it's changed from an earlier sociology or philosophy of science. And this new science studies has now turned again and changed literary studies. Now literature includes ecocriticism as a kind of science studies applied to literature itself.

HF *2140* imagines the '*Werteswandel*' you've called for elsewhere. In fact, it imagines a new idea of value itself. Is that what you're trying to do?

KSR For Marxism, '*Werteswandel*' is in dialectical relation with changes in material circumstances and systems, not just modes of production, but also modes of exchange, or modes of valuation. Mode of production isn't really the whole story anymore. I've been interested in some radical economists, like Dick Bryan, Randy Martin and others, who argue that we should nationalise the banks, that global finance is *the* great danger to the planet. They also suggest there's a way to trigger another crash and then, by nationalising the banks, you could both create and then solve the crisis. And by solving the crisis in this way you would actually have done something useful, rather than papering over the problems and going on as before, as we did in 2008. That's the storyline of *New York 2140*.

HF Capitalism disregards facts as well as non-economic values. Many Americans seem to ignore the findings of fact-checking, while many politicians ignore, or pretend to ignore, the facts themselves. Given this, what do you think of the schizophrenic role of science in capitalist culture?

KSR I think of them as in conflict for control. I'm very pro-science, but everything can be bought, and even science is in danger. I thought, because science was doing the real work, that capitalism was its parasite, like the puppet masters in the Heinlein story. I still think that's true, but in global capitalism, money really can direct scientific research; we still have the war machine, for instance. And big pharmaceuticals direct a lot of biological research, ignoring certain problems and paying attention to others, depending on the potential for profit. Just because science is doing the real work it doesn't mean it's in control; the puppet master can call the shots, the parasite could be strong enough to kill the host. That happens a lot in nature. It's a scary, scary century.

Science is a contested space. The AGU (the American Geophysical Union) is an example. Do they take money from Exxon or not? They voted on it, and they are still taking money from Exxon. They think it is better to have that money to put to good use than to make a symbolic statement against Exxon. This is just one small example of a constant battle.

The enormous, elaborate community of scientific institutions is trying to figure out how can they save the world without becoming revolutionaries, or without becoming political. This is funny, because they're acting politically without admitting it. What they're doing is intensely political, but they're still caught in a paradigm in which facts aren't political. Generally speaking, the psychological mindset of science is astonishingly naive, philosophically simplistic: 'What I do is very straightforward. I gather data, and then I analyse it, and I make a theory and I explain, then I go back and do more experiments.' On the other hand, many scientists are highly sophisticated and know more about the humanities than most people in the humanities know about the sciences. Many are actually more well-rounded intellectually than most people in the humanities.

The first wave of scientific efforts to alert the world to climate change was a painfully instructive moment for scientists. When scientists saw that just announcing the problem didn't change people's behaviour, they were shocked and dismayed because they thought that people would look at the facts and then change their values. Even now they are still trying to find a way to move forward, to be both scientists and effective political actors.

HF That's a nice segue to a question I want to ask about H.G. Wells. I know you're a fan. Anyone who works on Wells has a difficult task of trying to think through his visionary socialism alongside his authoritarian tendencies. Is there anything you want to say about *The Shape of Things to Come*, *The Work, Wealth and Happiness of Mankind* or, if by chance you've read it, *The Croquet Player*?

KSR No, I haven't read *The Croquet Player*, but I've read *Star Born*, another late work from the thirties. In the thirties they could see that another war was coming, and it probably felt apocalyptic to think that they were heading towards a war even worse than the First World War. I admire the way Wells tried to continue to be hopeful in that situation. It was a very totalitarian time; as with Leninism, people thought if you could just seize control long enough to do what's right, then democracy could come later. His version of taking over is usually a scientific meritocracy. It's almost like Silicon Valley today, which thinks 'If we could just ignore politics and tech our way out of all these problems …' Of course, Wells was much cannier than that. The libertarian Silicon Valley view is lame. They're not geniuses. I would say that your average scientist is more politically savvy than your average computer geek making tons of money down in Silicon Valley. But, again, it depends who you're talking to. I've seen computer world attitudes range from sophisticated concern to a siloed in [view of the world], 'We're so smart that we can ignore other problems; maybe we'll set up a colony on Mars, and then we'll be okay.' That kind of thinking is terribly inadequate.

HF 'Siloed in' is a good metaphor, because there's a solipsism that comes with living in an environment that is more and more human-made, more and more closed off to the complex more-than-human world. We're open organic systems, and all the normal 'input' we'd be getting from the universe is less and less present in systems of our own creation. How can we think politically, think about relations between subjects, human and nonhuman, when all we see is more of ourselves staring back at ourselves?

KSR It's a problem. People who sit on their butts looking at screens all day might think they're happy doing just that. But these people have problems with the third dimension, with ecology. This crowd thinks that they could live in a similar room on Mars, thirty feet underground, and be happy, that it'd be so cool to be Martians, and then there would be a lifeboat for humanity if by some impossibility all life on Earth were to disappear, which is another bad ecological thought. They aren't really thinking. It's more of a fantasy, and it goes back to the early science fiction fantasy of 'If only I could clear this situation and start over, and simplify it down to just what I like, everything would be okay.'

HF One of the horrible places in Wells has to do with population; Wells had phases of eugenic thinking. In *New York 2140*, there is a refugee crisis, but I don't recall seeing the word overpopulation in your novel. Did the first and second pulses (of rising sea levels) significantly diminish the population or are you trying to make people rethink the question of population in ecological terms?

KSR Population per se is not the problem. Population still matters, but it is only part of the equation. Ehrlich's 'IPAT' formula [$I = P \times A \times T$ or, impact is determined by population times affluence times the 'greenness' of the technology] shows that the ordinary westerner uses thirty times the resources of someone in Asia. When you do the math, 300 million people in the United States times thirty, you get a stupendous figure that makes India and China look like paltry little populations in terms of consumption or impact on the earth.

But it shouldn't be an A for affluence or appetite in that equation, it should be an E, for economics; in other words, the 'IPET' theory. I talked to Ehrlich about this, and he was interested. You don't want to talk about affluence or appetite, because everybody should have a refrigerator so they don't get sick, and what is true affluence is a value judgement. Thoreau was affluent. So, what's messy in this equation, between population and the cleanness or dirtiness of technology? What's the thing that makes us use too much? Our economic system, the middle term. It's more important than population per se, and tech is getting cleaner and cleaner. Re-rigging the economic system for our survival is the focus of *New York 2140*, but all my writing, going back almost thirty years now, has been about imagining various post-capitalisms. I don't characterise it with any one term because they're weighted with baggage from the past, so I'm perfectly happy to talk about any post-capitalist future, social democracy or democratic socialism, communism …

HF Social-anarchism?

KSR I'm a statist; I don't believe anarchism is a way to get through the next couple of centuries. I thoroughly approve of anarchism's ultimate goal of the total horizontalisation of power but, to me, anarchism is a horizon that is centuries out.

HF At least one literary critic has coupled your name with Murray Bookchin.

KSR I've read Bookchin and I admire his work. I'm thinking more of anarchisms that conflate capitalism and the state. I separate them, just as I separate capitalism and science. I'm also thinking of the anti-humanism of certain anarchisms, those that turn into libertarianism very easily in an ugly way, those that say it doesn't matter if six billion people die because then we'd have a sustainable number. What's good in anarchism is the idea of a complete horizontalisation of power and prosperity. It's a great long-term horizon to aim for. It's like utopia itself. I'm a utopian, but I wouldn't say I'm an anarchist because I don't think a state monopoly on violence is a bad thing at this point in history. It's better than the alternatives, better than chaos, better than the freedom to burn as much carbon as I want. I think that carbon use should be legislated and controlled and priced, and anarchy doesn't provide a way of doing that.

HF There are two new books out on post-capitalism that seem problematic in this regard, to varying degrees: *Post-Capitalism: A Guide to Our Future* by Paul Mason, and *Inventing the Future: Post-Capitalism and a World Without Work* by Nick Srnicek and Alex Williams. What did you make of these?

KSR They struck me as weak because they called for tech solutions only. In one, robots would do all the work ... but both failed to address the two big problems: what is the post-capitalist economic system, and how do we get there? The only good thing they're doing is putting the word out there. Ten years ago you could google the word post-capitalism and get practically nothing. We need [the concept of] post-capitalism. I'm not a theorist myself, but if you give me a theory I can turn it into a science fiction novel. I'm like a magpie.

HF Exactly what I thought when I read *New York 2140*. It's like New York itself, full of everything from everywhere: wide-ranging epigraphs, cultural history, economic history, literary history ... In places it felt a little like *The Arcades Project*.

KSR It was fun to use the city as a way to make all that stuff relevant to a single story. It's amazing what New York can do. I love it. But when you look for good post-capitalist plans, it's not that they're completely missing, because people like Robin Hahnel and Michael Albert have proposals, and a lot of them are co-ops, worker owned co-ops similar to the Yugoslavian industries, or the Mondragon cooperatives, or various successful city states, like Bologna. But we still lack global solutions, and this is one of the many complaints I have about the field of economics per se: it's not speculative. It doesn't try to imagine what would be better; it's just an analysis of a legal system. The spectacular lack of imagination in economics is painful because we need it. We need both a functional system people could believe in and a way to get there. It seems to me this should be the work of a school of economics. Yet many economics departments are completely hidebound, only analytical. It's painful because they're missing their necessary work: political economy. During the Cold War it was impossible to discuss political economy without being labelled a communist. And with the Milton Friedman crowd taking over during the Reagan/Thatcher revolution, we've lost thirty years to Ayn Rand stupidity. Whenever you see economics based on the ideas of a bad science fiction writer, you know you're in trouble.

HF Since we're on this terrain, you've mentioned the importance of interdisciplinary thought – not just political economy but leftist sociobiology – in the past. Could you talk a little more about this? Are you thinking of E.O. Wilson, often misread as deterministic, or his detractors, Richard Levins and Richard Lewontin, the authors of *The Dialectical Biologist*?

KSR No, I'm thinking of Wilson himself. I'm a big fan. The attack on Wilson by Levins and Lewontin after he brought out *Sociobiology* was mostly departmental politics. It was stupid, because he wasn't saying that biology is deterministic. It's not Social Darwinism. Wilson is, I think, like Ben Franklin or William James – he's going to be remembered as a major intellectual figure of our time, and the attacks on him were unfortunate because they made a lot of leftist humanists think, 'oh no, another Herbert Spencer,' without reading Wilson's text, without thinking it through. Some really useful work here was done by Sarah Hrdy, who was a student of Wilson. She taught here in Davis. In *Mother Nature*, she points out that if you look at the scientific evidence gathered by primatologists, you don't simply see alpha-male power; you see enormous female power, political power, power over things that really matter, like who gets born. She was a great corrective [to patriarchal primatology], and slowly but surely a leftist sociobiology, a feminist sociobiology, came into being under the umbrella of Wilson's first approaches, as elaborations and extensions, but not in opposition to him.

HF This brings to mind another undialectical relation. You've said in the past that capitalism is feudalism in disguise, that one of the problems with Marxist historiography is the sense that we've moved further in the dialectic than we actually have. Is it the case that we're stuck in feudalism or is it that capitalism never had any truck with democracy whatsoever?

KSR Capitalism is still very feudal in its distribution of wealth. One of the great triumphs of Marxist historiography is to describe accurately the transition from feudalism to capitalism, why it happened and the differences. At a presentation I once gave with Jameson, I said something like capitalism is just feudalism liquidified. In the break he said, 'Kim, it's actually a big accomplishment for Marxists to be able to describe the change from feudalism to capitalism.' I then brought up something he had taught me, Raymond Williams's concept of the residual and the emergent, and said, 'but there's a lot more residual than people have imagined.' That's one of the only times I saw Fred startled by something I said. Although I think there's an exchange of ideas between us, mainly he's the teacher, I'm the student. He's explained things that I never would have understood, and I treasure him for that. So it was nice to see him think, 'Mmm, that's an interesting thought.'

The residuals out of feudalism would be the power gradient and the actual concentration of wealth per se. In the feudal period, kings might not even have been as proportionally rich as top executives are now in relation to the poor. And if peasants weren't murdered by passing soldiers, they were living with their food source at hand and working a somewhat decent human life. That isn't largely true now of the dispossessed. So, capitalism is like feudalism in that, but worse.

HF *New York 2140* is an alternative future history. It tries to imagine, as you've said, how we get from a capitalist to a post-capitalist world, but through one building, the MetLife Building, and all the actors (people, human systems, ecosystems) in this network. Is the building also a microcosm of the relation between the money sphere and the biosphere?

KSR It was the way to tell that story, and it was an experiment in form, in the genre of the French apartment novel, used by Zola and others (recently by Thomas Dish, Geoff Ryman and John Lanchester). At the start of the story the characters don't know each other, but they live in the same apartment building. In my version of it, they eventually get to know each other to make the plot more interesting, rather than just a collection of short stories. It turned out to be quite a long novel, as you saw, because there were eight points of view and a dozen important characters, more than I usually deal with. Well, the Mars trilogy has scores of characters, but this was a single novel.

By the end of the story I try to make what's going on in lower Manhattan scale up to the national and the global. You can't have a local solution [to national and global problems]. You hear this focus on local solutions in Naomi Klein, in the work of all kinds of critics: 'At least there'll be resistance movements, there'll be these little pockets.' In global capitalism those are allowable discharge zones where energy gets dispersed; [they allow] people to think things are changing, while global capitalism continues its destruction. You need a global solution.

At the end of the novel the householder's union causes a financial crash; the crash causes the federal government to take over the banks. Essentially it's 2008 again, which indeed will happen again, and the question then will be, do we settle for a little fix or a big one? A big fix would be like what we did when we took over General Motors; we got it back to health and then sold it back to private ownership. When the banks crash again, instead of giving them a hundred cents on the dollar and telling them to go out and do more, we need to nationalise them. When I say nationalise them, there are specific plans as to how this might be done, how they might become fully owned subsidiaries of the American people, how finance might become a tool rather than a master.

What I like about *New York 2140* is that it describes something that could happen in the real world. The mechanisms are in place. Congress could make the laws and the president could enact them. It's not grossly dissimilar to what Bernie Sanders was advocating during his campaign.

HF Why do you think so many people don't seem or want to think globally? Is it a matter of fear and frustration, or has the systemic complexity and scale of global problems become truly incomprehensible?

KSR People want to be able to do something in their own lives. Also, [we suffer from] the feeling that the system is completely locked in. The story we've all been told is that the system is robust, permanent and massively entrenched, backed by guns and laws and prison sentences. If you resist it, you might spend the rest of your life in jail and nothing at all will change. And so you try to find a personal pocket utopia, where you can at least have a decent life for yourself and feel like you're not actively damaging the world compared to the ordinary capitalist life.

You need [places like] Village Homes, my own pocket utopia, that burn only 40% as much energy as an ordinary American suburb. But that's still ten times the energy of a peasant village in India, so it's not a solution. This place was built forty years ago, and nothing like it has ever been built since because it isn't as profitable as an ordinary suburb.

No local solution is sufficient. We need the World Trade Organisation and the International Monetary Fund, the World Bank and the G20, to do smart, ecological, democratic things. This sounds like a big task but, as I said in *New York 2140,* the number of laws that matter are few. They are human laws and laws change all the time, and a lot of these laws are heavily influenced by the USA, China, and five or six other really big national economies. So it could be done.

HF *New York 2140* depicts a constellation of connected systems, financial, biological, ecological, technological, and their analysis, from Gen's patterns of human behaviour and detection, Franklin's patterns of metaphor in numbers, Charlotte's patterns of emigration and Amelia's animal migration. If science fiction is the new realism, what constitutes the real in *2140*?

KSR The value of the apartment novel is that each of the eight points of view has a take on what is real. Combined, they're a mega-system. I suppose Jameson would just call it history, though it is important to include the planet, which I'm not sure that Fred often does; surplus value has always been appropriated out of the natural world in increasing circles, and now we've run out of circles, so the expansion crashes and the biosphere too. The real is too big of a term to be comprehended, and so you break it down into lots of smaller systems that are trying to explain the whole. Together, you get a mega-system or a stack of systems.

HF It's been theorised in many different disciplines that systems tend to formally mirror the organisational structures that produce them. For example, the systems created by IBM will mirror the organisational structure of IBM, or, in the sphere of Marxist philosophy, Neil Larsen would say the form of thought is the form of the social.

KSR Interesting. It is definitely the case, as Marxism [teaches], that ideology is crucial. To me, ideology is simply the stories that you believe in.

HF For *some* Marxists, capitalism is total and *totalising*. Nothing can change; nothing can happen.

KSR That's right in terms of what they believe, and this is something that Jameson is always wrestling with. But here it helps to keep science and its worldview in mind. Capitalism can't persist because it doesn't conform to the limits of physical reality. So, in every novel I write, I try to tell a story that's plausible, provocative *and* would allow everything to change. That's the utopian problem.

HF Capitalism has *natural* limits. Of course, it helps if there's sunken treasure, as in *New York 2140*.

KSR But there's always sunken treasure, right? That's the capital of the past. That is capital itself, freed from capitalism's system of ownership.

HF Literally, the gold without the ship? Because your canvas is the history of New York, you've also a wealth of literary treasure, writers from New York or visiting New York, which helps situate the text in a system of literary meaning. As your novel suggests, meaning is an alternative form of value. I was particularly interested in the way you use Melville; *Moby-Dick* comes up many times and Melville himself appears as a ghost. Two other things occurred to me as I read. The citizen sections seem almost like an Ishmael voice bearing witness to something. Also, *New York 2140* seems to invoke 'Bartleby, the Scrivener: A Story of Wall Street' as it does *Moby-Dick*. In the end, people speak with one voice to power, saying, 'I prefer not to.'

KSR I definitely wanted Bartleby [in the mix] since he worked right down in there, very close to my building, and Melville lived very close to my building. The first edition of *Moby-Dick* I read was abridged and I didn't know that. It had been thrown away, and I picked it up out of the gutter. I never looked at the title page, and so I had to re-read it later. Now I've read it many times. Melville is the Great Spirit of American Literature. In my mind I have a great novel about Herman Melville's life as a customs inspector, working on the docks. I may never write it, so I inserted it into this novel as a story told by a character.

HF In *New York 2140*, it's Jeff who claims that you could distil financial code into sixteen laws that could be altered to fix the global financial system. A coder might say it's the right order of magnitude, but might also invoke the notion of 'the great rewrite in the sky' for a system like this. Meaning that it is too complex to fix, that you'd have to start over.

KSR This is what Jeff finds out the moment that he tries. What he does with code, as eventually he admits, is more like graffiti than a hack. He marks what could be done but without actually doing it, like a note to the SEC [the US Securities and Exchange Commission]. It's a desperate gesture and it gets them in trouble, but it isn't real politics. This is what I'm saying to the tech community, the coders [who think] it's all just code. It's not all just code, because laws and codes aren't the same. They have formal similarities, but it's a question of power. What kinds of guns are behind them? How much do people live by them? How visible are they?

This is what's interesting about this Trans Pacific Treaty. How do we behave on a global scale between nations? How much do we try to enforce labour fairness and environmental intelligence into our global trading laws beyond the nation states? More would be better, and improvement by increments isn't to be scoffed at. So, the means by which that treaty was negotiated were obviously bad, a secretive little cabal. 'Let us, a few technocrats get it right, and trust us that we've got it right.' I haven't seen the details of what the Treaty would enact, so I don't know if I'm for or against the content, but I'm against the method of its coming into being. Nevertheless, I like the idea of international treaties, because we need to tie the bad actors into the good actors' value systems. We do not want liquid capital, global finance, to just slide into the worst [country], the worst actor in the network.

HF Speaking of liquid capital, I couldn't help but enjoy the pairing of global and financial liquidity (rising sea levels and financial crashes). Did you have the pairing, literally and metaphorically in mind from the start?

KSR Yes. People say I like floods. All of my big novels include floods, the Mars Trilogy, *The Years of Rice and Salt*, *Green Earth*, and now this book. And in *2312*, the drowned Manhattan appears for the first time as a set piece. It always struck me as funny that we might drown in our own liquidity.

HF In *New York 2140*, we have, on the one hand, dark economic pools and then, on the other, nature as Mother Ocean. In one of the Amelia chapters you invoke Aldo Leopold's land ethic, in which he exhorts us to think like a mountain. Is this novel trying, in places, to ask us to think like an ocean?

KSR Maybe. Leopold is very important. I think his phrase, 'What's good is good for the land' is a baseline value, a value that we should base everything else on. If you take care of the land, then people will also be okay. This is crucial, transformative ecological thinking.

KSR Essentially, what's good for the planet is good for the people who are co-existent with it. The inter-tidal is a great metaphor as well as a great real space. As a real space, it's complicated, messy, lively, and you can't legislate it. In many legal systems it's an unorganised public space.

HF Living in this post-second pulse, inter-tidal space requires some interesting future technology, including very resilient carbon negative building materials and infrastructure. Is any aspect of this technology in development?

KSR Right now it's at the level of venture capital, these graphene sheets, basically carbon nanotubes flattened out. It's science fiction tech right now, but people with money are interested in it because the source material is carbon.

HF *New York 2140* is a work of speculative fiction, speculating on the technology we need for a better future, which sheds light on another, related form of speculation: futures markets.

KSR 'The Volatility Index' is *already* a science fiction story set one month out! Risk assessment for investors is a matter of making predictions. Since it can't be done [accurately], the risk is high; the volatility is high. In that realm, what you want is to be able to win whether the market goes up or down.

HF This is interesting, because some of the earliest climate data we have comes from insurance companies.

KSR The insurance companies, especially the re-insurance companies, could be part of the story of post-capitalism, because they're going to be the ultimate holders of the costs. They are going to say to the world, 'Sorry, these are not payable costs.' I have friends in the Natural Catastrophe Division of Swiss Re who say, 'Wait, our whole industry is doomed, because we can't pay out what's going to come due,' and therefore [the world's now] uninsurable. They would have said, up to this point, everything's insurable, you just need to set the rate right. When you can't set the rate right, it would break civilization to pay the premiums. You get into the mass extinction event, you get into the stupidity of 'we can't afford to survive.'

HF *New York 2140* seems to reconfigure value as the products of the labour of inhabitation, of love. This is how real value is created in the inter-tidal space, by people who inhabit and stick it out. I was thinking of Gary Snyder's remark that ecology is a problem of love; they have the same root of course, ecology and economics, from the Greek *oikos*: home, dwelling. I was wondering if you were pointing to that by choosing the Householders Union for the very centre of the novel, not just this one big house, the Met Building, but the Householders Union.

KSR The Householders Union comes out of the work of the radical economists I mentioned earlier: the idea that everybody is a householder, everybody is illiquid. You want illiquidity, in that you want your house, your job and your health, but finance wants liquidity and can beat you at the game of liquidity. When you realise that global finance depends on us making our payments, there is hope for some kind of democratic control from below by way of a strike. But unions have been marginalised and turned into unimportant actors because they were always involved with one trade, a plumber's union.

But unions were important and still can be if you think that everybody's already in the union of the dispossessed. A Householders Union is a way of saying that everybody could be in the same union, and there's enormous power there. You become a *refusenik*, and if everybody were to do it at once, it becomes politics rather than personal default. This is, to me, a workable plan. Everybody would be really happy not to pay their bills one month and see what happened.

HF That would be interesting. If we're thinking about politics and transparency, I think it's clear to many people that we don't live in a democracy in the United States. Emma Goldman said a long time ago that if voting really mattered they wouldn't let you do it. What if everybody decided, 'In a two party-system monopolised by the same corporate money, I'm not going to vote.'

KSR I don't agree with Goldman. We could use the Democratic Party, as the one that is ostensibly closer to people's values, to elect a majority in Congress to enact a New Deal flurry of changes. Corporations could squeal but they couldn't make the army go onto the streets against the people. In this country the corporations can't do that. So voting does matter.

If you believe democracy is impossible, that corporations will always rule, money always rules, then that is self-fulfilling. Actually, corporations are massively overly leveraged, which is to say they're hanging over an abyss of bankruptcy. They often have fifty to a hundred times as much money out in loans as they do in assets in hand. If a call went out where they had to pay all their loans at once, they would instantly crash. That was 2008, so 2008 is analysable and reproducible, and it could lead to a different political result. This is not an entrenched, concrete bunker of a system. It's a house of cards, and the people at the bottom could bring the whole thing down. Do we then say, 'We do need capital, we do need banks, we do need investment, we do need some kind of market'? I'm not so sure what we do or don't need. But in post-capitalism, those things could all be transformed.

HF One reason people feel that the system is totalising is because we live in a surveillance society. People feel encompassed by power; their lives are collectible data.

KSR The surveillance that matters is your credit rating. The rest of surveillance is balkanised. It's also government. It's not all corporation's power. It's too much information to be analysed in human time. This is one of those science fiction fantasies of the computer that knows all, but there still need to be humans to process the data into useful information.

My feeling is that surveillance is a false issue, that there's no problem except for the credit rating. And this is where the Householders Union comes in; if everybody were to default at once, then everybody's credit rating would take a hit, but it's always differential value that matters. It's another case of we either hang together or we hang separately: the great American political realisation, which is that solidarity matters.

The real surveillance is your credit rating. It's public knowledge about you and it shouldn't be out there, but it is. The secret stuff, though, your private conversations, those don't matter because no one is ever going to listen, because there's too many of them, probably five hundred trillion conversations. What algorithm would they use to get data from them?

HF Speaking of problems of scale, the complex ecological effects of the industrial revolution and Great Acceleration, what do you think of the term Anthropocene, and the idea of Anthropocene literature?

KSR It's interesting to historicise it as a term. It began with scientists trying to say, 'Look, climate change is real, and we're having a profound impact as a species.' But when academia picked it up, it drops into the swamp of semantics, it loses political force. It's best as a geological term, but it has already been defused. It's become just another term like sustainability.

HF Yes, 'sustainability' has been co-opted. Do you think Anthropocene literature might rescue the term?

KSR Whenever science fiction gets interesting, then people try to give it another name. It's the anti-science fiction prejudice raising its head again. If its content becomes relevant, you call it cyberpunk, cli fi, Anthropocene literature or dystopian fiction. These are all science fiction. It's a very big, powerful genre. As soon as you say, 'we're going to talk about the future', you're saying you're going talk about history. You're going to talk about the planet. You're going to talk about everything. *That's what science fiction does.*

Helena Feder is Associate Professor of Literature and Environment at East Carolina University. She is author of Ecocriticism and the Idea of Culture *(Ashgate 2014, Routledge 2016).*

Reviews

Proletarianisation isn't working

Bernard Stiegler, *Automatic Society: The Future of Work, Volume 1,* trans, Daniel Ross (Cambridge: Polity, 2016). 341pp., £55.00 hb., £17.99 pb., 978 1 50950 630 9 hb., 978 1 50950 631 6 pb.

Despairing over the conditions of living and working in Foxconn's 'factory city' in China, a total of 14 workers leapt to their deaths from the rooftops of their plant in Longhua, Shenzhen in 2010. The company's stopgap response was to suspend nets between the plant's buildings so as to frustrate the efforts of the would-be suicides. Foxconn's long term solution, rather than improving the conditions of workers, is to remove them from the equation. Having reached some kind of upper limit in the tolerance levels of the human pysche they have moved to full roboticisation. Aiming towards the complete automation in the assembly of iPhones and other consumer electronics, Foxconn, like other major manufacturers, have turned in their pursuit of optimal productivity to replacing workers with machines.

Media reports on the 'Rise of the Robots' abound, as do warnings of job losses – projected at around 35% in the next 20 years for the UK, according to a Deloitte and Oxford University study of 2014. The effects of automation are, unsurprisingly, unequally distributed. That same report notes that 'jobs paying less than £30,000 a year are nearly five times more likely to be replaced by automation than jobs paying over £100,000.' Equally predictable is the opportunism of employers in using the threat of automation to suppress wage levels. In response to the current campaign being fought for by workers at McDonald's for a minimum $15 per hour the company's CEO, Ed Rensi, warned that this demand could only lead to greater automation. The Forbes article in which this was reported argues that what those involved in this campaign are 'really demonstrating for is accelerating the date at which their job disappears to a machine.'

Bernard Stiegler's *Automatic Society: The Future of Work*, the first volume in a projected series, is addressed to the implications of this turn to automation; concerned with the disappearance of work (or at least of 'employment'), but also with other, and equally troubling, consequences of automation. The algorithmic technics of contemporary capitalism, the ascendency of 'big data' as a mechanism of control, capture and subjectivation, threaten, according to Stiegler, human capacities for dreaming and reflection, even for thought itself. The book opens with a reference to Chris Anderson's often cited and tellingly titled essay 'The End of Theory'. In this text, published in *Wired* in 2007, Anderson enthuses over the displacement of human *knowledge* by computational *information*, as represented by the operations of Google. As Stiegler elaborates:

> The automated 'knowledge' celebrated by Anderson no longer needs to be thought. In the epoch of the algorithmic implementation of applied mathematics in computerised machines, there is no longer any need to think: thinking is concretised in the form of algorithmic automatons that control data-capture systems and hence make it obsolete. As automatons, these algorithms no longer require it in order to function – as if thinking had been proletarianised by itself.

For Stiegler, typically, the threat of automation, as it currently presents itself, is nothing less than apocalyptic. Its four horsemen - heralds of the 'becoming computational' of capitalism – are Google, Apple, Facebook and Amazon. These are '*literally disentegrating the industrial societies* that emerged from the *Aufklärung*.'

Stiegler draws substantially, though not uncritically, from Jonathan Crary's *24/7: Late Capitalism and the Ends of Sleep* (2013) in his critique of the technologically automated environments with which we are now functionally integrated. Continuously hooked up to these environments through portable and networked electronic devices, the subject subsists in a state of unremitting connectivity, eliminating the time of sleep, dream and daydream. Deprived of the intermittences that might afford time and space for states of reverie, the human subject is also dispossessed of its capacity for the kind of thinking necessary to individual and social transformation: 'The dream that thinks leads to realisations … technical inventions, artistic creations, political institutions'.

Antoinettte Rouvroy and Thomas Berns's conception of an 'algorithmic governmentality' performs a similarly significant role for Stiegler in articulating his critique of automation. For Berns and Rouvroy, the automation of governance enabled by big data obliterates the time and space of both politics and critique. In their 2013 essay 'Algorithmic governmentality and prospects of emancipation', they argue that 'legitimate authority has been displaced and distributed into things, making it difficult to apprehend or to question since it is imposed in the name of realism and loses its political visibility. Critique is paralysed because it seems to have been overtaken and rendered obsolete.' Algorithmic governmentality anticipates our every move, mapping out in advance an apolitical ideal of behaviour and perfomance – as exemplified in the 'smart city' – to which the subject must adapt and conform without reflection.

In addition to recent conceptions of 24/7 capitalism and algorithmic governmentality, Stiegler's critique of automation also takes in longer term perspectives with which readers of his substantial oeuvre will be familiar. He conceives of the 'proletarianisation of minds and spirits' effected in contemporary processes of automation, for instance, as the final culmination of a process of rationalisation originally identified by Weber, and by Adorno and Horkheimer in their *Dialectic of Enlightenment*, as the calculative instrumentalisation of reason within and for capitalism. Stiegler also builds here upon his longstanding engagement with the thought of the paleo-ontologist André Leroi-Gourhan – for whom the human is defined, as such, in terms of its 'originary technicity' – and his earlier synthesis of this with Derridean conceptions of 'supplement' and 'grammatisation' in his *Technics and Time 1: The Fault of Epimetheus*. Grammatisation, 'consisting in the duplication and discretisation of mental experiences', is a process conceived by Stiegler, following Derrida, as one in which human experience and knowledge are exteriorised and retained by technological means, including, but not limited to, those of writing. Digital technology is understood, within this schema, as only the 'most advanced stage' of a process essential to and inextricable from hominisation, one 'that goes back to at least the end of the Upper Paleolithic'.

These perspectives on technology and proletarianisation enable a more nuanced and in some ways more radical take on the political economy of automation than is offered by many other critics of its deleterious effects. Stiegler parts company with Crary, for example, over the issue of the relationship obtaining between capitalism and technology. For Crary, television and related technologies are 'part of a larger strategy of power', whereas, for Stiegler, capitalism is only ever the 'quasi-case' of technological development that is to be properly understood as 'fundamentally accidental'. While acknowledging that 'there are strategies and programmes directing and prescribing research and development', those devices which integrate us with Crary's 24/7 capitalism are better conceived as appropriated by capitalism – an advantageous 'windfall' – rather than as resulting from some pre-planned strategy. This point might be further debated, particularly given that state investment of tax revenues in technological research and development is often ultimately employed in devices supposed, for example, to be entirely 'Designed in California' by Apple. Whatever the intricacies of this particular debate, Stiegler's larger and effectively argued point is that the threat of automation is not best described as a 'rise of the robots' but rather as the capture of technics by capitalism within its ongoing project of rationalisation.

Stiegler's account of technics as exteriorisation, as an apparatus of human retention, also challenges conceptions of technology as an always externally posited and invasive threat to an essentialised humanity. Franco 'Bifo' Berardi, for instance, in his recent book *And: Phenomenology of the End*, argues that the human subject is currently threatened with 'neurological mutation'; that there is underway an epochal shift in the very nature of the human nervous system wrought by the rise of digital technologies that now makes possible 'the insertions of neuro-linguistic memes and automatic devices in the sphere of cognition, social psyche and life forms.'

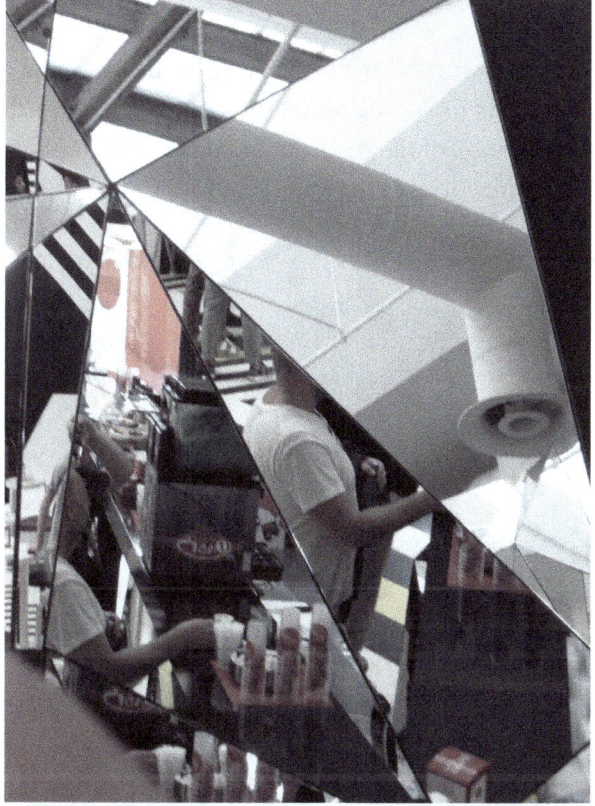

Through such insertions 'history is replaced by the implementation of a technological model, formatted by the networked machine.' Berardi's lament replays a longstanding trope in which newly introduced media technologies – writing, the printing press, television, the internet, social media – are held to threaten the supposedly given nature of the human subject. What Berardi describes negatively as the invasive and technological 'reformatting' of cognition is, for Stiegler, necessarily fundamental, and in some sense 'natural', to the human. '[S]ince the beginning of hominisation', he writes, 'the practice of tools and instruments has *disorganised* and *reorganised* the brains, minds and spirits of workers … of all kinds, which are formed during these practices.' On this basis, Stiegler is able to formulate an effectively critical response to a contemporary technics of automation rather than simply denouncing its supposedly inhuman effects.

Technics, then, is not itself the problem. What is at issue for Stiegler is rather the *proletarianisation* of the relationship between technics and the subject; the latter's *alienation from* rather than its *invasion by* processes of automation. When retention is digitised as data, as information algorithmically processed and circulated, it is no longer available to knowledge. Technics no longer serves as *pharmakon*. It is taken out of circulation as a site of social and psychic investment to be instrumentalised, instead, as the exclusive property of computational capitalism. In escaping and outrunning human cognition, automation leads to the 'disintegration of psychic and social individuals'.

As I have noted, the picture painted of the implications of an 'automatic society' subsumed to the rationalising and algorithimic logic of capitalism is apocalyptic. Stiegler is, though, equally concerned to grasp the possibilities of automation dialectically so as to envisage some exit from his catastrophic forecast. Whereas Berns and Rouvroy, for example, tend to present their 'algorithmic governmentality' as a done deal, in which critique has already been rendered impossible, Stiegler both insists on its possibility and demonstrates its necessity in *Automatic Society*. We are, he argues, placed at a critical juncture and his avowed purpose, rather than to paralyse thought through despair, is to 'anticipate, describe, alert, but also to propose'. 'The *question* this period poses', he notes, 'is how to make an exit from its own toxicity'. Stiegler's exit strategy is through automation itself. Automation as *pharmakon* might be turned to curative rather than poisonous ends. It is through a return to Marx's critique of the alienation of wage labour that Stiegler pursues this possibility here.

Stiegler is not alone in observing that automation will likely render much current employment redundant, but he is more original – while acknowledging here his debt to André Gorz – in arguing that we must not confuse employment with work in responding to this. Employment, as wage labour, necessarily implies proletarianisation and alienation, whereas for Marx, 'work can be fulfilling only if it ceases to be wage labour and becomes free.' The defence of employment on the part of the left and labour unions is then castigated as a regressive position that, while seeking to secure the 'right to work', only shores up capitalism through its calls for the maintenance of wage labour. Contrariwise, automation has the potential to finally release the subject from the alienation of wage labour so as to engage in unalienated work, properly understood as the pursuit, practice and enjoyment of knowledge. What currently stands in the way of the realisation of fulfilling work, aside from an outmoded defense of employment, Stiegler notes, is the capture of the 'free time' released from employment in consumption, as forms of entertainment and distraction equally devoid of knowledge or its real fulfilment.

Stiegler's critique of automation is inarguably dialectical and, in its mobilisation of the *pharmakon*, impeccably Derridean. Yet it leaves unanswered – for the moment at least, pending a second volume – the question of the means through which the transition from employment to work might be effected. This would surely require not only the powers of individual thought, knowledge, reflection and critique that Stiegler himself affirms and demonstrates in *Automatic Society*, but also their collective practice and mobilisation. What is also passed over in Stiegler's longer term perspectives is the issue of how such collective practices, such as already exist, are to respond to the more immediate and contemporary effects of automation, if not through the direct contestation of the conditions and terms of employment and unemployment.

Douglas Spencer

Unlikely hegemons

Angela Nagle, *Kill All Normies: Online Culture Wars From 4Chan and Tumblr to Trump and the Alt-Right* (Alresford: Zero Books, 2017). 136pp., £9.99 pb., 978 1 78535 543 1

Kill All Normies sets out to provide an anatomy of the internet spaces in which contemporary 'culture wars' are being fought out, and an account of how the alt-right rose to prominence and power. It examines the aesthetics of transgression, the symbiosis of sadism and sentimentalism, and the effects of alienation in modern life which have been reproduced and amplified by the internet. The text opens with the hope and optimism surrounding the 'horizontal', 'networked', 'leaderless' realm opened up by the internet, heralded by the 2011 Egyptian revolution (the so-called 'Twitter revolution') and the Occupy movement, before moving on to puncture the resultant hubris and complacency. If we let a thousand flowers bloom, some of them are bound to go rotten. It was a pervasive myth at the start of the decade that the methods of communication and organisation opened up by the internet were to the intrinsic advantage of the left. Subsequent events have shown otherwise.

On Nagle's account, Tumblr-liberalism, a form of politics focusing on identities and their recognition, mainly existed on social media before recently breaking out into what she calls 'campus wars'. For some time now, a more general version of identity politics has informed the prevailing world view of professional strata and the liberal press; Tumblr-liberalism is not coextensive with this but rather a radicalised offshoot that grew online. But the internet is a diverse place and, less noticed until relatively recently, on the message boards of 4chan and Men's Rights Activism (MRA) groups, the alt-right was beginning to emerge. Both the alt-right and Tumblr-liberalism are, Nagle argues, insular movements, possessing their own subcultural norms, their 'own vocabulary and style', raising barriers of entry in an effort to exclude the eponymous 'normies'. Both groups saw themselves as *transgressing* a mainstream orthodoxy, of rebelling against the status quo by violating social norms. But the kind of transgression that once sustained the left cut both ways: 'it was the utterly empty and fraudulent ideas of countercultural transgression that created the void into which anything can now flow as long as it is contemptuous of mainstream values and tastes.' One outcome of 1968 was, on this reading, a celebration of being outside the mainstream simply for the sake of being outside the mainstream. The politics themselves were of secondary importance, what mattered was the 'aesthetics of transgression'. The problem is, however, if opposition to the status quo is all you have, what happens when you start to win? You become a victim of your own success. When feminism goes mainstream, patriarchy becomes an act of rebellion.

Nagle's claim is then something like the following: in valorising identity as the essence of being, and its recognition by others as the political achievement *par excellence*, identity politics, with Tumblr-liberalism as its latest iteration, turned the left away from a project centred on structural critique, and a corresponding politics of transformative universalism that would overcome oppression and exploitation, to one of altering individual behaviours. The goal of ending oppression, by overcoming hierarchies of domination, become replaced by its celebration: to be oppressed was not a condition to escape, but the supreme virtue. A minoritarian political culture developed in which the politics of collectivity and solidarity, and 'bread and butter' issues, were replaced by 'obscure Internet spaces, subcultures and identifications', within which 'a culture of fragility and victimhood mixed with a vicious culture of group attacks, group shaming, and attempts to destroy the reputations and lives of others' was fostered. Nagle provides the example of the late Mark Fisher as someone who was mobbed online for challenging the politics and behaviour of Tumblr-liberalism in his essay 'Exiting the Vampire Castle'.

Kill All Normies' general account of a left that has turned from class to identity is a familiar enough thesis. What is distinctive about the book is the ways in which Nagle takes this analysis into the information age. That Tumblr-liberalism is deeply imbued with an exclusionary political culture is critical to her point. Tumblr-liberalism operates on an economy of virtue-signalling and shaming, and aspires to nothing beyond the accumulation of the former and the doling out of the latter. As she writes: 'virtue is the currency that can make or break the career or social success of an online user in this milieu'. Humiliation takes precedence over education. In doing so, it betrays not just the economic aspirations of the 'old left', but also those lofty aims of the post-68 social movements for gender, racial and LGBT equality. Countercultures can be productive – indeed Tumblr-liberalism and the alt-right are two countercultures that have defined the contours of our times – but they need to become common cultures if they are to endure. Tumblr-liberalism makes a virtue of its marginality, a virtue it has had to work harder and harder to hold on to as it has become more and more normalised.

Nagle's argument is that this marks a shift in the central battlefield from *politics* to *culture*. It was easy for neoliberals to co-opt Tumblr-liberalism precisely because it had ceased to offer any real political challenge. As such, it fell in behind Barack Obama and then Hillary Clinton who dressed up an anti-egalitarian project of distributing wealth upwards in all the correct identitarian terminology: 'In this style of politics, what a political leader actually does often seems entirely secondary to what cultural politics they profess to have.' Canadian Prime Minister Justin Trudeau is perhaps the most notable current practitioner of this 'style'. Once identity is thought of as the winning move on the political chessboard it is no wonder that the alt-right moved to claim the virtues of 'white identity', or doubled down on its assertions of a patriarchal masculinity in its MRA groups. As Richard Spencer, one of the alt-right's leading lights, has put it: 'if Donald Trump would ultimately become about identity, and he would ultimately understand America as historically a white country … he could just say this is ours, you are not us, this country is for us.' Thus identity becomes the organising principle for neo-Nazism, just as it was in its original form. Now, however, the left has ceded the terrain. If the battle is solely about assertion of identity, any identity will ultimately do.

The alt-right really hit the mainstream when it was harnessed by what Nagle calls the 'Gramscians of the alt-light'. This motley band of intellectual and media performers built an apparatus of online cultural dissemination that catapulted the alt-right from the message boards of 4chan to the centre of the national conversation. The incoherent rage of an anti-political correctness subculture was transformed into a political force when joined with a grand narrative vision (Steve Bannon, Richard Spencer) and youthful celebrity (Lauren Southern, Milo Yiannopoulos). In doing so, the alt-light carried the day not only over the centre-left and centre-right, but also the well-funded libertarian right. For although the alt-right intersects, in places, with the latter, it remains a decidedly different milieu to the Koch-funded Tea Parties that looked to be the future of the Republican Party only a few years ago. The real impact thus far has come from, in Nagle's view, a 'more mainstream alt-light' who 'made their careers exposing the absurdities of online identity politics'. But to make those careers they had appealed to a constituency of altogether more dangerous 'white segregationists and genuinely hate-filled, occasionally murderous, misogynists and racists.' They may not now be able to reign in what they unleashed. Yiannopoulos was the first casualty of that war.

There is a sense in which any advance of the left is going to inevitably be met with a response from the right – not everyone can be a winner in an egalitarian struggle. Even if it produces an overall collective gain, some are bound to try and defend their privileges. Nagle does not always make this elementary point clear enough, and if her thesis amounted to this it would be neither interesting nor novel. Having people oppose you is not an indictment; neither is having them emulate what made you successful. But Nagle's point is not just that: it is that the success of Tumblr-liberalism has deprived the left of the ideological weapons required to counter the resurgence of the right. Tumblr-liberalism's transgressions have become staid, censorious and authoritarian while the alt-right was able to become the new cool. Its adoption by the mainstream – in politics, in business, in liberal media – made Tumblr-liberalism the new orthodoxy. And this orthodoxy was enforced not by winning consent, but by the Twitter pile-on – a *modus operandi* now utilised to great effect by the alt-right as well. If you have never had to build a case, to explain precisely why this strategy is better than that strategy, to interrogate and justify your views and assumptions, how do you fight back when challenged? If identity is everything, the epistemic and ethical grounds, what do you do when people who come from oppressed groups start propagating an anti-egalitarian politics?

The socialist left were once the champions of science and reason, of the rationally planned society directed towards meeting the material needs of humanity. The neoliberals stole that crown. But it was, arguably, the poststructuralist collapse that led the left off down the garden path in this respect. When language is cast as the fabric of reality itself, how one *feels* became equivalent to what one *is*. For others to deny that those feelings constitute truth claims about the world is then to erase the core of one's being. The neoliberals' credentials for hard-headed rationalism have also undergone a slow rout since 2008, their supply-side economics shibboleths exposed for what they always were: wealth transfers from labour to capital and a managed decline for the vast majority. In this context the alt-right were able to portray themselves as the reasonable defenders of the ordinary person. And so the great insurgent force of our times came not from the left, but from the fringes of the right.

Nagle makes much of how 'Milo and his 4chan troll fans are in many ways the perfect postmodern offspring, where every statement is wrapped in layers of faux-irony, playfulness and multiple cultural nods and references', but this is really only half the story. It is an important half, because it was no mean feat to make the aged tropes of the far right cool again. The other part is, however, precisely an appeal to rationality and reason. Witness *Rebel Media's* Lauren Southern mobilise science in her anti-feminist crusade. Or how Bannon packages the various motivating concerns of the alt-right into a compelling story of Western decline and how it can be reversed. In an anecdote indicative of the intellectual deprivation of Tumblr-liberalism, Nagle tells of how Buzzfeed published an interview with Bannon 'presumably thinking this was a ready-made hit-piece that would destroy his reputation', but instead he 'came across in the interview as darkly fascinating and, relative to many Buzzfeed listicle writers, as quite a serious and intriguing person.' *Vice* journalist Elle Reeve's interview with Richard Spencer, in which Spencer is awarded open season to portray himself as a wronged and misunderstood individual, might also be cited here. The bar has been set so low, and the left's resources become so depleted, that Bannon, a Z-list pseudo-intellectual, found himself cast as a luminary of the zeitgeist and a household name across the Anglophone world.

But for all the success of the alt-right in reaching the mainstream, as Tumblr-liberalism did, it remains, as Tumblr-liberalism has, an *elitist* formation. They may have helped catapult Trump to the White House, but 'behind the "populist" president, the rhetoric of his young online far-right vanguard had long been characterised by an extreme subcultural snobbishness toward the masses and mass culture.' It is this conception of the popular that underpins the shared problematic – the ordinary person is either an unreformed racist or a feminised loser, depending on which side you ask. The effect is to decisively undermine the currently circulating view that the socialist left should be re-branded as 'alt-left'. Nagle demonstrates that, if anything, the commonality lies in the other direction. But she, rightly, never goes so far as to make the move and dub Tumblr-liberalism the alt-left. It is implicit, although never adequately stated, that for all its weaknesses Tumblr-liberalism draws from emancipatory discourses. All the edgy gloss of the alt-right should not be permitted to conceal that it remains, by contrast, firmly anchored to a long tradition of dangerous reaction.

Jen Isakson and Ross Speer

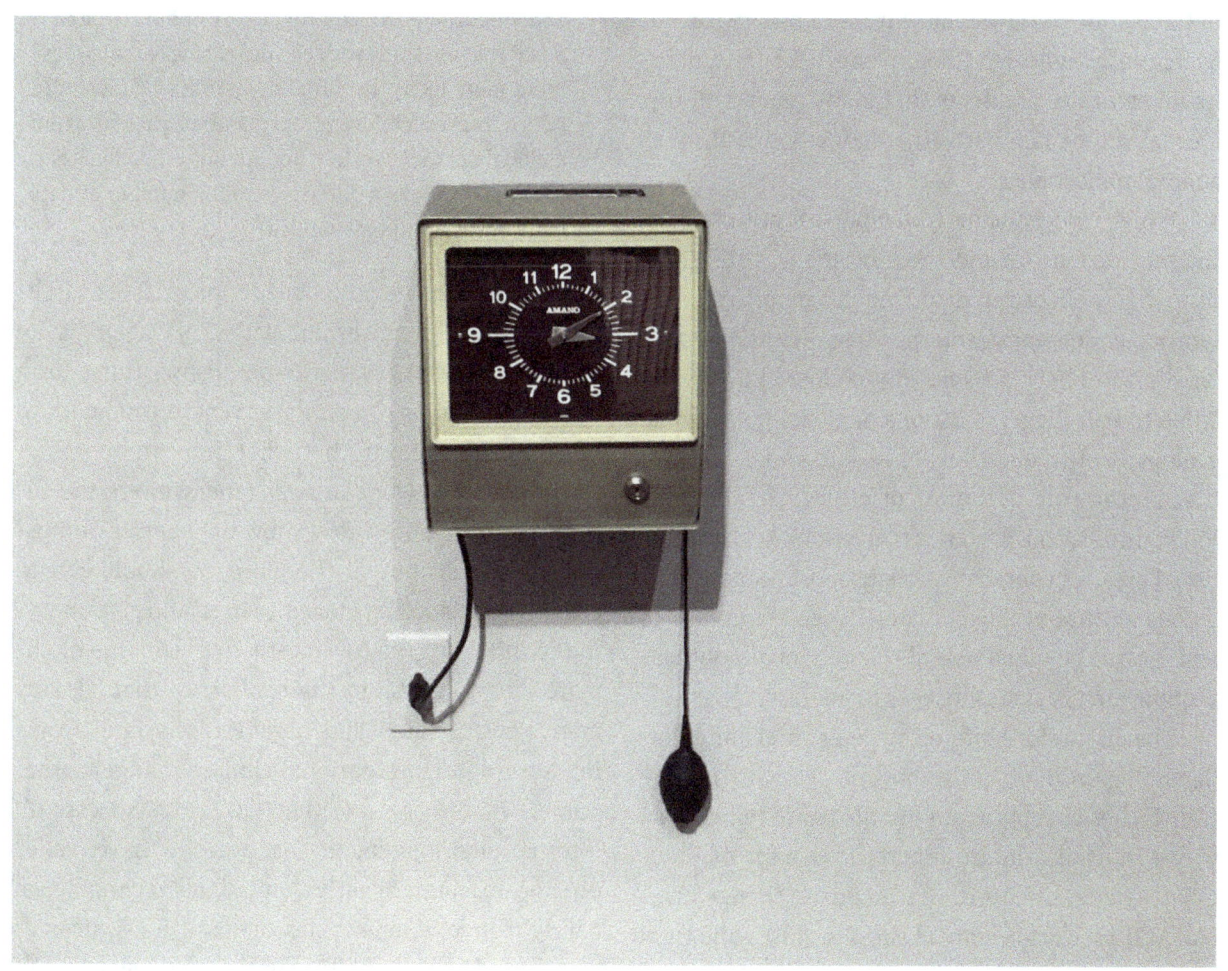

Must do better

William MacAskill, *Doing Good Better: Effective Altruism and a Radical New Way to Make a Difference* (London: Faber and Faber, 2015). 336pp., £8.99 pb., 978 1 78335 051 3

Peter Singer, *The Most Good You Can Do: How Effective Altruism Is Changing Ideas About Living Ethically* (New Haven: Yale University Press, 2015). 272pp., £14.99 hb., £12.99 pb., 978 0 30018 027 5 hb., 978 0 30021 986 9 pb.

The Effective Altruism (EA) movement stresses cost-effective philanthropy over carelessly throwing effort or money behind any old cause. It is motivated by the laudable, selfless desire to maximise global happiness. It might have been called 'Consequential Altruism' or even 'Consequentialist Altruism': it demands that any intervention be judged not by its deontology nor by the agent's virtue or otherwise, but by its consequences, its effectiveness. EA thus inherits many of the problems that many readers of this journal will be familiar with in consequentialism as a moral philosophy.

While it is possible to deeply admire many of the motivations behind the movement, and recognise that well-targeted individual giving can certainly have demonstrable positive effects, EA falls far short of offering a solution to global poverty, let alone to still-bigger questions of global politics and ecology – or to questions of how to choose to live; that is, the true questions of ethics. In its quest for quantification, EA tends to overlook key, foundational areas of concern – perhaps most notably dangerous anthropogenic climate change – and fails to appreciate the fundamental role of global political-economy in the issues it seeks to address.

The discussions offered by Peter Singer and William MacAskill of anthropogenic climate change throws these doubts about EA into sharp relief. Start with MacAskill. In an important chapter of *Doing Good Better* entitled 'Poverty vs climate change vs ...', MacAskill seeks to compare various causes and their scale, level of neglect and tractability. Of '2-4 degrees of climate change', he writes that its scale as a problem is 'fairly large'; the same level of scale he assigns to the issue of 'US criminal justice reform'. This is a catastrophic under-estimation. Four degrees of climate change would mean the end of the world as we know it; it would involve heat-waves in large land-masses for instance at 10 to 12 degrees centigrade above the hottest levels current. Of course, we don't know just how bad it would be; it could be much *worse* than this (or, indeed, less bad). It's simply not *measurable* in the way that EA prefers things to be. And it involves a constitutive time-lag; by the time the climate threat is fully measurable, it will be too late to stop it.

Now take Singer, who writes:

> [C]ompare climate change and malaria. On the basis of what the overwhelming majority of scientists in the [field] tell us, the need for an international agreement to reduce greenhouse gases is extremely urgent. There are, however, already many governments and organisations working toward getting such an agreement. It is difficult for private donors to be *confident* that anything they can do will make that agreement more likely. In contrast, distributing mosquito nets to protect children from malaria is, at least from a global perspective, less urgent, but individuals can more easily make a difference to the number of nets distributed. (emphasis added)

Singer's conclusion: tackle malaria, leave climate change to governments. This again is an epic fail (as well as a truly perplexing thing for a former Australian Green Party senate candidate to say). Notice the way that what one can be *confident of* skews Singer's answer (and skewers the future). We can more easily show the *number* of mosquito nets distributed: therefore, we should give to charities distributing mosquito nets, and give up trying to influence the too-big-to-succeed issue of climate. We can bask in the confidence that 'already many governments and organisations [are] working toward [an international climate change] agreement'. Ignore the fact that Paris, the 'successful' international agreement that we now have, relies on non-existent negative-emissions technologies, barely *mentions* renewables or fossil fuels, doesn't mention animal agriculture or the vast downsides of large-scale agrofuels, commits us, even on its own terms, to 3-4 degrees of global over-heat, and has literally no enforcement mechanisms.

The complacency of Singer's response to probably the greatest issue of our time makes one worry about what the effects of 'Effective Altruism' may actually be. The climate issue is *determinative*; it will either make possible or utterly undermine effective action on a host of other issues. The key methodological flaw here, and one that is common to much of EA, is the elision of 'effectiveness' with 'evidence-based'. It makes the EA methodology little better than the infamous drunk looking for his car keys where the streetlight happens to be shining. Lack of certainty should not be a reason to delay strong precautious action in the face of potential catastrophe; but EA cannot take the precautionary principle seriously, because of the dogmatic insistence upon evidence.

Focusing largely on health in the way that most EA does (a focus explicitly defended in MacAskill's book) is also hopelessly short-sighted; catastrophically so. EA largely occludes the systemic threats bearing down on us in favour of more visibly 'effective' interventions ultimately conceived of as interventions by individuals to help individuals. Consequently, EA tends to boil down largely to relatively short-term / manageable projects. (Life-projects are discussed, and I will come to this in a moment; but of course these are bound to be far harder to 'measure'.) Activities with long-term consequences tend to be eschewed in favour of such short-term projects. Failing to award climate change the premier global threat status it deserves, on the grounds of its being calculus-unfriendly, represents a grave discrimination against future generations. But perhaps this tacit 'moral future discount rate' is not entirely unexpected from a utilitarian model that is closely linked to classical economic theory.

Dealing only with extreme poverty as it exists *now* boils down to storing up a constant stream of emergent destitution into the future, rather than tackling its root causes. If philanthropy is solely focused on the most egregious manifestation of symptoms, then the underlying causes are allowed to fester and intensify. EA's fixation on the symptoms creates the impression that they arise spontaneously, and are not reflective of structural problems of the neoliberal socio-economic imaginary. In fact, geo-political and historical forces are chief causes of ongoing poverty in the Global South. Whether we are talking about land grabs, toxic waste dumping, labour and consumer exploitation from Western multinationals, massive environmental degradation, health impacts of resource plundering, local government corruption, ongoing regional conflicts, and the escalating environmental consequences of Western economic activity, all of these deep causes of poverty are unresolvable through scientistic philanthropy and single-issue projects. They require a deeper (philosophical) look and a harder (political) struggle. MacAskill's defence of carbon-offsetting as an allegedly affordable, allegedly potentially effective way for caring Western individuals to help deal with the climate crisis evinces an almost total failure to be willing to take such a look.

The point is that most of the causes of deep poverty (including, strikingly, anthropogenic climate change) are *structural* and can therefore only hope to be alleviated through systemic (global) measures. Such systemic thinking is what (real) politics is all about. But being holistic in one's approach, unfortunately, seems in practice inimical to EA, which is necessarily balkanised because of its 'evidence-based' nature. Singer in particular focuses almost exclusively on charity (i.e. on charities), and virtually ignores the bigger frame: political change.

At this point an EA-advocate would doubtless say that we should have an 'evidence-based politics'. Yet, while it is true that it would be a good thing for evidence to be less blithely ignored in politics, it would be a depoliticising disaster to substitute 'evidence-based politics' for real politics. Many of the problems we face are rooted in systematic uncertainties, of a type that 'evidence' alone cannot possibly deal with *effectively*. Any need whose causes or solutions are complex or political is thus likely to come out badly from an EA approach. In this sense, it is not only the case that, say, love and fellow-feeling (as opposed to the spirit of calculation) are important dimensions missing from the EA analysis, but that there are also 'harder' political dimensions that EA systematically misses. For example, if responsibility for sharing the 'burden' of refugees were more equitably shared then the political incentives to address the underlying drivers of displacement would be likely to increase – though not certainly so: there might be a political reaction instead, à la UKIP/Trump – regardless of how much fellow-feeling there was or is.

Perhaps the most crucial political lack in EA is its tendency not to question the overarching political-economic frame of (neo)liberal capitalist individualism. Singer's defence of capitalism on the grounds that it increases wealth misunderstands the grave consequences of inequality (on which, see Wilkinson and Pickett's 2010 book *The Spirit Level*); he ignores the value of community or society in itself. Instead, he likes a system which 'increases the ability of the rich to help the poor, and some of the world's richest people, including Bill Gates and Warren Buffett, have done precisely that, becoming, in terms of the amount of money given, the greatest effective altruists in human history.' Never mind that such wealth massively suborns democracy, nor that such inequality is intrinsically harmful. Similarly, consider MacAskill's extraordinary support for the unbelievable level of inequality involved in what we allow to accrue to entrepreneurs: quoting ultra-neoclassicist William Nordhaus favourably, MacAskill praises entrepreneurs for allegedly generating $50 for society for every $1 they take themselves. The conventionality of MacAskill's economics is matched by the conventionality of his admiration for 'conventional' (sic) agriculture – that is, for industrialised agriculture dependent on pesticides, artificial fertilisers etc.; agriculture that is leading towards a situation in which we have only about two generations worth of soil left. MacAskill attacks the movement for local food, and issues ill-informed calls to substitute foreign-grown tomatoes for home-grown ones, ignoring the possibility of a system-change which would, for instance, once more re-centre our food-production on what is seasonably growable, where we live. He signs up uncritically to an agenda of 'developmentality', looking forward to the replacement of agrarian societies by a 'universal' mode of industrial growth.

If this perhaps allows us to understand better why it is impossible for the likes of MacAskill to get the threat and causes of human-induced dangerous climate-change into focus, it also makes it easier to understand how he can make the extraordinary claim that sweatshops are the most humane form of employment for many people in the '3rd world'. His '1st-world' narrow-mindedness cannot conceive of any other future for most people in the world than that set out by the path of the industrial revolution. He quotes standard pro-growth economists of capitalism such as Krugman and Sachs singing hymns of praise to standard industrial-growth pathways in general and to sweatshops in particular. The idea that people in 'developing countries' might conceivably have been sold a false prospectus about what life in cities is like – or real alternative possibilities such as a Gandhian culture of self-reliance, or outright political revolution – is simply not considered. Nor, of course, once again, is the straight line between industrial growthism and looming climatic cataclysm.

The extent to which EA is thoroughly in hock to something remarkably akin to the standard capitalist industrial-growth model perhaps helps to explain also something EA has become famous for: recommending many people to take high-earning jobs in business or finance and give away much of their earnings to charity. The consequences of the career-consequentialism of EA are more startlingly visible still at a revealing moment in Singer's book when he writes that 'on a plausible reading of the relevant facts, at least some of the guards at Auschwitz were not acting wrongly', for nastier people still would have taken their places, if they hadn't nobly stepped forward to kill Jews 'humanely'. We see at a moment like this the depths to which the logic of the lesser evil – the logic of consequentialism, the logic of EA – will take one. It seems a long journey from the utopian aspirations of EA to an apologia for serving as a Nazi guard at Auschwitz. But, for one who accepts the logic of EA, it is apparently no distance at all.

It is admirable to be willing to break social norms to improve the lot of other beings, and encouraging that significant numbers of people are willing to give selflessly and systematically to others far away, and that they care enough to work to check that their money is used effectively. And for comparing the effectiveness of a few commensurable charities, EA is, as I have said, of use. Yet there needs to be far more thinking here on the relationship between effective altruism and effective *democracy*. Rich people can choose what they give to. Bill and Melinda Gates are not technology-neutral: their charitable work focuses on techno-fixes and ignores anthropogenic climate change. Indeed, its only major climate-change dimension, worryingly, is Gates's interest in buying up geo-engineering patents. I am not encouraged by MacAskill's warm words for those looking into this. At the very least, it is alarming that MacAskill seems almost to pass over what is by far the most vital element of the climate issue – namely, cutting down on our GHG-pollution of the atmosphere – in favour of carbon offsets on the one hand and reckless technophiliac enthusiasm for geo-engineering on the other. Doing good better? I think that philosophy can help us do much better than this.

Rupert Read

Gender without identities

Judith Roof, *What Gender Is, What Gender Does* (Minneapolis: University of Minnesota Press, 2016). 280 pp., £78.00 hb., £21.99 pb., 978 0 81669 857 8 hb., 978 0 81669 858 5 pb.

In queer theorist Annamarie Jagose's book, *Orgasmology* (2012), she argues that orgasm has been an overlooked aspect of queer critique. Part of a larger recent interrogation of queer theory's relationship to normativity, Jagose suggests that orgasm, often a seemingly normative aim of sex, has, for the most part, escaped the purview of queer thought. In turning to orgasm, Jagose also attempts to turn queerly to the stuff of sex without turning it into metaphors for queer kinship or sociality. Sticking with the material and literal orgasm, Jagose, in a challenging methodological move, insists that sexuality studies has difficulty thinking about sex outside of identity. There is a similar challenge in Judith Roof's recent rethinking of gender. In *What Gender Is, What Gender Does*, Roof suggests that gender is too tightly bound to identity – it is too often imagined as something that one can fashion, claim, or 'be'. She asks instead after what gender might be without subjectivity, offering readings of popular culture (television, film, celebrity) that decentre gender as a process of subjectification. She reads gender not through subjectivity but through a variety of other concepts, including the taxonomical, the ethical, the narratological, the temporal and the non-human. In this way, Roof aims to rearticulate gender away from 'masculinity and femininity', insisting on the non-binary, processual nature of gender. Genderings, for Roof, are 'infinite and perpetually changing'; not tied to 'any original theme or desire in subjects', nor in any way stable.

When Judith Butler published *Gender Trouble: Feminism and the Subversion of Identity* in 1990, it was, as goes without saying, a game changer. It both challenged the foundations of a feminism that seemingly required 'woman' as its political referent and helped to inaugurate the field of queer theory. In

Butler's conception, gender is a stylised repetition of acts, acts which both give the illusion of an internal truth and produce the subject as legible. Butler's thinking intervened in theories of subjectivity by insisting that the subject comes into being through gender, even as she suggested that there is no subject that 'does' gender; the doing is what produces the subject. It remains by far the most influential and most often cited text when it comes to theorising gender. Moreover, its ideas have crossed over from the academy into a more popular vernacular – most recently, Sasha Velour, the Season Nine winner of *RuPaul's Drag Race*, quoted Butler's ideas on the show. The degree to which Butler's theory of performativity has dominated the field of gender studies could hardly be overstated.

It is precisely in opposition to this dominance that Roof positions her work. As she asks in her introduction, what happens when performativity has become not 'a' way to think about gender, but 'the' way? In this, Roof seems less concerned with Butler's concept of gender performativity itself and more with its legacies, or with the various ways that her complex theory has been translated and taken up by others (particularly, it seems, non-academics). Part of Roof's concern is about the way in which performativity seems to bestow agency upon subjects – the crude interpretation of Butler that imagines gender's performativity means anyone can choose their gender at will. This, of course, has been something that Butler has, again and again, clarified, most notably in *Bodies that Matter: On the Discursive Limits of Sex* (1993). However, Roof suggests that performativity has so attached us to gender as an identity that we cannot see the way it exceeds this logic of 'being' or 'having'. Drawing on Gilles Deleuze and Félix Guattari, as well as Lacanian psychoanalysis, Roof suggests that a more systems-inspired model better gets at what gender is, or, better gets at gender outside of identity. She suggests that gender is a 'machinic process that perpetually reorganizes multiple sets of regimes and operations that link the psychic and the social.' Along with her suggestion that the legacies of performativity have resulted in gender being anchored to identity, her more machinic account of gender is meant to counter what she reads as performativity's production of gender as binary. For Roof, the conceptual problem with performativity is that it appears to be secondary to a subject's 'primary sexuation'; it is locked then within binary categories, even if these categories appear to be 'wieldable'. For Roof, Butler's theory of performativity too heavily tethers gender to binary sex, even as she aims to separate them as critical objects; gender remains, in some sense, 'masculinity and femininity', even as it becomes loosened from 'men and women'.

What feels unsatisfying in *What Gender Is, What Gender Does* is the way genders become at times untethered in Roof's work – a crude reading would summarise the book by saying that Roof multiplies the meaning of gender without an anchor or any political stakes. The bold warning at the end of the book's introduction seems to bear signs of this anxiety: 'MOST IMPORTANT, THIS IS NOT SIMPLY AN EXTENDED LIST OF CATEGORIES, NOR IS IT AN EXPANDED TAXONOMY.' Yet, Roof's theorisation lacks the anchor that heteronormativity provides for Butler's theories of performativity. In my understanding of Butler, heteronormativity is central to her analysis of gender – this is partly why her theory has been so influential for queer thinking. Her analysis is careful to connect gender with desire and sexuality, where heteronormativity is the driving factor behind the cultural demands for binary gender identity. For Butler, this is what gender does: binary gender produces the seeming naturalness and inevitability of heterosexuality (or, heteronormativity requires the production of binary gender). It is also this point that both makes genders something other than free-floating possibilities and connects gender to subjectification, producing heterosexual identity as the only recognisable subjectivity. In Roof's insistence that gender is neither identity nor binary, what is lost is the critique of heteronormativity that has been so generative from Butler's account. What do we get instead? In some sense, what we get is a thorough account of gender as non-binary. In this, Roof's repeated insistence that gender is a machinic process that is neither binary nor essential seems to come out of, and sit within, a contemporary mainstreaming of non-binary identity. As 'man' and 'woman' are increasingly displaced, rejected and forced open by queer, intersex and trans activists and theorists alike, it is as crucial a moment as any to keep thinking through what gender might be outside of 'masculinity' and 'femininity'. Indeed, as I write this, the singer/songwriter Pink has just given a speech at the MTV Music Awards in defence of her child's non-normative gender expression, which is being praised on multiple internet news outlets as a rallying cry for non-binary gender. 2017 also saw MTV rename its iconic 'Moonman' trophy the 'Moon Person' award, as well as erase all gender-specific awards categories in both its Music Awards and its Movie & TV Awards. Yet, these are not the discourses that Roof's work contributes to, precisely because she wants to wrest genders away from identity.

It becomes clear that the real target of Roof's work is not Butler, but those (mostly unnamed) others that are responsible for the legacies of Butler's work; those who insist on gender as an identity, particularly those, it seems, who are claiming identities outside of the binary. While there are, I think, good reasons to be sceptical of a neoliberal mode of subjectivity that privileges an 'I' that is seemingly 'free' to make itself (where this is always an imperative framed as a choice) – and Roof offers some insightful analyses of makeover paradigms in this regard – there is a deeply difficult refusal in Roof's work to engage with any of the seeming targets of her critique (those contemporary activists and theorists who are opening up binary gender identity). In a book that advocates gender as nonessential and non-binary, many will be surprised to find that Roof does not engage in any sustained way with trans theories or theorists. Instead, activist Riki Wilchins, author of *GenderQueer*, is made to stand in for all 'gender activists' and Jan Morris' now dated autobiography, *Conundrum* (1974), is made to speak to all trans people's experiences of gender. Had she engaged with any trans theorists, for instance, she might find that many of them are also deeply suspicious of a neoliberal model of subjectivity.

The particular violence of Roof's refusal to engage becomes most marked, however, in the concluding castigation of 'younger "queer" advocates' who, she charges, are misguided in their play with gender, attempting to 'shock ingrained structures out of existence by simply appearing to fly in the face of the surface signifiers by which they believe such structures persist.' Here, finally, are the stakes for Roof: 'Gender is a lure', a lure away from the problem of sexual difference. Playing around with signifiers and multiplying gender identities is imagined as a kind of distraction from the real and more difficult problem of sexual difference, which, for Roof, seems to name the real problems of asymmetries of power that 'continues no matter how liberated, proliferative, or varietal we might be about either gender or identity'. If sex becomes gender – as in Butler's suggestion that we take gender as a sign of sex, when in actuality sex is always-already gender (all there is is gender) – then 'play' with gender seems to destabilise the binary logic of sexual difference. Roof's project is to separate once and for all genders from sex. As Roof would have it, 'young "queers"' today are distracted with gender, thinking they are doing the work of dismantling sexual difference, when really they are playing with signs, subscribing to 'a fantasy of whisking away the symptoms of the binaries of which they seem oddly unaware.' Here though, we must take Roof at her word that 'they' are 'oddly unaware' – as nowhere do 'they' appear. Helpfully though, Roof lists all the things that 'they' don't know: anything of patriarchy, anything of capitalism or anything of politics (specifically the Fourteenth Amendment of the US constitution). It becomes difficult, in the end, to salvage the more convincing aspects of Roof's arguments, entrenched as they become in a generational admonition of what she sees as the failures of a younger, contemporary gender activism and queer politics; a politics caricatured but never engaged in dialogue.

Robyn Wiegman writes in *Object Lessons* of the desires attached to 'gender' as a critical object, tracing in particular the way in which 'gender' has supplanted 'woman' in university departments and centres across the US – where the shift itself is meant to achieve something, desire attaches to 'gender studies' as being able to do work that 'women's studies' cannot. More broadly though, she asks after the kinds of desires invested in critical terms and objects: what is it that we want or think 'gender' can do? I kept thinking about Wiegman's insights as I was reading Roof's book. In Wiegman is a suggestion that asking gender to 'do' anything tells us as much about the desires we invest in critique as it does anything about gender. Here, what gender 'is' might also then be a critical term that is invested with certain desires for political transformation, or, a paradigm that is invested with the desires to make certain lives more liveable. Roof's evisceration of the politics of gender performativity, in the end, falls flat. A book dedicated to describing and reworking gender is finally offered as a book that will take us back to sexual difference – yet what this might look like remains unclear. In a book that painstakingly describes, and yes, endlessly lists and taxonomises genders, Roof hopes that this 'better' description of gender will do the work of refocusing us back on sexual difference. But description, in the end, just feels like description, and the politics of this project seem to end here – leaving me thinking less about the problem of sexual difference and more about the ongoing desires we have for gender to do so much work.

Sam McBean

Move it

Bojana Cvejić, *Choreographing Problems: Expressive Concepts in European Contemporary Dance and Performance* (Houndmills: Palgrave Macmillan, 2015). 280pp., £58.00 hb., £22.50 pb., 978 1 13743 738 9 hb., 978 1 34955 610 6 pb.

A generation of recent artists have shared the conviction that choreography and dance think. Bojana Cvejić's book seeks both to theorise and defend this conviction. Such artists could defy Susan Sontag's argument against 'assimilat[ing] Art to Thought' because the thinking that they wanted to see was very different from those clichés that Sontag had declared herself sick of in the 1960s ('Phallus', 'Oedipus', 'Decline of the West', and so on). While, however, the Deleuzian critique of 'recognition' provided, for instance, one influential way to escape Sontag's false alternative between thought and feeling, it could only provide a negative criterion for the kind of thinking that art can do. The frustration of recognition is not in itself thoughtful. As Cvejić rightly notes, we need other concepts, positive concepts, therefore, if we are going to understand what is going on in contemporary choreography. Elaborating one such concept is Cvejić's primary achievement in *Choreographing Problems*: what she calls 'problem-posing'.

Take, for example, Jonathan Burrows and Jan Ritsema's *Weak Dance Strong Questions* (2001). The germ of the piece was a line of poetry: 'neither movement from nor towards'. The first problem is then: how to imagine such a movement. As an initial approach, let us say we're trying to imagine a movement without spatial or temporal structure; or, again, to imagine 'a movement that internalises "the still point"', as Cvejić puts it. This first line of experimentation is imaginative, and the fantasies that it produces constitute, in this way, the starting point for a new problem: how to actually move, work it out in dance. A third problem superposes itself, however, on the first and second. Here, the negated 'from' and 'towards' reveal another aspect of themselves, not as spatio-temporal but rather as syntactic operators. What kind of teleology is involved in the notion of a 'phrase'? Does a phrase go 'towards' punctuation? What kind of punctuation? Burrows and Ritsema ask themselves: If every movement is a statement, is it possible to ask a question by moving? What makes it possible to ask a question? They begin hollowing out the implicit enunciative dimension of their movements, making room for deviations from an assertoric mode.

The artists translate this third problem into two rules, both prohibitive: their movements will not be mere tasks to accomplish, and they will also not become statements. Because the artists are now focused on the refusal of aesthetic teleology in dance (with all of the accent given to the 'towards'), improvisational dance seems to become a crucial part of the 'solution'. But this solution creates the same problem: the dancers must resist their own tendencies 'towards' remembered forms and gestures while improvising. By this point, their research itself becomes problematic, as they resist the tendency to reuse the movements that they discover. So, again, this new problem generates new rules for side-stepping the automatisms that keep turning their movements into tasks or statements. Burrows and Ritsema write rules *ad personam*, specific to the sorts of automatisms that each of them slip into. Starting from the initial citation, a series of new problems, questions and rules unfolds, progressively determining the conditions of the performance.

Weak Dance Strong Questions is an unusually simple case in one respect. A single, continuous process of problematisation seems to encompass both the making and the performing of the work. That the performers are the same people as the choreographers is irrelevant here. The point is that, under this unusual improvisational protocol, the performance is just further research (endless, progressless, amnesiac research) into the same problem that Burrows and Ritsema began with. But problem-posing doesn't always take the form of research or questioning.

Ezster Salamon's *Nvsbl* provides a good counterpoint in this respect. The performers of the piece are faced with the problem of producing a smooth movement that is too slow to be seen, and even too slow to be felt. At this duration, it's actually impossible to produce a continuous, smooth movement through a continuous, smooth effort. The performers learn to produce an appearance of continuity through a multiplicity of minute fragmented flashes of attention, by imagining sensations rather than by willing movement. At the same time, the audience members are faced with other problems. For one thing, they have to learn to perceive on a new time-scale (which means looking away, covering their eyes, and so on). But the more radical problem is that they are prevented from performing the function traditionally assigned to them (that of seeing) within the theatrical division of labour between display and spectatorship. As such, *Nvsbl* poses distinct problems for its audience and for its performers, and these problems are also distinct from those through which it was created. However, all three activities are processes of problem-posing.

This example allows us to see just what it means, for Cvejić, that a performance or choreography *thinks*. The point is not that the work articulates a thought, or that it is thought-provoking, but rather that performing it or attending its performance involves posing specific problems, and that the creating it involved posed other problems. In homage to Spinoza, the author dubs the processes of making, performing and attending the 'modes' of the performance. The performance itself comes into being only through these three 'parallel' processes of problem-posing. Cvejić refuses to subordinate performing to making as copy to model, or attending to performing as perception to reality. Every performance emerges three times at once. Consequently, for Cvejić, thinking is a process. More specifically, it is a process of emerging (as opposed to decaying, disappearing). This is a book about art that thinks primarily about the way the art is made - not as a supplement, ancillary to more serious questions of meaning or form, but because art thinks, and because art only thinks through its emergence.

The genesis of a work has no place in aesthetics, which, as its name suggests, thinks art in terms of the perceptual encounter with a finished work. However, Cvejić is not concerned with the artwork as object of perception, judgment or thought. Instead, *Choreographing Problems* is a poetics, in the sense that it is a book about the process of *making* (*poïesis*). Still, it is an unusual poetics. In the western philosophical tradition, *poïesis* has most often been understood teleologically. Aristotle's *Poetics*, for example, subordinates the process of making to fixed genres (e.g. tragedy) and their proper functions (e.g. catharsis). Marx's architect, like an Aristotelian carpenter, starts from the idea of the chair. As he writes in *Capital*: 'What distinguishes the worst architect from the best of bees is this, that the architect raises his structure in imagination before he erects it in reality. At the end of every labour-process, we get a result that already existed in the imagination of the labourer at its commencement.' The teleological frame thus disjoins imagination and process: the architect imagines before the labour-process begins, and the bees labour without imagination. By contrast, to get an idea of the idea of *poïesis* at stake in *Choreographing Problems*, we would have to conceive of an artwork that thinks through its emergence.

Cvejić's book has two main ambitions. On the one hand, it is a poetics of problem-posing, and, on the other, it attempts to articulate the condition of contemporary choreography in general. This latter ambition goes, of course, beyond the seven pieces Cvejić analyses in detail in *Choreographing Problems* itself. Since the end of the 1990s (with, of course, some antecedents), choreography has been grappling with what the author calls the 'body-movement bind', or the 'organic regime in dance'. This regime is specific to the twentieth century, and determines two antithetical positions within it. The organic regime emerged when modernism reinvented dance as self-expression. This reinvention was so influential that in subsequent generations even non-dancers grew up with it. Even today, dance is a key ideological operator in popular culture and the construction of the self. That's why it is worth insisting on its originality with respect to the preceding centuries. On the surface, one could see some common ground between *Sturm und Drang* in theatre and modernism in dance, where, too, form broke with classical convention to become the organic expression of raw emotion. In *Sturm und Drang*, these emotions still belonged to the characters presented – not necessarily to the author or the actor – whereas, for modern subjects, dance expresses the emotion of the dancer him- or herself. Indeed, more radically, it expresses the dancer's individuality, which is thus identified with his or her body.

Cvejić calls this the 'organic regime of dance' because movement is supposed to emerge spontaneously from the body as locus of individuality. Such an idea of self-expression allowed body and movement to be treated as one medium rather than two. The body expressed itself in movement, and movement expressed the self. The critique of this ideology leaves us with 'a new condition', Cvejić argues, a 'set of minor questions as to how, why, when and in which case the body should move, if it is to move at all - which is conspicuously at odds with the prolific dance culture of self-expression and auto-affection in entertainment and social media.' I move because I'm at work, because it's cold, because the bar is closing, or because I am taking care of somebody. In such cases, the unity of body and movement is compulsory. The heteronomy of bodies is beyond remedy.

A second form of the 'body-movement bind' manages to ground the autonomy of the artwork in the supposed autonomy of form. Thus, in 1960s and 1970s postmodern dance, the body becomes an instrument *of* a movement, rather than the other way around. The relationship between body and movement is reversed, but the unity of the two is re-established. As such, self-expression and formalism, modern and postmodern dance, are, for Cvejić, two ways of maintaining the same body-movement bind. Her crucial move is then to show that contemporary European choreography – not only in the seven pieces she analyses, but in an extended list including BADco, La Ribot, Antonia Baehr and others – breaks with both forms of the body-movement bind. Its medium is no longer the unity of body and movement, but their disjunction; the field of all possible disjunctions between them, all the delays, phasings, discordances, artifices, questions and experimental constructions that compose or disjoin them.

Every analysis in *Choreographing Problems* begins with a virtuosic description, which is addressed, like Diderot's *Salons*, to those who couldn't be there.

The same goes for the compact lessons provided on the history of choreography that punctuate it. In this way, the book functions simultaneously as a philosophical intervention and as a textbook. Among its other achievements, the book should be able to give readers in thirty years a sort of historical experience of the period in question. It is partly for this reason that, reading *Choreographing Problems*, one feels out of time. However, there are other reasons, too. Since this is a book about *European* contemporary dance, it is worth recalling that the subprime crisis, and the sovereign debt crises that followed it, developed over the time of this book's composition from 2007-2012. The funding cuts and wave of precaritisation that ensued have changed the possibilities of artistic production in Europe, and will continue to do so. None of the performances analysed in the book were more than nine years old in 2007, when Cvejić began work on the project, and the most recent, Mette Ingvartsen's *It's in the Air*, had made its debut only a few months before. But today, they all belong to the near past, between ten and twenty years ago; not 'now' but 'just now'. This recent past saw the emergence of a new 'set of practices' and a new 'method of creating', which the author theorises and names 'problem-posing', and whose implications she pushes to the limit. But what is the relationship between these practices and this period? One might answer that problem-posing can never become 'dated' because it will always remain a possibility for choreography. In that case, it belongs to its period insofar as it originated there, but transcends it as a possibility. I wonder if we can be happy with this answer, however, which hitches the autonomy of art to the hot air balloon of possibility. At the very least, it provokes the following (productive) doubt: what if, since 2007, these practices have not had a future, or have not yet had a future? What if we have been unable to maintain the conditions that made them possible? What were those conditions?

Cvejić is a powerful thinker of the geneses of works of art, which are classically considered irrelevant to aesthetics, but, when it comes to endings, she is very oblique. Perhaps this is her Deleuzian side: to see more that is remarkable in the emergence of a thing than in its ending. The last chapter of the book promises to inventory the legacy of problem-posing post-2007: 'As I write these lines, six years after this project began…' The tendencies and works she goes on to mention continue to problematise live presence and the theatrical apparatus, but none of them, so far as I can tell, carry on with problem-posing as a method of creation. The crucial afterward that would explain and give the measure of this absence is missing.

Austin Gross

Gridlock!

Rosie Warren, ed., *The Debate on* Postcolonial Theory and the Specter of Capital (London and New York: Verso, 2016). 304pp., £60.00 hb., £19.99 pb., 978 1 78478 696 0 hb., 978 1 78478 695 3 pb.

'To leave error unrefuted is to encourage intellectual immorality.' Attributed to Karl Marx, this dictum prefaced E.P. Thompson's infamous 1978 polemic against Louis Althusser, *The Poverty of Theory*, but it might equally have adorned the opening pages of Vivek Chibber's 2013 book *Postcolonial Theory and the Specter of Capital* (hereafter *PTSC*). The conceptual and empirical errors Chibber was out to refute belonged to a number of historians and political theorists gathered around the journal *Subaltern Studies*, which was formed in the early 1980s and initially dedicated to its own form of Gramscian-infused 'history from below' that aimed at displacing both colonialist and elitist historiographies of Indian nationalism. In *PTSC*, arguments made by Ranajit Guha, Dipesh Chakrabarty and Partha Chatterjee were consecutively reconstructed and dismissed as inadequate attempts to theorise the relation between power and capital in a global perspective that at times would tend toward cultural essentialism. With its focus on historiography and historical sociology, Chibber's intervention read both as an echo of and compliment to Aijaz Ahmad's 1992 *In Theory: Classes, Nations, Literatures*, which explicitly challenged the forms of 'theory' that had prevailed, especially in comparative literature departments, in the wake of Edward Said's *Orientalism*. Disciplines (and transdisciplinary objects) are important here, since the polemics against postcolonial theory often come with the charge of unwarranted generalisations and obfuscating transpositions of linguistic registers. As Chibber frames it, the most problematic issues with 'subaltern historiography' stem from an opposition to the 'naïve' global extension of analytic categories generated in a specifically 'Western' context. In a dispute where both sides have seemed intent on 'bending the stick' to straighten up the theory, how one defines 'naïvety' itself is both crucial and, in part, what is being fought over.

Aside from acerbic comments about 'High Theory', Thompson, Ahmad and Chibber shared another concern: the easily inveigled youths of grad schools who, then as now, were incapable of resisting the temptations of convoluted language and complicated ideas with ties to French philosophers. In Chibber's case, the cure is presumably to be found in a clearheaded and rational(istic) rundown of the central arguments, a quick assessment of their empirical premises and the big reveal of 'inconsistency', designed to bring us all back from follies of subjectivation, traces, archives, traditions and erasure to a more tangible conception of 'class'. The standout response to Thompson remains Perry Anderson's book-length reply, *Arguments within English Marxism* (1980). In the case of *PTSC*, its publication was followed by a centre-stage confrontation between Chibber and Chatterjee at a *Historical Materialism* conference in New York (April 2013), picking up on a panel at the launch of the book at another *HM* conference in Delhi earlier that month. Lines were sharply drawn in the ensuing online and printed responses and the tone seemed to tend irreparably towards disdain on both sides: those defending the subaltern historians, or the different lineages of postcolonial theory, and those congratulating Chibber on having composed the final 'riposte' against their supposedly corrupting effects. Nonetheless, Chibber's critique carved out a space marked by a number of important questions. First, is the globalisation of capital relations co-extensive with their universalisation? And, second, how does our grasp of this possible overlap affect the traction and translatability of theoretical frames grounded in certain streams of the European Enlightenment?

With such questions in mind, a collection of review essays, symposium papers and previously published commentaries has now been published by Verso (the publishers of Chibber's original book). The stated purpose of the collection, edited by Rosie Warren, is to bring together 'the major critics of Chibber's work to assess the efficacy of his arguments from differing perspectives'. With little done to alter or elaborate the pieces for this publication, a great deal of space is given over to reiterations of the argument Chibber originally presented, concerning what he considered to be mistaken assumptions regarding the specificities of colonial capitalism reflected in the work of the Subaltern Studies historians. This might be fair, given that the ambition of the collection is a recapitulation not an elaboration. But then the question becomes whether this is really a debate worthy of so *much* unelaborated recapitulation.

The book is structured in sixteen chapters divided into three parts and prefaced by Achin Vaniak's introduction to the debate, its context and the central claims that sparked it. As another opening feature, a fairly fawning interview with Chibber from *Jacobin* is reprinted – in which the drive-home point is that the manner in which the Subaltern Studies historians conceptualise the difference between 'East' and 'West' (Chibber's terms) entails an endorsement (however unintended) of 'the kind of essentialism that colonial authorities used to justify their depredations in the nineteenth century.' Of the book's three parts, the first is presented as the debate proper, with responses by Chatterjee, Gayatri Chakravorty Spivak and Bruce Robbins contrasted in each instance with Chibber's reply. Name calling is ample and tiresome, and Chibber fares no better than his critics; to lament the tone of an academic debate while calling the replies offered by your opponents 'hysterical' and 'shrill' frankly doesn't cut it. The second part gathers the scholarly and mostly careful papers from a review symposium dedicated to *PTSC* (previously published in *Journal of World-Systems Research*), while the third consists of slightly longer articles and reviews framed as 'commentaries'.

The core concerns of the debate can be gathered

in three clusters, each centred on a specific question. First, how might we trace the lineage of postcolonial theory and relate this lineage to the possible cohesion of a field of inquiry with a distinct vocabulary and methodology? In other words: what do we mean when we talk about postcolonial theory? Second, within a broadly construed Marxist perspective, how are we to understand the globalisation of generalised commodity production and its relation to universalist political categories and terms of analysis – especially regarding the distinctions to be drawn between the globalisation of the wage relation, the homogenisation of labour conditions and the notion of bourgeois hegemony? Third, to what extent does Chibber's own form of social theory, counterposed as it is to the arguments he reconstructs and denies, provide an adequate frame by which to address global capitalism, with its high tolerance towards (or even reproduction of) so called 'cultural difference'?

The first of these – the lineage of postcolonial theory – is perceived by the contributors, subject to affiliation, either as a red herring or a central issue. Several of the responses (notably Spivak's, Robbins's and Timothy Brennan's) give a much needed, if cursory, map of the histories of (as well as overlaps and divides between) anti-colonial Marxists, the Subaltern Studies group and post-colonial theory as it took shape largely in Anglo-American comparative literature departments. The chronology of theoretical influences matters, but as George Steinmetz suggests in his contribution, a title like *The Subaltern School of History and the Specter of Capital* certainly has less panache and would probably have created much less of a response.

The questions posed in relation to the second issue – that of the relation between the globalisation of the wage relation, the homogenisation of labour conditions and the notion of bourgeois hegemony – grapple directly with Chibber's critique of Guha, Chatterjee and Chakrabarty. Since Chibber's argument (brutally reduced) is composed first as a critique of Guha and then, in different forms, as a critique of derivative claims based on Guha's initial assumptions, I'll limit this summary to Chibber's assessment of the work in question: Guha's 1997 *Dominance without Hegemony*. Here, Guha proposes that the specificity of capitalist modernity in India might be grasped in terms of the dominance of a subaltern class without a political and ideological hegemony on the part of a national bourgeoisie, contrasting this with a standard image of bourgeois hegemony at the inception of European modernity.

The notion of dominance without hegemony also reflected Guha's proposition from the first edition of the *Subaltern Studies* journal, of a structural dichotomy between the politics of the subaltern classes and the politics of a national bourgeois elite which in no way should entail a conception of the former as 'pre-political'. Chibber counters this argument by insisting that even in Europe the bourgeoisie did not attain the form of hegemony Guha alludes to and that, paradoxically, the counter-image of the 'Western' achievement of liberal democracy and political freedoms misrepresents and elides the role of working-class struggles in the realisation of this political change. In short, Chibber attributes an essentially Whiggish conception of the English and French bourgeois revolutions to Guha, arguing that this impedes the validity of his claims regarding (a lack of) hegemony in the Indian context.

The central term of the debate here is that of capital's universalising 'drive', or 'tendency', and the question that of how this drive is to be conceived in relation to proclaimed universalist political projects. The degree to which Guha and others were dependent upon an implicit comparative historical method to make claims of historico-geographical difference with regard to how this drive was realised largely structures the exchanges. A certain blurring of terms between capital and capitalism, capitalists and bourgeoisie is unfortunate here (as Spivak also notes), and perhaps also what colours the lack of clarity regarding the distinctions and mediations between the subjects of political actions and the subject(s) of economic relations.

In fact, the category of the subject is largely absent from the debate altogether, and perhaps an explicit reckoning with it might have brought a bit more clarity to matters at hand. With Chatterjee's defence of Guha, it becomes clear that both sides speak past each other, as the former flatly denies the validity of Chibber's critique by arguing that 'getting one's European history right is not the magic formula that will solve the problems of historical change in the non-Western world.' On this issue, especially, Willian H. Sewell, Jr's measured (but again, brief) commentary on the historiography of the bourgeois revolutions functions as a good mediator by emphasising that perhaps the best way to 'provincialize Europe' is to insist that it, too, consists of a number of provinces, nations and histories.

On the final issue, regarding Chibber's only proposal for an adequate form of social theory, several of the symposium papers criticise the appeal to a modified analytic Marxism espoused by Chibber; the prominent term of derision here being 'rational choice Marxism'. The rather bombastic call in *PTSC* for a twofold 'universal history' – a history of capital and one of worker struggles read as the expression of a struggle for the fulfillment of basic needs and rationally-comprehensible interests – wasn't fully worked out therein, nor was it of course intended to be (although if his recent article 'Rescuing Class from the Cultural Turn', is anything to go by, this is a task he will take on in time to come). But the claim that there is an unbridgeable gulf between postcolonial theory and Marxism (or, between identity politics and class struggle) is one we've heard before; Ahmad's 1992 book is a case in point.

The current volume does much to elucidate the terms of this 'debate' but little to push the stakes further. The exception is the final (and by far the longest) essay by Viren Murthy. Here, the limitation that one faces when insisting on either side of a dichotomy between postcolonial theory and Marxism is skilfully sidestepped in an immanent critique of both Chibber and Chakrabarty that interrogates their respective conceptions of capitalism by way of value-form theorist Moishe Postone. Unfortunately, as a whole however, if the criteria of assessment for intellectual debates should go beyond leaving either side with a sense of having been both misunderstood and right all along, the Chibber debate offers, in the end, only a limited contribution.

Marie Louise Krogh

Remain in light

Finn Brunton and Helen Nissenbaum, *Obfuscation: A User's Guide for Privacy and Protest* (Cambridge, MA: MIT Press, 2015). 136pp., £16.95 hb., 978 0 26202 973 5

Since the beginnings of Enlightenment era struggles against absolutism, one of the most prominent concerns of progressive politics has been to tear away the veils concealing the operation of power. Publicity and openness have long been the overriding values in Western democracies and, although they do not necessarily take a liberal form, such ideals are now deeply ingrained. Political discourse constantly references the importance of 'transparency', while suspicious publics are ever vigilant with regard to the secret machinations of their representatives. At the same time, a competing tendency, according to which progressives and radicals strove to protect privacy and foster secrecy, has been equally important but arguably less prominent. In the early days of Enlightenment, those with unorthodox ideas needed to be sheltered from scrutiny; thinking against the grain required the space to do so. Thus, Habermas has described how in the eighteenth century it was from within the private space of the family that the bourgeoisie set out into the newly formed public sphere. Perhaps the most striking example of this strand of opacity is the way Masonic lodges promoted equality and Enlightenment partly through ritualised secrecy, helping to undermine the status quo from Bavaria to Haiti as they did so. Rather than ever-increasing illumination, then, modern struggles for liberty and progress began with a combination of transparency *and* obstruction.

Contemporary conditions appear to call with increasing urgency for a renewal of the latter part of this equation. The Snowden revelations concerning the extent of government surveillance capabilities and, at a more mundane level, the unprecedented capacity for corporate giants such as Facebook and Google to harvest our data are well known. Awareness is one thing, however, knowing how to respond quite another. Many are not concerned at all – shocking as the Snowden revelations were, 'if you've done nothing wrong, you have nothing to fear' is the easiest response. It is easier still to surrender 'our' data as we access social media or shop online. In keeping with the more obvious appeal of publicity and popular determination to see behind the veil, perceived obfuscation and mendacity by elites incur far greater popular ire than these incursions on our privacy.

As Finn Brunton and Helen Nissenbaum point out, the problem is that when it comes to the politics of knowledge most of us are on the wrong side of a massive epistemic asymmetry. Our relative lack of power arises not only, or even predominantly, from the way information is concealed, but also from the fact that the data we produce as we shop, socialise, travel and work – as we do just about anything, in fact – is collected and analysed using methods and in pursuit of ends which remain mysterious to all but a few experts. Complex algorithms use data harvested from everyday activity to determine our access to insurance, credit, housing, healthcare. As the authors put it: '"They" know much about us, and we know little about them or what they can do.' We know even less about the uses to which this data might be put in the future by actors who may not yet exist. In many respects, as the authors point out, the result is a prison from which it is hard to see any possibility of escape. There is little prospect of grand acts of resistance, and 'opting out' is, for most, simply not realistic. We seem to have little choice but to allow ourselves to be subjected to constant scrutiny using methods which we cannot hope to understand – a fact which perhaps explains the apathetic reaction of many to invasions of privacy.

If we are to retain our dignity and autonomy under these conditions, Brunton and Nissenbaum argue, we must look to 'weapons of the weak'. The forms of resistance most easily adopted, and therefore most likely to prove effective, are 'foot-dragging, slowdowns, feigned ignorance, deliberate stupidity, and the pretence of compliance.' A significant source of such humble but revolutionary – and, as the book shows, frequently ingenious – action lies in 'obfuscation', the essence of which is 'getting overlooked and adding to the cost, trouble, and difficulty of doing the looking'. This is the quintessential tactic of those who cannot avoid being observed.

The first part of this 'user's guide' provides examples of obfuscation drawn from nature, military strategy, espionage and technology. It opens with a description of World War II planes using 'chaff' to confuse radar: an Allied plane could not avoid being detected, but by dropping hundreds of pieces of foil it could become one dot among many on a Nazi radar screen. In the natural world, the orb-weaving spider must spin a large web if it is to eat but in doing so exposes itself to attack from predatory wasps. Its response is not to fight or to build shelter, but the more efficient solution of creating decoy spiders from silk and leaves. Like the plane or the spider, we cannot avoid exposing ourselves to surveillance. Like them, however, we are in a position to make life difficult for those watching us. In the context of gross epistemic asymmetry, data obfuscation represents a realistic means of defending privacy. Through obfuscation we can retain some dignity and autonomy, along with some hope of expressing dissent or concealing resistance. Nissenbaum herself has designed the TrackMeNot browser extension, which obfuscates in the face of attempts to observe the user's search history or mine it for data. Rather than relying on encryption or concealment, the program generates a stream of random searches in which the genuine are lost. Other examples include FaceCloak, which hides genuine social connections from Facebook by producing a plausible 'non-person', and Anonymouth, a tool for anonymous authors to avoiding stylometric identification by producing 'statistically bland prose.'

Part II of the guide deals with the implementation and justification of obfuscation. Chapter three describes our contemporary informational asymmetry, whilst drawing on James C. Scott's account of power relations in a Malaysian village to explain why obfuscation is necessary. The authors are rightly careful not to push the comparison too far, but use Scott to support their claim that in the face of power asymmetries the weak must often rely on modest forms of resistance. The book's fifth chapter presents a series of questions through which potential users might determine what kind of obfuscation they need. In keeping with the practical purposes of the book,

Brunton and Nissenbaum emphasise that successful obfuscation must be highly sensitive to context and purpose: do you want to buy time, cover your tracks or conceal your identity? Your answer to such questions should shape the tools you employ.

The most complex questions are addressed in chapter four, which considers how obfuscation can be justified. The authors' primary aim is clearly to provide those practicing and designing obfuscation with a ready means of responding to objections that they are engaged in antisocial, destructive behaviour through free-riding on online communities or using up valuable bandwidth. Rawls' maximin principle provides a neat response to such criticisms: in assessing data practices we should favour those which maximise the position of the worst off; the status quo clearly does not meet this requirement and obfuscation is therefore justified. Perhaps more insightful, however, is the suggestion that informational asymmetry involves a violation of autonomy of the kind described by Philip Petit in his account of republican freedom. On this view, obfuscation is justified because we are currently subjected to the arbitrary will of those who control data collection and analysis and, as a result, are not truly free.

Perhaps because of the concern to be concise and practical, the book rarely ventures beyond the possessive and distributive epistemology that has come to represent an article of information age common sense. Knowing involves holding information and transmitting it from actor to actor, and obfuscation appears as a strategic move in a field structured by the circulation of data. This is, of course, an at least partly true representation of our current predicament. However, it risks marginalising those aspects of obfuscation which might involve the assertion of a fundamentally different subjectivity to that imposed by the data-harvesters. The power asymmetries identified in the book are not simply a matter of the possession and control of information; they relate to the very nature of the subjectivity available to us. Before information can circulate, be fought over or distributed, individuals must be moulded into the right kinds of actors and their relationships, actions and preferences rendered into fungible data – into exchange values. This occurs at the cost of their autonomy, individuality and spontaneity. Obfuscation is potentially an act of resistance in the face of this process, rather than a strategic move on the pre-existing terrain of information. The dangers of pursuing obfuscation in the absence of such considerations are apparent in Brunton and Nissenbaum's concern that Anonymouth's 'statistically bland prose' would prevent the emergence of a modern Tom Paine. Nevertheless, by reviving a tradition of progressive opacity, *Obfuscation*'s call to throw sand in the gears shows the degree to which we can turn systems of data-mining against themselves and begin to exercise the autonomy which they serve to supress.

Matthew Fluck

Blinded by surveillance

Simone Browne, *Dark Matters: On the Surveillance of Blackness* (Durham, NC and London: Duke University Press, 2015). ix+213pp., £70.00 hb., £19.99 pb., 978 0 82235 919 7 hb., 978 0 82235 938 8 pb.

Surveillance is not blind. Massive, generalised and indiscriminate surveillance might nowadays be pervasive, but the blanket nature of some surveillance practices should not make us forget that they are governed by specific purposes, and that they produce distinct impacts in relation to race and gender. Surveillance is not fortuitous, and its technologies are not neutral, undiscerning or colourless. Simone Browne's *Dark Matters: On the Surveillance of Blackness* documents the non-blindness of surveillance with vibrant detail. It bridges the (cosmic) gap between the fields of surveillance and black studies, guided by a cultural studies' will to embrace potentially anything as a source of edifying light. Bringing into her discussion heterogeneous historical records, contemporary art and Hollywood blockbusters, the book travels through the history of black lives under surveillance, so illuminating its connections with anti-black racism. Indeed, *Dark Matters* connects the roots of surveillance itself with the transatlantic slave trade, drawing parallels between Michel Foucault's reading of Jeremy Bentham's notorious prison model, the Panopticon, with the plan of the Brooks, a slave ship. It links *The Book of Negroes,* as cardinal archive of fugitive slaves, to the contemporary regulation of mobilities, and traces the ties between lantern laws in eighteenth-century New York City and the disciplining force of hypervisibility, as well as between slave branding and biometric border technologies.

All these accounts are used to display what Browne calls 'racialising surveillance', that is, enactments of surveillance that reify boundaries along racial lines, potentially resulting in discriminatory and violent treatment. Racialising surveillance would not just be surveillance that sorts out, but an exercise of power that reifies race, as well as possibly gender – the surveillance that puts things in a certain order and a racialised order in place. As a mirroring concept, she mobilises the notion of a dark *sousveillance*, which would relate to those tactics used to move out of sight, the strategies underpinning a flight to freedom, and, more generally, the charting of modes to respond to, challenge or confront surveillance. Yet, *Dark Matters* also aims to do more than throw light on all these issues. It argues that the very genealogy of surveillance is grounded in blackness, and that its historical foundation is contained inside the historical foundation of slavery. Surveillance is in truth the fact of antiblackness, Browne contends, alleging that an understanding of the ontological conditions of blackness is thus integral to developing any general theory of surveillance. The argument is as illuminating as it is provocative, albeit built, in part, upon some obscure assumptions, and occasionally casting some deep shadows.

It is unclear, for instance, why any coupling of slavery and surveillance should primarily be settled on American chattel slavery, disregarding any other of its previous and later manifestations, most notably Roman slavery. The life of Roman slaves is conceivably at least as equally suited to portray the embodiment of life without freedom and to testify to the inscription of the commodification and disciplining of human beings not only on and through their bodies, but also through other means, including the architecture and practice of law. Roman law, indeed, considered slaves to be property, and silenced their voices by preventing them from informing about any crimes unless interrogated under torture; men and women were dispossessed of themselves and rendered as inaudible and invisible as convenient. While this could lead to relevant insights on the interconnections between surveillance, slavery and their various techniques, Browne prefers to look at them exclusively through the lens of the American slave trade, so concluding that everything is, fundamentally, about a commodification of blackness.

Blackness is certainly the critical focus of Browne's concerns, and her insistence on more or less exclusively tracking its legacies eventually affects the whole analysis of how surveillance operates, especially the intersectional dimension of her investigation. Browne's rendition of the experiences of black women in the context of aviation security, expounded on the basis of a reading of the TV series *South Park* (cultural studies etiquette *oblige*), eventually tells us very little about contemporary surveillance and women. A better insight could probably be obtained by listening to Chino Amobi's *Airport Music for Black Folk*, even if Amobi might be rather less popular than Eric Cartman. A more thorough understanding of the challenges faced by feminism in light of modern surveillance would need to follow Safiya Umoja Noble, whose extensive research on algorithms and female oppression clearly shows that misrepresentation in online search engines is not a problem exclusively affecting the lives of black women and girls.

As blackness is constantly put forward as the main issue at stake, *Dark Matters* also ends up turning a blind eye to the numerous settings where modern surveillance is not fundamentally about reifying anything at all, but, on the contrary, about dismantling the possibility for the subject to reclaim any personal territory or identity. The case of the language testing of asylum seekers, lightly touched upon by Browne, has been further dissected by British-Lebanese artist Lawrence Abu Hamdan. His work on the analysis of speaking in the procedures to obtain refugee status puts on record the policing of belonging through laws and science, showing that in many instances the problem is not to be ascribed to blackness, or to anywhere in particular, but to the pseudo-scientific dispute of self-identification by the apparatus of the state. This is directly related to the question of how to conceptualise resistance to racialising surveillance. If surveillance is about slavery, escaping might be a good option. *Dark Matters* hints that we should ask ourselves whether we wish to constantly surrender our bodies as data, as if that was in fact an option. If surveillance is framed as anti-blackness, going back to black(ness) might be a decisive counter-surveillance trick, but, then, performing whiteness or trying to pass in terms of race and gender (to the extent this is inspired by the narratives of runaway slaves) could also be regarded as genuine revolutionary moves. After much travelling through the dark side of surveillance and its sufferings, Browne ends up somehow oddly celebrating the sharing of style tips to confuse artificial intelligence, along with some other accidental counter-performances and symbolic gestures of defiance in the face of the white gaze, without really questioning the limits and effectiveness of these confrontations.

In this context, what really stands out as a perplexing gap in the argumentation of *Dark Matters* is a deeper reflection on the relationship between surveillance and the Black Lives Matter movement. Triggered by the murder of Trayvon Martin in 2012 by a Neighborhood Watch volunteer, Black Lives Matter is unquestionably rooted in a reaction against surveillance's violence, a visible answer to the barbarity of the gaze. Additionally, the movement has, since then, been regularly reignited by images of brutal anti-black racism, often obtained from police car and body cameras, as well as smartphone and CCTV footage, that incarnate a paradigmatic instance of complicated (non-exclusively dark, non-exclusively white) *sousveillance*. Thinking about surveillance from this standpoint could have made more explicit the tensions between the blackness of surveillance, on the one hand, and on the other, what the Dutch research and design studio Metahaven term 'black transparency': that is, the potentially disruptive uses of counter-information. Oscillating between the accidental disclosure of secrets and the systemic concealing of information, black transparency is not a straightforward remedy, and certainly not the contrary of surveillance. It is rather a counter-weapon acknowledging that surveillance is an exercise of power, and a reminder that, because it is not blind, surveillance can never be subverted by simply being dodged, played around or reversed.

Gloria González Fuster

French philosophy today

Christopher Watkin, *French Philosophy Today: New Figures of the Human in Badiou, Meillassoux, Malabou, Serres and Latour* (Edinburgh: Edinburgh University Press, 2016). 272pp., £24.99 pb., 978 1 47441 473 9

Following an earlier study of 'post-theological thinking' in the work of Alain Badiou, Quentin Meillassoux and Jean-Luc Nancy (2011), Christopher Watkin's new book on several contemporary French philosophers considers the way in which they approach human beings. It explores both how they understand what is distinctively human, and how they present this distinctiveness in relation to broader forms of life, existence or being. The more open and inclusive their figure of the human, Watkin argues, the more successfully it evokes the peculiarly elusive and multi-faceted nature of its object.

Watkin structures his account of the five thinkers named in the subtitle of his book in terms of a broadly linear story of progress; one that begins with a relatively closed and thus relatively limited and exclusive figure of the human, and that culminates with a maximally open celebration of human actors as part of an all-inclusive relational field. The beginning and end points of this trajectory are marked by Badiou and Bruno Latour, respectively, with Meillassoux, Catherine Malabou and Michel Serres marking so many successive stages along the way.

Watkin rightly sees how Badiou's conception of truth-affirming subjects, despite the 'inhuman' austerity of his underlying ontology and the 'immortal' or 'super-human' inflection of the truths that they seek to uphold, nevertheless relies on basic human capacities like the ability to think, to reason, to wager, to commit, etc. However universal the scope for affirmative thought might be, such abilities themselves serve to distinguish, for Badiou, a genuine human life from the 'merely animal' dimensions of our worldly existence. This ability to affirm a universal truth exemplifies what Watkin calls, throughout his study, a delimiting 'host capacity', possession of which serves to police the line between human and animal forms of life. Reliance on such a 'gatekeeper capacity' immediately raises the problem of what to make of human beings who, for whatever reason, have been dispossessed of it – for instance 'neonates, the senile, those with severe mental disabilities'. What is the status of such figures who lack the capacity to affirm, in the purportedly universal affirmations of both Badiou and then Meillassoux?

The value of Latour's 'polyphonic and multimodal' approach, by contrast, is that it embraces a myriad diversity of human figures as an integral part of an all-encompassing relational network of other figures, without relying on a specific capacity, substance or story that might demarcate the hosts that carry it from those that do not or cannot. The reason why Latour figures effectively as the pinnacle of the field Watkin surveys is that he finds a way to acknowledge human capacities like language and thought simply as local instances of more properly universal phenomena of 'translation and mediation' which appear to apply to *all* modes of existence. Actors' identities are then free to evolve without reference to any underlying or identifying essence, and in extremis to confront those tipping points where, as a result of changes in their capacities and relations to other actors, they might become truly other than themselves. As a result, the paradigmatic figure of self-assertive humanity, the modern subject championed by Descartes and the scientific revolution (to say nothing of Rousseau, Marx and subsequent political revolutions), is here 'completely unmoored, dislocated, distributed, divided up' (citing Latour). Of all those Watkin surveys, Latour's figure of the human is thus the most open and varied, and 'the least prone to dangerous exclusions'.

Serres comes close to similar heights, with his recognition that the difference between human and crystal, or mammal and mineral, is only 'quantitative' rather than 'qualitative' – but he still falls a little short of Latour insofar as his conception of humans as uniquely 'undetermined' or de-differentiated self-fashioning animals remains tied to this very uniqueness, and consequently to a 'host narrative' that restores a gatekeeper exclusivity to the figure it upholds. Although Meillassoux's emphasis on contingency and possibility opens his conception of the human up a little more than Badiou's, his reliance on rational thought and affirmation still positions him, on Watkin's spectrum, much closer to Badiou than to Latour.

Malabou, finally, is the central and most thoroughly studied figure in this account, since her conception of plasticity stretches any notion of a host capacity past its limit, and replaces it by a 'host substance'. Malabou's determination to think mind and brain together allows her to evade the exclusive confines of mental operations like affirming or reasoning and to explore a biological field that disperses humanity in the midst of a much wider, more ecological frame of reference, but she nevertheless stops short of that leap into a fully 'polyphonic', fully post-anthropocentric cosmos which Watkin associates with Latour.

Each of Watkin's readings is admirably clear and impressively thorough, and his decision to approach the field in terms of a single over-arching movement lends his book both a coherence and a momentum that distinguish it from the great majority of survey-style overviews. Needless to say, readers with different political and philosophical priorities may well see, in the overall movement from Badiou to Latour, something rather different than the broad opening and progression that Watkin applauds – but there isn't space for this argument here, and in any case politics isn't one of this book's central concerns. Two other question, however, seem harder to avoid.

First of all, given Watkin's determination to avoid any reliance on a specifying host capacity or substance, combined with his determination to expand the frame of reference as far as possible, the question of what exactly still serves to demarcate a distinctively human figure seems hard to pin down. That is Watkin's point, of course, in his appeal to 'multiple, layered accounts of the human' over any 'single-aspect' identification. Nevertheless, in his recurring reference to the neonates or the severely senile, what seems to recur are indeed *figures* in the most literal sense, figures that we might recognise as human because, presumably, they appear to conform to a recognisably human shape. But this begs the question of why this should be so, and of where (or why) we should locate the points at which any figure per se might cease to *look* human, in order to appear as something else.

Second, the more thoroughly Watkin purges his human figures of their reliance on a host capacity such as reason or affirmative thought, the more his own appreciation of the humanity of senile or disabled figures seems tacitly to rely on a form of just such affirmation. Total elimination of every host capacity deprives these figures of any opportunity to affirm their *own* humanity, of course, as actors in their own right, and like some of Malabou's 'new wounded' they can appear here only as the objects of others' benevolent concern. But no matter how inclusive and diversified our categories of apparently human-shaped objects might become, doesn't their affirmation as human still depend, as ever, on some actors' capacity first to recognise them as such, and then to do what is required, at the level of social organisation, to affirm and look after them? Watkin's book certainly helps us to escape the conventional limits of humanist affirmation, but to my mind its celebration of an effectively 'unlimited humanity' seems to rely on precisely the sort of affirmative thought it seeks to undermine.

Peter Hallward

Paper trails

Kate Eichhorn, *Adjusted Margin: Xerography, Art and Activism in the Late Twentieth Century* (Cambridge, MA: MIT Press, 2016). 216pp., £21.95 hb., 978 0 26203 396 1

The punning title of Kate Eichhorn's book refers to the 'somewhat audacious argument' at its core: that the xerographic (or dry photocopying) machine played an overlooked but decisive role in the formation of alternative artistic and political communities in North America during the late twentieth century. As Eichhorn notes, however, evoking the over-signified margin 'remains a somewhat perilous endeavour'; perhaps as a consequence, this thoroughly researched study of the emergence and decline of xerography tends towards a romantic celebration of the subcultural, alternative or peripheral.

The book begins by providing a succinct history of xerography's technological development from the late nineteenth century onwards; including unexpected details such as Edison's 'electric pen' of 1895, a motorised stencilling device that would eventually morph into the modern tattoo needle. Post-Fordist regimes of work hastened these machine advancements, and yet, as Eichhorn demonstrates, the burgeoning countercultural movements of the mid-twentieth century promptly abraded the administrative and bureaucratic world of white-collar office employment. The wildly successful North American copy shop Kinko's provides a neat framing device for Eichhorn's story, a grassroots business founded in 1970 that generated 'the space and equipment to turn an administrative task (copying) into art and anarchy and social practice.' Copy shops like these are cast as liminal social spaces in *Adjusted Margin*, integral to a shared 'experience of public culture and the production of non-localized networks and communities.'

Eichhorn explores the creative repurposing of a mass administrative technology, tracing the Xerox machine's allegorical relocation from the office to artist's studio. The prevailing use of these machines served to challenge established notions of copyright and alternative publishing networks flourished (often at the expense of employers whose machines were quietly exploited), circulating everything from fan fiction to mail art to avant-garde poetry. 'Visual artists and writers', Eichhorn tells us, 'embraced xerography as a way to produce books and booklike objects quickly, cheaply and collaboratively.' The activities Eichhorn describes here complement those anthologised by Gwen Allen in her 2011 study *Artists' Magazines*, where she connects the emergence of dematerialised modes of art to experiments in alternative publishing culture. Eichhorn's technological excavation provides a welcome counterpoint to Allen's earlier art historical perspective, enriching a growing field of historical research concerned with late-twentieth-century art, politics and print.

The book considers copy shops as sites of permitted illegality, where under-age IDs are produced and copyright laws openly flouted without recourse. The impossibility of enforcing copyright as a result of technological advancement adds a valuable historical dimension to current debates regarding 'open source' online publishing and illegal digital sharing within the humanities. However, this line of enquiry takes a darker turn as Eichhorn points out how copy shops' association with illicit behaviour functioned in association with their high numbers of immigrant staff to construct a space of 'imagined terrorisms' in the post-9/11 consciousness. The heightened surveillance and state aggression against Muslim workers at Best Copy in Toronto is taken as a case study to explore how public opinion arrived at 'the point where simply frequenting the shop was eventually posited as potential evidence of a terrorist link.' Eichhorn further proposes that a notable increase of photocopying businesses in close proximity to university campuses from the late 1980s onwards can be tied to education cutbacks and the rise of adjunct faculty members without access to institutional resources, an interesting contention that would, to become wholly credible, benefit from further research.

Xerography's critical role in the production of publics and counterpublics is a major theme in the book, which particularly concentrates on the history of subcultures in disinvested urban centres prior to enforcement of gentrification schemes in the later 1980s and 1990s. While similar ground has been covered before, Eichhorn looks beyond the illustrious subcultural urban centres of this history to suggest that xerography and zine production permitted the 'deterritorialisation' of those downtown scenes. The circulation of photocopied materials allowed for activist and subcultural values to spread far beyond the limited physical space of, for example, New York's East Village. That this stands as a pre-digital form of social media is a convincing claim: 'Beyond revolutionizing printing by enabling one to photocopy anything on a wide range of surfaces in myriad contexts, then, xerography anticipated the mobile, high-speed, real-time forms of communication that would be taken for granted by the end of the century.' Drawing on conceptualisations of the public sphere from Jürgen Habermas to Michael Warner, it is, she writes, a pressing question of mediation: 'what types of publics become imaginable through xerography that would have otherwise remained unimaginable?'

The book moves on to a discussion of AIDS and queer activisms, via which the organised production of graphic posters, flyers, zines and large-scale demonstrations strikingly intervened in prominent public spaces. The significance of xerography is shown to go beyond solely reprographic mechanics, being instead bound up with the very fundamental 'freedom to be public' for which queer groups were advocating. In concurrence with other writers including Sarah Schulman and Tara Burk, Eichhorn discusses photocopying and postering in terms of the visual character of cities, where the urban landscape is evocatively transformed into a peeling papered canvas, in some parts an inch thick. Eichhorn conveys the sheer volume of Xeroxed materials circulating under the official radar, from illegally copied university texts to scientific reports on new AIDS drugs, and her enthusiastic prose evocatively captures a tactile sense of inky materials being passed from hand to hand. If the book risks repetition at times this might be attributable to the endlessly reproductive technology under discussion.

Eichhorn concludes by pointing out the almost total replacement of xerographic machines with digital photocopiers by around 2000, an occurrence 'most people didn't even notice'. This, she contends, is significant because the original machines enabled replication without a master copy, whereas the new technology consists of a scanner and data bank: 'While people no doubt continue to use copy machines in subversive ways, in the digital era they can no longer do so with a guarantee that they won't leave a trace.' A visit to a technology museum in Berlin reveals that, as objects, copy machines are 'bereft of design considerations'. As such, unlike the stylish typewriters, turntables and Polaroid cameras that continue to change hands as desirable retro commodities, these machines have been completely abandoned. However, the technology lives on in what Eichhorn calls the 'xerox effect', a DIY aesthetic that is digitally reproducible and functions in dialogue with new forms of social media. As she puts it: 'If photocopied posters, flyers, and zines still quickly found a place in Occupy, it is because the aesthetic of these forms continues to signify something that exceeds a method of document reproduction.' The significance of the photocopied aesthetic is that it 'is anarchic and punk, radical and queer', a bold claim that needs, possibly, to be situated in relation to less optimistic readings of analogue media and nostalgia, as discussed, for example, in the 2014 collection *Media and Nostalgia* edited by Katharina Neimeyer.

Eichhorn's lucid 'media archaeology' persuasively situates the photocopier as a new technology essential to the production of alternative communities in late twentieth-century North America. In this it achieves the outcome of good material culture research by taking an object of such ubiquity that it had become practically invisible and rendering it fresh again. As in her previous book, *The Archival Turn in Feminism: Outrage in Order* (2013), Eichhorn weaves insightful cultural analysis with personal and practical observations, treading a line between scholarly and activist registers. Although her celebration of radical xerographic practice flirts with hyperbole, the tone is exciting. The clean design of the book itself remains thankfully free of 'xerography's gritty aesthetic', but it also hints at the inherent contradiction of writing a scholarly-press history of activist materials. The copyright page clearly states: 'no part of this book may be reproduced'.

Victoria Horne

Smart writing

Sarah Kember, *iMedia: The Gendering of Objects, Environments and Smart Materials* (London: Palgrave Macmillan, 2016). vi+122pp., £45.00 hb., 978 1 13737 484 4

Sarah Kember's new book positions itself in a field of theory dominated by an often masculinist discourse that privileges conceptualisations of its research objects as things or environments in-themselves, instead of as the conflicted and hypermediated objects-in-time that they are. Im/mediacy is a recurring theme throughout the book, which bears both a political and conceptual charge. In particular, Kember targets the theoretical practices stemming from Object Oriented Ontology (or OOO), arguing that disavowing processes of mediation and problems of subjectivity leads to a disturbing complicity between the media industry and iMedia theorists. Her contention is that if we stop asking the question 'who writes?', while positing a flat ontology as the ground on which materials, environments and objects appear as equal, undifferentiated and neutralised, then we run the risk of erasing the structural and epistemological hierarchies which constitute those objects. This negation can do little to counter the current post-political, neoliberal consensus, especially if it goes hand-in-hand with a dismissal of critique as something outdated and redundant.

The task of *iMedia* is to unpack and undo such covert complicities between theory and the post-political. She does this in a skillful, albeit sometimes frenetic manner, by assembling the work of a variety of scholars and storytellers. The book deploys critique, humour and ambiguity to offer a decisively feminist perspective on the stakes involved in mediating and narrativising the 'i' in iMedia. Storytelling and writing, as practiced by writers such as Donna Haraway or Hélène Cixous to whom Kember often returns, can become methods for reclaiming territories which are already seemingly lost to the post-political world of the iMedia industry. Writing is deployed as a 'queer feminist praxis' and simultaneously as '*the* deconstructive mechanism' that pertains to movements and displacements, while also being always both mediated and situated. I am wary of attempts to envisage any technique as somehow positioned on a privileged level of criticality by virtue of its adherence to a supposedly inherently subversive set of practices (in this case, deconstruction). Nonetheless, in the feminist setting within which Kember operates and positions herself, writing can indeed only ever be conceived as a *practice*. As such, it cannot claim a privileged access to worlds and situations with which it is not already in a tenuous relationship. Instead, it must acknowledge its responsibility in the co-creation of these (i)worlds.

Kember performs the heterogeneity and partiality of writing by experimenting with different genres such as the manifesto, the sci-fi novel and the monograph. She inserts disparate fragments into her text, including a somewhat confused debate on an Apple forum, a detailed description of a Corning glass promotional video and a diagram that refigures the conceptual points of the book. These techniques seek to demonstrate that there is no writing in-itself just as there are no objects or environments-in-themselves. Indeed, it becomes apparent that being a skillful storyteller does not necessarily imply an ethical or politicising position. As the case of the materials manufacturer Corning makes apparent: it 'subsequently reveals its own own effectiveness as a storyteller and how effective stories themselves are at in-forming their audience, writing them into the futures that are told.' Her intention is to unscrew and loosen the mechanisms that secure this efficacy, a political practice which, Kember insists, can and should be performed by means of writing: 'this question of "what should we do as citizens" has an answer: "write".' The industrial logic that is behind the narrative mode of promotional videos of companies such as Corning and Microsoft demonstrates its preference for neutralised, naturalised and loosely sexed protagonists, at the same time as it reinstates a traditionalist vision of gender roles, offering a vision of the future that looks more like the past. A feminist reading of these stories aims to reclaim the 'i' in iMedia, in its necessary ambiguity, and to shift attention towards the processes of constitution and erasure of political subjectivity.

According to Kember, glass is the *i*material which most persuasively demonstrates the tension between mediation and immediation, transparency and ambiguity. She argues that glass has always worked 'towards the endpoint of mediation', but in the present moment, imbued with its own future fantasies, it is starting to become information technology itself, and, via a ubiquity akin to plastic, now acts as an intelligent skin, becoming one with human bodies. Glass' transparency and seeming capacity to present 'the world as if it just is' is, however, not neutral but complicit with the neoliberal fantasy of an invisible information infrastructure that negates its own 'contribution to the world'. Here equality is understood in terms of access to the market. As Kember puts it: 'Glass itself might make everything clear to everybody equally, but its design and architecture, its cultural and technological working is never neutral but rather imbricated in power and social divisions.' In this discussion, expressions like 'glass itself' sometimes give the impression that we are being transported into the realms of ontology. Kember, however, decisively aligns herself here with Ezio Manzini, who underscores that the question at stake is not what glass *is*, but rather what it *does*. He consequently argues that what is needed is an onto-epistemology of the material. Cinderella (with her glass slipper) becomes Kember's way of approaching the problems associated with the gendering of this increasingly smarter material and the ways in which it is co-opted by tales of the iMedia industry about the future.

The book is ambitious in its attempts to enter and problematise a number of seemingly disparate theoretical fields and to orient them around its main concern: the question of mediation and subjectivity in iMedia, and the political implications of their erasure or reinstatement. With the exception of Cixous and Jacques Derrida, there is barely a thinker who is not subjected to critical scrutiny by the author. Moreover, the adoption of such a stance is the practice Kember envisions as a means of situating herself in the quest of producing and diffracting iMedia knowledge. The polemical tone of the book, however, sometimes leads to imprecision and obscurity, as in the discussion of the tension between *potentia* and potential in the end section of chapter three. Kember criticises vitalist feminist thinkers Rosi Braidotti and Elizabeth Grosz for their reinstatement of oppositionalist logics and utilises their discussion to introduce the question of time as a ground for a feminist political intervention and story-telling. Yet it remains unclear how her own distinction between potential (the 'finely grained and ingrained clock time that carves out women's work') and *potentia* ('the life-times of women's diverse becomings') can provide an alternative.

If Kember's argument about the politics of time(telling) remains underdeveloped, its charge can nevertheless be retraced by attending to her preoccupation with the way in which the book is crafted and structured. The publication consists of a montage of disparate parts, including a sci-fi novel in progress (in which the implementation of Global Democratic Capitalism has resulted in the perfection of citizenship as defined by people's actual and potential capacity to consume) and a two-part iMedia manifesto. These different genres convey their own temporalities and velocities, their own fidelities to the contemporary and the future. Perhaps then the book performs its most enigmatic point formally, by navigating different ways of organising and experimenting with time in writing. The book invites its reader to rethink the future of critical praxis and of feminist media theory and to explore their potential to create iWorlds. Their protagonists would actively undertake the task of politically and materially refiguring the current neoliberal, masculinist logic of iMedia theory and industry. It becomes apparent that the politico-theoretical project for a *movement towards* a post-dialectical feminism as proposed by Kember would go hand-in-hand with the development of a writerly praxis which acknowledges its own responsibility in matters of decision-making or 'cutting'. It is precisely this commitment to experimentation which transmits a sense of urgency to the reader to adopt practices of threading, storytelling, parody and cutting.

Neda Genova

www.ingramcontent.com/pod-product-compliance
Lightning Source LLC
Chambersburg PA
CBHW050445090526
44586CB00038B/2145